Shakespeare for Young People

Shakespeare for Young People

Productions, Versions and Adaptations

ABIGAIL ROKISON

The Arden Shakespeare

1 3 5 7 9 10 8 6 4 2

First published in 2013 by The Arden Shakespeare

The Arden Shakespeare is an imprint of Bloomsbury Publishing Plc

The Arden Shakespeare
Bloomsbury Publishing Plc

49–51 Bedford Square
London WC1B 3DP

www.ardenshakespeare.com

Available in the USA from Bloomsbury Academic & Professional,
175 Fifth Avenue/3rd Floor, New York, NY 10010.

A CIP catalogue record for this book is available from the British Library.

ISBN: 9781441172280 (hardcover)
9781441125569 (paperback)
9781441188052 (PDF)
9781441175298 (ePub)

This book is produced using paper that is made from wood grown in
managed, sustainable forests. It is natural, renewable and recyclable.
The logging and manufacturing processes conform to the environmental
regulations of the country of origin.

CONTENTS

ACKNOWLEDGEMENTS

I am extremely grateful to everyone who has worked on this book, in particular Margaret Bartley at Arden and David Avital, Anna Fleming, and Laura Murray at Continuum where the book began its life before it moved to Bloomsbury.

Particular thanks must go to those who allowed me to interview them for this book – Anthony Banks, Clive Bryant, Bill Buckhurst, Babou Ceesay, Vince Leigh, Michael Lesslie and Tam Williams, and those who gave permission for the use of their work – Lucinda Coxon, Globe Education, Carl Heap, Michael Lesslie, Sharman McDonald, Shakespeare 4 Kidz and the Young Shakespeare Company (Sarah Gordon and Christopher Geelan).

I would also like to thank Tim Crouch, Globe Education and Archive, the National Theatre Discover Programme, Pocket Propeller, RSC Education and Literary departments, and my colleagues in the Centre for Children's Literature in the Faculty of Education and Homerton College, Cambridge.

I am, as always, eternally grateful to my family, friends and loved ones for their support.

Introduction

Writing in the *Independent* in 2009 Caitlin Davies asks the questions 'Should children be introduced to Shakespeare at the tender age of four? Or should we wait until they are eight, or even better, the teenage years, when they are able to understand some of the seventeenth-century language better?' These are questions over which critical opinion continues to be divided. Some argue that primary school children are perfectly capable of grasping elements of Shakespeare's work, gain pride and pleasure from an understanding of his language and enjoyment from his stories. Such advocates of the early introduction of Shakespeare to children argue that if they become familiar with his work before its study in school becomes compulsory, they are less likely to feel intimidated by it. Other critics, however, assert that many of the themes and plot elements of the plays are unsuitable for children, the language too difficult, and that introducing Shakespeare to children too young may make his work all the more intimidating.

Shakespeare is the only writer whose work is a compulsory part of the curriculum in British schools, and policymakers, teachers, theatre practitioners, writers, illustrators and film makers, irrespective of whether they agree about the centrality of the bard in prescribed education, continue to try to find ways of engaging young people, who are often perceived as struggling with his work. Jennifer Hulbert, Kevin J. Wetmore, Jr, and Robert York suggest that similar concerns and efforts are at play in America where all too often, 'the usual first encounter with Shakespeare by youth is in secondary education, in which the classroom becomes a site of resistance' and where 'an entire industry has sprung up for the purpose of marketing Shakespeare to youth' including 'books, videos, graphic novels, software, CD-ROMs, "translations" of the plays and other activity-based products' (2006, pp. 1–2).

This book is concerned less with the teaching of Shakespeare in the classroom, and more with the various means – theatrical, filmic and textual – through which young people encounter his plays. It examines a range of work aimed at children from as young as 7 to those studying the plays for GCSE and A Level, considering the debates outlined above concerning the most appropriate time for the introduction of Shakespeare to young people, and the means by which such an introduction might be made. Focusing exclusively on texts in the English vernacular, it explores full-scale theatre productions and feature films of the plays aimed at young audiences; picture books, graphic novels, cut-down theatrical and animated versions of the plays and adaptations of Shakespeare for children and young adults in the form of novels, original plays, teen movies and animated features that take the plots, themes and characters of Shakespeare's plays and rework them to create original pieces of work. Each chapter is necessarily selective – focusing either on particular productions or on a particular play – *Macbeth* in the case of graphic novels, *A Midsummer Night's Dream* in the case of cut-down theatrical versions and film adaptations and *Hamlet* in the case of young adult fiction. These texts are selected because they are the most frequently adapted plays for young people alongside *Romeo and Juliet*, *Twelfth Night* and *The Tempest*.

The terminology surrounding the area of adaptation is fraught with difficulty. Daniel Fischlin and Mark Fortier in their book *Adaptations of Shakespeare: A Critical Anthology* (2000) acknowledge this problem, conceding that 'adaptation is not the right word' for the theatrical works inspired by Shakespeare that they collate, but asserting that this is because 'there is no right name' (p. 2). They survey the variety of terms that have been applied to pieces and that rework Shakespeare's themes, plots and characters, including 'spinoff', 'offshoot', 'transformation' and 'appropriation' (pp. 2–3). The last term forms the title of Christy Desmet and Robert Sawyer's book *Shakespeare and Appropriation* (1999), which deals with works from Kenneth Branagh's *Hamlet* to Disney's *The Lion King*. However, Fischlin and Fortier find this term aggressive, suggesting 'a hostile takeover' and not doing 'justice to other, more respectful, aspects of the practice' (p. 3).

This book follows Michael D. Friedman's proposed categorizations of 'version' and 'adaptation', which Friedman uses in relation to film, but which can be equally applied to the genres of drama and prose narrative. In Friedman's words, 'versions' are works that 'primarily use Shakespeare's original language for a particular play, although the dialogue may be heavily cut, redistributed, and occasionally summarized or modernized' (2008, p. 3). Friedman cites 'Zeffirelli's and Luhrmann's *Romeo and Juliet* films, as well as *The Animated Tales*' as belonging in this category (p. 3). I also apply this term to storybook narratives, which retell the plays, in a similar manner to *The Animated Tales*, summarizing the plot, but adhering closely to its structure, characters and occasionally language; graphic novels that employ Shakespeare's dialogue in either edited or modernized form; and heavily edited theatre productions.

The term 'adaptation', according to Friedman, may be used to refer to a film that 'borrows the basic plotline, characters, and thematic issues from a particular play, but employs the contemporary vernacular almost exclusively in its dialogue' (p. 3). Friedman cites *West Side Story* (1961), *10 Things I*

Hate About You (1999), *Never Been Kissed* (1999), *Get Over It!* (2001) and '*O*' (2001) as instances of adaptations. I extend the category to include plays and novels, as well as films, that rework Shakespeare plots, themes and characters, some adhering to the plays more closely than others, but all being recognizable, like the films cited by Friedman, as modernizations, sequels, prequels or as offering a different perspective on a Shakespeare play.

There are, of course, a number of other ways in which Shakespeare's work has been adapted and reworked for young people, in particular in the field of popular culture. The Hip Hop Shakespeare Company is a perfect example of the sort of work that is being done, not only to engage young people with Shakespeare, but also to use his work as a means of inspiring creativity and a more adventurous use of language. The company was established in 2008 by hip hop artist Akala, with the backing of Sir Ian McKellen. Initially established at the Limehouse Youth Centre in East London, and predominantly working with young people in the London boroughs of Tower Hamlets, Newham, Hackney and Enfield, the company now runs workshops and mounts productions around the United Kingdom and abroad. Its main objective, as expressed by Akala, is to challenge 'perceptions of both hip hop and the Bard' (Arts Council, 2009) showing young people that there are a fewer differences than they might imagine between the rap lyrics of hip hop and Shakespeare's verse. In doing so the company seeks to 'create social cohesion between young people from varying social/economic backgrounds and enable all young people to be creative through the use of all art forms' (Hip Hop Shakespeare Company, 2008). As Akala explains, for many young people, Shakespeare is 'the most unattainable things they can think of'. Once they realize that 'Shakespeare is attainable to them then how can a job not be attainable, how can anything not be?' (Guest, 2009). While Akala's statement may seem like wishful thinking given current rates of youth unemployment, the results of the project have been extremely impressive, with young people creating imaginative and expressive hip hop lyrics based on Shakespeare's plays that combine contemporary language, hip hop slang and Shakespearean imagery. Indeed, Guest reports that one young person who took part in early workshop 'has been commissioned to write a play for the Young Vic' (2009), seemingly confirming Akala's assertions about the potential role of the project in job attainment.

Another project that encouraged young people to engage with Shakespeare through their own contemporary mediums of communication was the Royal Shakespeare Company's (RSC) *Such Tweet Sorrow* (2010), which used Twitter, alongside the other digital media of Twitpic, YouTube and Facebook, to create a 'production' based loosely on *Romeo and Juliet*. The project, which emerged in real time over 5 weeks, revolved around a script by Bethan Marlowe and Tim Wright, set in the present day and featuring six characters based on Shakespeare's – Romeo (aged 19); Juliet, a 15-year-old schoolgirl; Laurence Friar, 'the 38-year old owner of the local internet café & alternative bookshop' (Mudlark and the RSC); Mercutio, a gap-year student; Tybalt, Juliet's disturbed older brother and Jess, Juliet's older sister, otherwise known as 'Nurse'; as well as the additional character of Jago Klepto, who functioned as a choric figure. The story gradually unfolded through the characters' tweets (posts of 140 characters or less improvised by the actors) between 12 April and 13 May 2010, with viewers able to respond to the posts and take part in certain sections. The reviews of the project were mixed, Michael Billington writing in Twitter-style: 'Isn't the real WS more about poetry than plot? Give me Baz Luhrmann's movie any day' (quoted by Kennedy, 2010), while Charlotte Higgins declared: 'A plague on the Twitter Romeo and Juliet' expressing incredulity as the use of the medium; 'Twitter's public right? So it somewhat stretches credibility to think that Romeo and Juliet would use it to conduct their secret love affair' (2010). However, research carried out after the production showed that it attracted over 30,000 followers from all over the world (Figaro Digital, 2011), fulfilling the RSC's aim of attracting 'a much younger, more ethnically diverse and less upmarket audience' (Leapfrog Research and Planning, 2011).

In addition to such active and interactive projects, Shakespeare has been consistently present in popular culture through the medium of cult television series including *Star Trek*, *The Simpsons* and *Doctor Who*. In *Star Trek*, visual and verbal references to the playwright and his work abound, most notably in season one, in the episode entitled 'The Conscience of the King' (1966) in which a travelling troupe of Shakespearean actors, the Karidian Company, mount a performance of *Hamlet* on the Starship Enterprise. Shakespeare references similarly appear throughout the long history of *Doctor Who*, with the Bard himself appearing in two episodes – in season 2 in which the Doctor briefly sees Shakespeare in conversation with Elizabeth I and in series 3 of the revived *Doctor Who*, which featured an entire episode, 'The Shakespeare Code' (2007), based on Shakespeare's lost play – *Love's Labour's Won*. These references are significant in confirming the pervasive presence of Shakespeare in a range of popular media. However, they fall outside the remit of this book, since none involves the adaptation of plays in the Shakespeare canon.

The Simpsons, however, in addition to containing numerous references to Shakespeare and his work, and an appearance by Shakespeare as a zombie in the episode 'Treehouse of Horror III' (1992), also features satirical adaptations of two of Shakespeare's plays, albeit only as parts of larger episodes. 'Tales from the Public Domain' (2002) and 'Four Great Women and a Manicure' (2009) contain reworkings of *Hamlet* and *Macbeth* respectively. The former sees the Simpson family and their friends transformed into characters from *Hamlet* as Homer reads to them from the inaptly titled 'Classics for Children', while the second portrays Homer and Marge as an ambitious couple whose lives partly mirror those of Shakespeare's Macbeth and Lady Macbeth. Both episodes present humorous parodies of the plays, which, although they begin by following Shakespeare's tragic stories, albeit loosely and extremely speedily, soon descend into farce. Much of the humour of 'Tales from the Public Domain' derives from the absurd ways in which the characters die in comparison with their deaths in *Hamlet* – Rosencarl and Guildenlenny (the equivalents of Rosencrantz and Guildenstern) by high-fiving one another while covered in poison, Laertes by stabbing himself accidentally, Hamlet by slipping on some blood and Gertrude by knocking herself on the head with a mace because she doesn't want to clean up the mess. Similarly in 'Four Great Women' Homer, unlike Macbeth, does not die on the field of battle, but kills himself when Marge suggests the many Shakespeare plays for which he could audition, stating – 'Me having to read all those plays would be the real tragedy' – a comment that undermines not only the tragedy of *Macbeth*, but also the notion of Shakespeare's greatness. The simultaneous undermining of Shakespeare as something difficult while presenting his stories and characters in an accessible and entertaining manner is similarly evident at the end of 'Tales from the Public Domain', when Bart asserts that he 'can't believe that a play in which every character is murdered can be so boring' only to be countered by Homer who informs him that *Hamlet* is 'not only a great play, but also became a great movie called *Ghostbusters*' at which point the family leap up and dance to the theme tune of the film. This strategy of both venerating and undercutting Shakespeare is one which is found in a number of the teen film adaptations discussed in Chapter 9, in which characters often assert the incomprehensibility of a Shakespeare play while mirroring the actions of its characters. Presumably the aim is to challenge similar preconceptions in the viewer through the evident irony of the characters' assertions.

While, as the Museum of Broadcast Communications reports, the 'key viewing group for *The Simpsons*' is 'the "tween" demographic, those between 12 and 17' (The Museum of Broadcast Communications, 2011) many of the series' parodies of social and cultural institutions appear aimed more at adult viewers. The Shakespeare parodies discussed above, for example, are dependent for their humour on a fairly solid knowledge of the original text and a reasonably sophisticated understanding of the concept of satire. This is a phenomenon also evident in the animated movies discussed in Chapter 9, which, though ostensibly aimed at children, contain Shakespearean references that are only likely to be recognized by viewers readily familiar with Shakespeare's work. These references presumably function not only to invite the approval of parents who perceive cultural value in the animation, but also to encourage family viewing by providing parents with something that they can find entertaining even if their children do not recognize the allusions.

While this book cannot pretend to be exhaustive, it aims to cover many of the ways in which young people encounter Shakespeare's plays. Part 1 examines productions and feature-length film versions of Shakespeare that are aimed particularly at a young audience. The first chapter is concerned with the Globe's 'Playing Shakespeare' project, which, since 2007, has produced yearly full-scale Shakespeare productions for a Key Stage 3 audience. 'Playing Shakespeare' productions differ from those more typically mounted for schools in that they are more than an hour in length, performed in a main house theatre space – Shakespeare's Globe Theatre – with a cast of around 10–12 actors and production values, in terms of technical support, music, set, props and costumes, which one might expect to find in the theatre's main repertoire. Chapter 1 examines the 'Playing Shakespeare' productions of *Much Ado About Nothing* (2007 and 2008), *Romeo and Juliet* (2009) and *Macbeth* (2010 and 2011), looking, in particular, at the features of the productions designed to appeal to young people and the range of supporting materials intended to support study of the plays at Key Stage 3. Actor and director Bill Buckhurst has been involved with all of the 'Playing Shakespeare' productions, initially as an actor (in *Much Ado About Nothing*) and subsequently as the director of *Romeo and Juliet* and *Macbeth*. The chapter concludes with an interview with Buckhurst, in which he discusses the aims behind the project, the different productions and their design concepts, the challenges and benefits of working in the Globe Theatre and the nature of the audiences' engagement with the productions.

Chapter 2 moves to a discussion of three feature films of Shakespeare's plays, all of which seem designed to have a particular appeal to young people. Baz Luhrmann's William Shakespeare's *Romeo + Juliet* (1996) is described by Emma French as marking the beginning of the 'teen filmed Shakespeare phenomenon' (2006, p. 101), and though not made for an exclusively teenage audience, is, according to French, 'the first filmed Shakespeare adaptation that positions itself towards the teen market in such an exclusive manner in its marketing campaign' (p. 107). French identifies a similar marketing strategy for Michael Almereyda's *Hamlet* (2000), also discussed in this chapter. Although, again, Almereyda's film was not aimed solely at young people, his extensive cutting of the text, casting of adolescent protagonists and incorporation of modern media combine to form a movie with an evident appeal to the teenage market.

The target audience of Christine Edzard's *The Children's Midsummer Night's Dream* (2001) is made explicit in its title, which refers both to the film's prospective viewers and to its cast of 8–12-year-old children. Edzard's film is unique in having all of the play's roles performed by young people, and while there are obvious disadvantages in having a cast who are unfamiliar with Shakespeare's language and inexperienced in the art of film acting, the experiment encourages a sense of ownership of the play among children for whom Shakespeare may otherwise seem intimidating. The results may be uneven, but, as Douglas Lanier comments 'as an interpretative essay on the virtues of children's productions of

Shakespeare, Edzard's film has enormous value and cumulative power' (2006, p. 170).

While Edzard leaves most of the text of *A Midsummer Night's Dream* intact, there is an overriding tendency when producing Shakespeare for children to cut the plays severely in a way that privileges the story over the language. Part 2 of this book deals with versions of Shakespeare for young people in the form of prose narratives, graphic novels, theatrical productions and animated films, many of which are severely edited, reflecting both the perceived attention span of young people and the notion of what is accessible and suitable for them. Two major questions emerge from these four chapters – the suitability of many of Shakespeare's plays for children, and the extent to which the stories of the plays can be said to be representative of the works as a whole. The question of suitability arises both in terms of what adaptors choose to cut or alter, and what they leave in. While some adaptations of *Pericles*, for example, including Charles and Mary Lamb's *Tales from Shakespeare* (1807) avoid mentioning Marina's sale into prostitution, something that significantly alters the journey of the character in the play, when Carl Heap chose to retain this moment in his National Theatre (NT) adaptation of the play, some concerns were raised about its appropriateness for an audience of primary school children. One might question, as I do, whether *Pericles* is simply an inappropriate choice of play for an audience of under 12 years.

In Chapter 3, I explore storybook versions of the plays from those of Charles and Mary Lamb in 1807 to a wide range of twenty-first-century editions. I examine what I perceive to be a move from an emphasis on the morally didactic potential of Shakespeare's work to a focus on the entertainment value and theatricality of the plays. However, I also note that despite a less overtly expressed desire to employ Shakespeare's plays as moral exempla, editions of the past 10 years continue to remove morally complex and sexually explicit elements from the stories in order to make them more 'suitable' for young readers.

The overriding assumption inherent in the continuing production of short narrative versions of Shakespeare's plays is that children are best introduced to Shakespeare's work through his stories. I question this assumption, arguing that while storybook adaptations of Shakespeare may serve a useful introductory function prior to seeing or reading a play, much of the meaning and indeed appeal of the plays is lost when their language is reduced to modern prose narrative. Reading narrative adaptations of the plays is also a passive activity, which cannot compare with the active and interactive experience of viewing or performing the plays.

Although the major focus of Chapter 3 is on the texts of the storybook Shakespeares, I also examine the potential impact of the accompanying illustrations on young people's perception of the plays' characters. I focus particularly on the depiction of Caliban in *The Tempest* as an example of the tendency of these illustrated prose narratives to provide overly simplistic impressions of inherently complex characters. A similar inclination is evident in the increasingly popular graphic novel editions of Shakespeare discussed in Chapter 4. With their use of dialogue emanating from the mouths of characters, rather than narrative, graphic novels might be said to create a reading experience closer to viewing the plays in performance. However, while viewing the plays in performance is often an adjunct to studying them in the classroom, graphic novels are often used in place of more conventional texts. Although this may serve to bring the play alive for readers, the often quite extreme interpretations of characters provided by the illustrators of these texts may, I argue, close down other potential interpretations of the text.

I focus on five different graphic novel editions of *Macbeth* examining in particular those that feature either a cut-down version of the Shakespearean text, or an edited 'translation' of the plays in the modern prose vernacular. I consider the arguments behind each and the potential gains and losses for young readers, exploring the nature of the cutting and translation and its effect on the transmission of meaning. I also comment on the potentially misleading layout of the dialogue of the graphic novels as prose, a layout which, I argue, obscures the vital distinction between verse and prose in Shakespeare's work. Finally, I examine the wide range of resources that accompany the graphic novels, looking at inherent assumptions about what young people need to know and what they find attractive in a learning environment.

Chapter 5 looks at the recent profusion of cut-down stage versions of Shakespeare aimed particularly at primary-aged children which have emerged over the past few years from some of the country's leading Shakespeare-producing companies, including Regent's Park Open Air Theatre, the NT, the RSC and Propeller. It also explores the work of the Young Shakespeare Company (YSC) and Shakespeare 4 Kidz, both of which have a long history of mounting Shakespearean productions exclusively for young people. I explore the work of these companies, focusing on Pocket Propeller and YSC's productions of *A Midsummer Night's Dream*. I examine the style of the productions, the companies' approaches to the text, their relationship with their young audiences and the accompanying educational materials provided. I consider what these companies elect to cut from the texts and what they retain and the apparent rationale behind such decisions. The chapter includes an interview with Tam Williams, Babou Ceesay and Vince Leigh, members of the cast of Pocket Propeller's *Pocket Dream*, in which they discuss their interpretative decisions, the reactions of their audiences and the challenges and benefits of performing Shakespeare for young people with an all-male cast.

The final chapter of Part 2 is devoted to a discussion of *Shakespeare: The Animated Tales*. The chapter examines the most frequent criticisms levelled at the *Tales* – their focus on the stories of the plays rather than on character and language, and their oversimplification of the complexities of the plots and characterization. However, it also takes up Gregory M. Colon Semenza's call for the *Tales* to be considered as films rather than 'adapted literature' (2008, p. 37), exploring the varying styles of animation used in the films, and examining the often sophisticated relationship between style and thematic content; verbal and visual imagery. I also consider, as with the storybook and graphic novel Shakespeares discussed in Chapters 3 and 4, how the interpretative choices of the animators may impact on young viewers' perceptions of the plays, particularly when the *Tales* serve an introductory function as is suggested in their advertising materials and the rhetoric surrounding their release.

The final section of the book – Part 3 – is concerned with adaptations of Shakespeare's plays, and the role that these play in mediating children and young people's encounters with Shakespeare. I examine the extent to which original works, drawing on the themes, characters and plots of Shakespeare's plays, can stand alone or rely on an awareness of the original for a full-appreciation of elements of their intertextuality and humour or pathos. I argue that, at their best, these prose, theatrical and filmic reworkings of the plays can encourage a more in-depth interrogation of the plays' themes, help young people to see connections between their own lives and those of the characters and encourage debate surrounding the ambiguities inherent in Shakespearean drama. At their worst, they use the figure of 'Shakespeare the cultural icon' to provide artistic validity to something that has little creative merit.

Both Megan Lynn Isaac in *Heirs to Shakespeare* (2000) and Sarah K. Herz and Donald R. Gallo in *From Hinton to Hamlet* (1996) argue that Young Adult (YA) novels provide one of the most fruitful means of engaging teenagers with Shakespeare's work. Herz and Gallo look at a myriad of YA literature, citing books that share thematic links with Shakespeare's plays, and asserting that 'by linking YAL with the classics . . . students become developing readers, connecting, comparing, and drawing parallels' (p. 25), while Isaac explores books that have a more direct connection to Shakespeare's work, arguing that such novels, when 'read in tandem' with Shakespeare's plays 'reveal multiple layers of meaning' (2000, p.xi).

In recent years, Shakespeare's *Hamlet* has provided the inspiration for a number of YA novels. Chapter 7 explores these recent adaptations, looking first at Matt Haig's *The Dead Fathers Club* (2006), Alan M. Gratz's *Something Rotten* (2007) and John Marsden's *Hamlet* (2009) all of which update the story of *Hamlet* to the twentieth or twenty-first centuries, making the characters, situations and settings more familiar to young readers. I examine the novels' treatment of the themes and characters of *Hamlet*, considering ways in which the authors make these relevant and accessible to their young readers. While Marsden's novel follows quite closely the plot of *Hamlet*, both Gratz and Haig depart significantly from Shakespeare's play – both in terms of setting and plot. I argue that Gratz and Haig have created novels that can be enjoyed independently of *Hamlet* while also exploring the function of dramatic irony in these texts for readers familiar with Shakespeare's play. The second part of the chapter interrogates novels that place Ophelia at their centre, often in the role of the narrator – Lisa Fiedler's *Dating Hamlet* (2003), Rebecca Reisert's *Ophelia's Revenge* (2003) and Lisa M. Klein's *Ophelia* (2006). I explore the ways in which these writers subvert certain episodes in *Hamlet* in order to give Ophelia a more assertive voice and, most significantly, a life beyond Shakespeare's play, arguing that such a strategy encourages the interrogation of the role of Renaissance society in the fate of Ophelia and encourages readers to think about the similarities and differences in societal expectations regarding the behaviour of young women in Renaissance and the twenty-first century.

Chapter 8 looks at original plays that take their inspiration from Shakespeare's work, in this case in the form of prequels and sequels to his plays. I look at three plays that have emerged out of the NT's Education department – Sharman MacDonald's *After Juliet*, written in 1999 for the NT Connections programme, and Lucinda Coxon's *The Eternal Not* (2009) and Michael Lesslie's *Prince of Denmark* (2010) both commissioned by the NT Discover programme. Both *After Juliet* and *The Eternal Not* (2009) are prequels to Shakespeare's plays – *Romeo and Juliet* and *All's Well That Ends Well* respectively, while Michael Lesslie's *Prince of Denmark* (2010) is a prequel to *Hamlet*, a strategy that has been seen in adult literature – in John Updike's *Gertrude and Claudius* (2000) and Myrlin Abrosia Hermes' *The Lunatic, the Lover and the Poet* (2010) both of which novels narrate the events at Elsinore prior to the start of Shakespeare's play – but not in literature for young people.

Importantly for this study, in addition to being predominantly aimed at young audiences, each of these plays focuses almost exclusively on the younger generations of Shakespeare's plays, allowing them a voice independent from that of the older generations who frequently play a controlling role in their respective source plays. In doing so, I argue, they have a particular appeal to young audiences, not only in presenting characters like Ophelia and Helena as more assertive and capable figures, but also in voicing some common concerns of adolescence and early adulthood and encouraging young viewers to explore the themes of Shakespeare's plays in relation to their own experiences. I examine the relationship between these new plays and their source texts – their themes, characters, gaps and ambiguities – exploring their potential to encourage discussion on and interrogation of Shakespeare's work and to see his themes and characters in a new light. I also consider the extent to which the plays can be understood and appreciated independent of the Shakespearean plays on which they draw. Chapter 8 includes an interview with Michael Lesslie, author of *Prince of Denmark*, in which he discusses the relationship of the play to *Hamlet*, his exploitation of dramatic irony and his deliberate focus on the younger generation of Shakespeare's play.

As this book goes to press, some of the most entertaining and sophisticated Shakespeare-based pieces for children – Tim Crouch's *I* plays – are coming to prominence, and certainly merit mention. The series consists of four plays – *I, Caliban*; *I, Banquo*; *I, Peaseblossom* and *I, Malvolio* – in each of which the title character tells the story of their respective Shakespearean play – *The Tempest, Macbeth, A Midsummer Night's Dream* and *Twelfth Night* – from their own perspective. Although Crouch's writing of the series began in 2003 with *I, Caliban*, commissioned by the Brighton Festival, the plays had, until 2011, mainly been performed at Arts and Shakespeare Festivals. As I write, however, the Bristol Old Vic Theatre and Company of Angels are mounting a production of the first three plays, under the title *FairyMonsterGhost*; *I, Peaseblossom* and *I, Malvolio* are set for inclusion in the RSC's 2011 Autumn/Winter season; and the four plays have just been published under the title *I, Shakespeare* (2011).

The RSC's Autumn season also includes performances of Michael Rosen's new play – commissioned by Little Angel Theatre Company in association with the RSC – *The Magician's Daughter* (2011) – a sequel to *The Tempest* aimed at children as young as 3 years old. Using puppetry and song, the play tells the story of Miranda's daughter and her return to the magical island of Shakespeare's play and will tour the country before taking up residency at the Albany Theatre in London for Christmas 2011. These instances of new writing for young people as part of the RSC's repertoire are, perhaps, indicative of a growing interest in finding new ways of encouraging young people to engage with Shakespeare's work.

One of the main ways in which children and young people have engaged with Shakespeare's plays through original pieces of drama is in the genre of film. Chapter 9 explores two types of film that make use of Shakespeare's stories, themes and characters – the Shakespeare teen film, which has become a familiar staple in Hollywood mainstream cinema and the Shakespeare-based animated feature. The first section of the chapter explores adaptations of *A Midsummer Night's Dream* aimed predominantly at a teenage audience – *Get Over It!* (2001) and *Were the World Mine* (2008). I explore the ways in which the two films use the story of *A Midsummer Night's Dream*, in particular the love plot and magically induced transfers of affection, to explore issues of adolescent identity, in the case of *Were the World Mine*, more particularly the issue of teenage homosexuality. The motivation behind such adaptations is also examined – the extent to which the films seem designed to mediate teenagers' experience of Shakespeare's plays or appropriate Shakespeare 'as a vehicle for accruing capital, power, and cultural prestige' (Desmet and Sawyer, 1999, p. 2).

The second section explores the animated feature films *The Lion King 2* (1998), *Romeo and Juliet: Sealed with a Kiss* (2006) and *Gnomeo and Juliet* (2011), all of which rework *Romeo and Juliet* with the young protagonists transformed into non-human figures – lion cubs, sea lion cubs and garden gnomes respectively. I look at the various ways in which these animations both adhere to and depart from Shakespeare's story, in particular in the inclusion of a more assertive female heroine, in line with recent developments in Disney's princesses, and in a subversion of the genre of tragedy with the inclusion of a happy ending, presumably deemed necessary for an audience predominantly comprised of children. In addition to examining these and other elements apparently designed to appeal to a young audience, I also argue that these animations, in particular *Sealed with a Kiss* and *Gnomeo and Juliet*, include elements intended to appeal to adults – in particular in their use of parody. The dual appeal of the animations to children and adults encourages family viewing by combining some adult humour with appealing characters, while the Shakespeare connection serves to encourage the perception of the films as having some educational potential. Indeed, as I explore, *Gnomeo and Juliet* has been used on the primary curriculum in order to encourage an early engagement with Shakespeare's work, as well as to stimulate a range of literacy, numeracy, history and DT activities.

There are, of course, numerous books, plays, films and, as discussed above, television programmes that allude to Shakespeare's work, but are not devoted exclusively to the reworking of his plays, and thus fall outside the remit of this book – what Friedman calls 'citations' (2008, p. 3). There are also a number of pieces, including the *Doctor Who* episode mentioned above, that use the performance, study or reading of a Shakespeare play as the focal point of their story, notably Jan Mark's highly praised *Heathrow Nights* (2000), Suzanne Harper's *The Juliet Club* (2008), Kate Gilmore's *Enter Three Witches* (1990) and Nancy Charles Linehan's play *A Midsummer Night's Dream or The Night They Missed the Forest for the Trees* (2001). However, the distinction between these works and the films discussed in Chapter 9, which also revolve around a performance, is that the lives of their protagonists do not mirror those of Shakespeare's play and thus, there is no obvious reworking of the themes or plot elements.

Gary Blackwood's *The Shakespeare Stealer* trilogy (1998–2003) and Susan Cooper's *King of Shadows* (1999) are similarly not discussed in this book, focusing as they do around the writing and performance of plays by Shakespeare and the Lord Chamberlain's Men at the original Globe Theatre. However, all four books merit mention as superb stories which provide the reader with insight into the world of the Elizabethan playhouse, Cooper's book through the eyes of a young American boy, Nat Field, who, while working on *A Midsummer Night's Dream* at Shakespeare's Globe, is whisked back in time to act in the play with Shakespeare and his company and Blackwood's books through the eyes of orphan Widge, who becomes a member of the Lord Chamberlain's Men having tried to 'steal' the play of *Hamlet* during a performance.

Blackwood and Cooper's books are just some of the many novels, comic books, plays and films for children and young people in which Shakespeare himself appears as a character, as he does in the episodes of *Doctor Who* and *The Simpsons* discussed above. Like the texts that revolve around productions of the play, those that are mainly concerned with the figure of Shakespeare rather than his plays are also excluded from discussion in this book, since they cannot reasonably be said to fall into the categories of performance, version or adaptation. However, it is worth noting the trend for young adult novels centring around the women in Shakespeare's life – Grace Tiffany's *My Father Had a Daughter: Judith Shakespeare's Tale* (2003) told from the point of view of Judith Shakespeare, Peter W. Hassinger's *Shakespeare's Daughter* (2004) in which the protagonist is Susanna Shakespeare, Carolyn Meyer's *Loving Will Shakespeare* (2006), narrated by a young Anne Hathaway, later to become Shakespeare's wife and *Mistress Shakespeare* (2009) by Karen Harper in which Shakespeare's childhood friend and later mistress Anne Whately tells her story. These novels can be compared to the adaptations discussed in Chapter 7 that give a fuller voice to the often marginalized female characters in Shakespeare's plays, allowing them to tell the events of the plays from their own perspectives.

This book is merely a snapshot in time of the work that is being done to engage young people with Shakespeare and to extend their enjoyment and understanding of the plays. As this introduction has made evident, as it goes to print, new productions, versions and adaptations of the plays are emerging, confirming Shakespeare's ongoing centrality both in education and popular culture. With the advent of the Cultural Olympiad in 2012, the programme for the World Shakespeare Festival is being announced, featuring workshops, online education programmes, recital competitions, productions and adaptations for and by young people, as well as the 'World Together Conference' in association with the RSC, British Museum, British Council and Tate Modern, which seeks to 'explore the place of Shakespeare and the arts in young people's lives across the world' (World Shakespeare Festival), a place which will continue to be explored and debated for many years to come.

PART ONE

Shakespeare Productions for Young People

CHAPTER ONE

Full-Scale Stage Productions for Young People

Shakespeare's Globe: 'Playing Shakespeare with Deutsche Bank' – *Romeo and Juliet*, *Much Ado About Nothing* and *Macbeth*

In 2008 the Royal Shakespeare Company launched 'Stand Up for Shakespeare', a manifesto for the teaching of Shakespeare in schools, which calls for children to 'do it on their feet', 'see it live' and 'start it earlier' (RSC, 2008, p. 3). Shakespeare's Globe and the National Theatre (NT) have also lent their voices and support to this project, and although I would question the motivation behind the exhortation to study Shakespeare 'earlier' (the themes being not always appropriate for children of 7 or 8 years old) there can be little doubt that seeing Shakespeare's plays performed live, and engaging with his work in practical workshops are the most desirable forms of early encounter with Shakespeare.

The main producing houses around the country all regularly include Shakespearean productions in their main repertoires, and most provide online educational resources to accompany their productions. A number of these theatres also have education departments that produce heavily abridged and adapted Shakespeare, predominantly for primary-aged pupils. It is, however, rare to find full-scale Shakespeare productions created specifically for young audiences. Presumably this is partly because such productions are seen as having a limited appeal, insufficient to fill a theatre for a run. It is also the case that, for many schools, attending full-scale professional productions is too great an expense and, for those not based in towns or cities with theatres, a practical difficulty. Most productions for young people are therefore designed to tour to schools with a limited cast, often necessitating the cutting of a number of characters and by extension a substantial amount of the text. However, despite the fact that Shakespeare is performed in theatres around the country and by a number of small-scale touring companies, a survey carried out by Shakespeare's Globe of over 1,200 Year 9 students found that 'four out of five (82.5%) have never seen a Shakespeare play' (Shakespeare's Globe, 2010).

In 2007, inspired by issues of accessibility and an acknowledgment of the valuable impact of seeing live performance on young people's perception of Shakespeare, the Globe Theatre launched 'Playing Shakespeare', a project dedicated to creating full-scale Shakespeare productions on the Globe stage specifically for young people. The project was launched with a production of *Much Ado About Nothing (Ado)*, which was restaged in 2008, followed by productions of *Romeo and Juliet* (2009) and *Macbeth* (2010 and 2011). As Fiona Banks, Globe Education's Head of Learning and Teaching Practice, explained when launching the project, the productions have two key features – first, 'all aspects of the production' are designed to 'consider the young people we hope to engage' and second, the 'production values mirror those in the Globe's theatre season, even though the run of this play is considerably shorter' (2008a, p. 16). Each of the productions was created for Key Stage 3 students from London schools, and supported by a range of online resources and in-school workshops. Although the productions ran for only one week, each had a cast of around 10–12 actors (slightly fewer than in the Globe summer season productions that habitually have around 15) and a full production team, many of whom work regularly on the theatre's main repertoire.

The Playing Shakespeare project coincided, as Banks notes, with a shift in emphasis in education policy in the United Kingdom, with the National Curriculum recognizing both the importance of 'creative learning' in the classroom, and the value of 'watching plays in performance' as part of their study (2008a, p. 15). The government's 'National Strategies' publication of 2008 – 'Shakespeare for all Ages and Stages' – recommended that pupils studying a Shakespeare play at Key Stage 3 should 'see, if possible, a professional production of a Shakespeare play', while at Key Stage 4 they should ideally 'see, if possible, alternative productions of the same play' (Department for Children, Schools and Families, 2008, p. 8).

In March 2010 the Qualification and Curriculum Development Agency (QCDA) launched a new teaching initiative entitled 'Active Shakespeare: Capturing Evidence of Learning'. Working alongside the RSC and Globe Education, the government has developed materials for Key Stages 3 and 4, designed to encourage 'lively and active approaches to teaching and learning that see the text as something to be performed' (QCDA, 2010). The Globe's Playing Shakespeare project, and in particular its online resources, adhere closely to these aims, and in 2010 the Department for Education National Strategies created 'Macbeth: From the Globe to the Classroom', a resource comprising ten lesson plans, with supporting materials, based on the Playing Shakespeare production.

The three plays were selected with young audiences in mind. The choice of *Ado* (2007 and 2008) was mainly due to its presence, at that time, on the National Curriculum. As Banks explained in 2007, 'approximately 70% of 14 year-old students' were studying the play 'for their National Tests at Key Stage 3' (2008a, p. 16). Although *Romeo and Juliet* and *Macbeth* were not prescribed texts, given the abolition of compulsory Key Stage 3 tests, both have a widely recognized appeal to young audiences. In 1993 'before the recent specifications of Shakespeare texts' for particular year-groups (Wade and Sheppard, 1993, p. 268), John Sheppard carried out a questionnaire, designed to investigate what texts English teachers were selecting for study at different stages of the curriculum. At Year 9 *Macbeth* and *Romeo and Juliet* were the second and fifth choices respectively, and at Year 10 these two plays had become by far the two most popular (pp. 270–71). With its teenage protagonists and central themes of generational conflict, violence, rebellion and first love *Romeo and Juliet* seems an appropriate choice for a contemporary teenage audience. As Buckhurst elucidates, 'Shakespeare touches on subjects that still spark debate in 2009, from arranged marriages, to family warring, parent/ child relationships to teenage suicide' (Globe Education, 2011j). *Macbeth* has the appeal of the witches, and a clear, quick-moving storyline that is relatively short and easy to follow and is described by Buckhurst as 'written like a fast-paced thriller' (Lambert, 2010).

Although substantially longer than most versions for young people, the productions were cut to around an hour and 45 minutes in length, partly, as director Jo Howarth explains, because 'three hours is a long time for an audience to stand in the cold' (Globe Education, 2011g) and partly in order to make the productions 'short and punchy' getting 'to the core of the story' (2011l). In cutting the text, Howarth states that she 'identified moments that didn't drive the story forward and cut jokes and phrases that a modern audience might find obscure or difficult to understand' (2011g). These principles of cutting do not differ significantly from those employed by most directors, the plays rarely being performed in their entirety in the professional theatre. For Buckhurst, it is very important that Playing Shakespeare is 'about giving young people a full-scale production' rather than trying 'to tell the story in as few words as possible' (2010a). Like Howarth, he removed mostly elements of the text that seemed particularly obscure, and those necessitated by having only 10–12 actors available. This approach seems to acknowledge young people's capacity to appreciate largely unexpurgated productions of Shakespeare's plays even if, like many of their adult counterparts, they do not understand every word.

What was immediately noticeable about the productions of all three plays was their simplicity of style and embracement of the Globe Theatre space. As Buckhurst explains, being aware that the young audience members might be visiting the Globe for the first time, he and his designer wanted to ensure that the design didn't 'take away from the architecture of the space' and the audiences experienced 'the Globe as well as the play' (2010a). All of the productions used only a few set items, keeping the action flowing without a break, and fully incorporated the key features of the Globe – the pillars, the balcony and the stage trap – into their staging. The productions also made use of the entire auditorium in order to submerge the audiences in the drama, with characters appearing in the yard and upper galleries, shouting to one another across the auditorium. Howarth explains that her design for *Ado* was shaped by a desire to fully involve the audience, imagining the whole theatre as Leonato's house – 'a house that just happens to have a thousand people inside!' (Globe Education, 2011l) – connecting the stage to the yard and the yard to the first-level gallery with steps and ladders. *Macbeth* similarly made use of the whole auditorium, with zip wires from the second-floor gallery and ladders leading up to the first, creating a feeling that events might happen anywhere, the close proximity of the actors and element of surprise keeping the young audiences alert.

Although, as Alan C. Dessen notes, 'no evidence exists that the yard was used for entrances, exits, processions or special effects at the first or second Globe' (2008, p. 48), not least due to the number of people likely to have been standing in the yard (at least double the number of groundlings permitted in the new Globe),[1] the use of the yard for elements of the action, most notably actors' entrances and exits, has been characteristic of numerous productions at Shakespeare's Globe, and was a feature of all the Playing Shakespeare productions, ensuring that the young audiences were consistently surrounded by the action. In all three productions, the actors entered through the yard almost as frequently as through the doors in the frons scaena, delivering their lines as they pushed their way through the groundlings, opening up the action beyond the stage and implicating and involving the audience in the world of the play.

In addition to establishing close proximity with the audience through the use of the yard, the actors frequently involved the spectators through direct address. One of the central discoveries of the reconstructed Globe, and one of its lasting legacies, has been the realization that, with the actor and audience in a fully lit auditorium, with groundlings sometimes only inches away from the stage, asides and soliloquies work most effectively when spoken directly to the audience. In *Romeo and Juliet,* apart from the Chorus, and the Friar's brief speech at the beginning of 2.2, Romeo and Juliet are the only characters in the play who deliver speeches alone on stage. The delivery of their soliloquies directly to the audience helped to establish a bond between these characters and the young viewers. In *Macbeth,* James Garnon, in the title role, delivered all of his soliloquies as direct addresses, moving across the stage to speak to different groups of audience members, enabling him to target disruptive elements or refocus groundlings whose concentration might be waning.

As Tim Carroll notes, in the Globe space, 'the audience members are not passive recipients' (2008, p. 40) – they can act as a character's conscience, as their closest ally or as an extension of the onstage world, implicated directly in the action.

The audience were cast in a range of roles in *Macbeth*, implicated, for example, as Macbeth's court in 3.1, when Macbeth and Lady Macbeth emerged through a cloud of ticker-tape to shake their hands. Garnon expressed some shock at the enthusiasm with which the audience reached up to touch the protagonists:

> I was very much expecting the audience to boo, or react to him negatively. They don't. They all join in, very happily, I reach down to shake the hands of the children and they all merrily shake my hand. (Department for Education, 2010c)

The young audience were clearly caught up in the moment, fully accepting their assigned roles as Macbeth's supporters. A similar reaction was evident in the final moments of the play. When Malcolm entered to the cry 'Hail King of Scotland' (5.11.25) and a huge Scottish flag was unfurled at the back of the stage, the audience cheered and applauded, now playing the parts of Malcolm's loyal subjects. This willing and indeed vocal acceptance of their change in identity coheres with Carroll's assertion that 'the audience is . . . capable of being different people at different times' (2008, p. 41). It also exemplifies the way in which the architecture of the Globe space and well-lit auditorium seem to encourage the audience, in particular the groundlings, to respond to the plays in ways that are rare to witness in darkened auditoriums where audience and actors are separated by a proscenium arch. Mark Rylance, the first artistic director of Shakespeare's Globe, refers to a 'collective spirit' (2008, p. 109) generated by the space, a spirit that the young audiences clearly felt.

Some of the responses of the Playing Shakespeare audiences – the affectionate 'aah' when Romeo turned away from the balcony, head in hands, after first bidding farewell to Juliet (*Rom.* 2.1.202); the booing that followed Capulet's verbal assault on the Nurse in 3.5; and the wolf whistles that greeting Juliet parading around the stage to show off her wedding dress in 4.3 – while perhaps a little pantomimic, evidenced their engagement with the characters and stories. Buckhurst acknowledges that the Globe gives the audience 'a kind of ownership of the play' permitting and even encouraging the audience to respond (2010a). However, as he admits, there are points at which such vociferous reactions can become unhelpful in the transmission of the story (2010a). While generalizations cannot be made about the behaviour of the young audiences, words or action of a sexual nature invariably generated quite disruptive responses that obscured passages of dialogue. All of the kisses in the three plays were met with wolf-whistles, laughter, whoops and applause, followed by chattering, which often took at least 30 seconds to die down. While some actors, notably the more experienced members of the casts, were able to pitch their lines above such raucous responses, at other points the lines became obscured. The extreme reactions to the kisses from audience members seem surprising given the age of the attendees. One might expect most 14-year-olds to have become immune to seeing actors locking lips or indeed indulging in more explicit sexual activity; however, the entry of Romeo and Juliet in 3.5, thrust forth from the central opening in a bed, was greeted with virtual hysteria. Once again, maybe such reactions are the result of a space in which the audience are acutely aware of their fellow audience members and consequently feel more self-conscious, or, like a crowd at a football game, compelled to vocalize their reactions in a rather crude way.

What was most noticeable, however, about the reactions of the audiences was their utter involvement in the productions. Despite the lack of an interval, there was little evidence of boredom or lack of engagement, and the final moments of each of the productions – the 'jigs' characteristic of most productions at Shakespeare's Globe – were met with rapturous applause and cheers. Online reviews of *Ado,* written by pupils from St. Saviour's & St. Olave's School, attest to their utter involvement in and enjoyment of the production:

> I went to see the performance of *Much Ado About Nothing* and enjoyed it so much!! . . . Seeing this play has encouraged me to get more involved with Shakespeare's works and has shown me that they can be fun and understandable. (Hannah Judge)

> I thought the play was outstanding and a major reason for this was the twist of modernization which was incorporated in the play. Using the songs from Grease made the play incredibly fun and enjoyable, for me being in the audience it made me get up on my feet and join in with the songs which shows the performance was really engaging. (Demi Eleftheriou) (Globe Education, 2011h)

Howarth asserts her view that a production for young people 'needs to be energetic and, most importantly . . . look at the issues in the play that are relevant to that audience' (Globe Education, 2011l). This issue of relevance is one that emerges consistently in the rhetoric of the directors and in the resource material. One of the most obvious ways in which the productions sought to appeal to the young audiences was through the use of contemporary costumes, scenery, props and music, emphasizing the proximity between the worlds of the play and contemporary society.

Although not specific in their modern setting *Ado* and *Macbeth* were both unequivocally twenty-first century, the use of modern dress serving as a means of inferring elements of characterization through a shared contemporary understanding of codes of dress. In the 2008 production of

Ado, for example, Beatrice, beginning the play in grey stretch jeans and a black leather jacket, was immediately identifiable as cool, tough and unfeminine[2] in contrast to Hero who was initially clad from top to toe in pink, with a pink wool jacket and pink skirt. Characters' occupations were similarly made apparent through the use of recognizable uniforms – the soldiers arriving back from the war in modern fatigues, and the Watch wearing workmen's hard hats and florescent jackets. The soldiers in *Macbeth* were similarly clad in modern fatigues, emphasizing both the connection to contemporary wars and to the genre of the action movie on which the production seemed to draw. Buckhurst notes the startling parallels between the political situation in Renaissance Britain and that of 2010, parallels enhanced by the contemporary setting – 'When Shakespeare wrote the play the country was being run by an unpopular Scotsman at a time of economic turmoil, fear of terrorism' (Department for Education, 2010b).

Romeo and Juliet, by contrast, featured an anachronistic combination of modern and Elizabethan elements, which Buckhurst dubbed 'Period-Urban' (2010a), justifying this decision on the basis that since Shakespeare himself was unspecific about his setting – 'it's Verona, but it's Verona / England in the 1590s' – it seemed appropriate to employ 'a mix of worlds and styles' (2010a). The effect of this design choice was, like *Ado* and *Macbeth,* to highlight parallels between contemporary London and Renaissance Verona while not pushing them too far – 'it's not about young people in London in 2009. I didn't want to be sort of cramming in today's world into this situation' (Department for Education, 2009a). The costumes of the young Montague and Capulets alluded simultaneously to Elizabethan doublet and hose and modern 'hoodies', providing a clearly recognizable analogue to contemporary teenage gang culture while avoiding the Baz Luhrmann-like temptation to alter the sword play to gun fights.

Buckhurst's production made the headlines when the press reported that he had consulted the police about the play's fight scenes, a story that Buckhurst stresses was completely untrue. The *Telegraph* suggested that such a meeting had taken place because the 'producers' were 'so concerned that it could be seen to glamorize knife violence and gang violence' (Irvine, 2009) while the *Guardian* suggested that the motive was in fact to 'discuss how to make the play more relevant to its intended audience of 14-year-olds' (Walker, 2009), in particular the parallels between the play's fight scenes and recent teenage stabbings in London. Although this purported meeting never took place, the reaction of the press exemplifies the striking proximity of themes in the play to the lives of young people living in contemporary London.

All three productions made use of modern popular music, enhancing the sense of contemporaneity and further engaging the audience in the action. Most of the music was composed specifically for the productions by Alex Silverman (*Ado*) and Olly Fox (*Rom.* and *Mac.*). Silverman explains that he was inspired by a range of contemporary music, from 'K.T. Tunstall' to the 'Bollywood Brass Band' to 'Africa Sound System', the diverse nature of the music reflecting the ethnic mix within the audience (Globe Education, 2011k). Fox's music was similarly modern and eclectic, the opening music for *Macbeth* played on electric guitars having the flavour of punk rock, while that of the Ball scene in *Romeo and Juliet* had the feeling of popular jazz. A particularly striking inclusion of a contemporary song occurred in 2.3 *Ado*, where, in place of Balthasar's 'Sigh no more' (2.3.56–71), Claudio and Hero performed a rendition of 'You're the one that I want' from *Grease*. This musical number was met with rapturous applause, cheering and squeals of approval at Claudio's adept street-dance moves, and served as an opportunity for the audience to relax and let off steam. However, the choice of song is not, perhaps, as appropriate as Shakespeare's, which neatly foreshadows Claudio's imminent rejection of Hero by raising the issue of men's inconstancy:

> Men were deceivers ever
>
> One foot in sea and one on shore,
>
> To one thing constant never (*Ado.* 2.3.57–9)

In *Macbeth,* in addition to highlighting the parallels between contemporary Britain and that of the Shakespeare's play through the use of modern costume and music, Buckhurst and actor Russell Layton, who played the porter, also rewrote the porter's speech in 2.3, making direct reference to the constituencies in his audience. The porter's speech is complex, its humour largely dependent on an understanding of Jacobean 'gags' such as the one about the greedy farmer who 'hang'd himself on th' expectation of plenty'[3] and of contemporary events, such as the equivocation of Father Garnet.[4] However, it also serves both a practical and dramatic function in the play – allowing the actor playing Macbeth to wash his hands and change his clothes and providing relief from the dramatic intensity prior to the discovery of Duncan's body. Buckhurst followed in the footsteps of others who have decided that the porter functions best as a kind of stand-up comedian performing observational comedy.[5] With Shakespeare's farmer and equivocator changed to a schoolboy and a teacher, the speech elicited laughter from the audience who clearly gained pleasure from self-recognition:

> Here's a schoolboy, a schoolboy replete in blazer and tie-very nice. Demonised by society as a feckless, workshy, knife-wielding thug. They saw you coming. Just remember everyone; a pencil-sharpener in the wrong hands is a lethal weapon. Come on in schoolboy, have napkins enough about you, here you'll sweat for it. Knock, knock, knock, who's there in the other devil's name. Here's a teacher, a teacher. She's spent her extended summer holiday sunning herself on the beach. Christmas

and Easter holidays abroad and the rest of the time moaning about how much work she's got to do and how little time she's got to do it in. You want to get yourself a proper job. Security. It's 24–7 – never stops. Things I've seen, you wouldn't believe. Come on in teacher, it's always half-term here. (Buckhurst and Layton, 2010)

Self-recognition and empathetic connection was also utilized by Buckhurst in his creation of the witches for his production. As the audience entered the theatre space, they encountered two school children, much like themselves, wearing uniform, sitting on the stage. These figures disappeared at the start of the production, only to emerge, dishevelled, in the second scene, as the witches. This concept emerged, as Buckhurst explained from a discussion that the witches might have been victims of the war, planting the seeds of ambition in Macbeth's mind as a means of vengeance. Thus two of the witches became school children, killed in the conflict, and the third their grieving mother. This concept generated a feeling of the 'uncanny' about the witches – figures eerily both familiar and strange. It also allowed Buckhurst to create a palpable sense of magic surrounding them, one of the major challenges for a contemporary production where most audience members, unlike their Jacobean counterparts, are unlikely to believe in witchcraft. Buckhurst reversed the order of the first two scenes, allowing the actors who had appeared on stage at the start to exit, change, and secrete themselves onstage. Thus, as the soldiers exited, apparently leaving the stage empty, the second witch emerged out of one of the army boxes left on stage and the third witch out of a body bag. The latter of these entrances was particularly alarming, generating terrified squeals from the audience as the body bag suddenly began to move and sit upright before the witch materialized from within it.

The second appearance of the witches in 4.1 similarly managed to thrill and alarm. After Banquo's death, his body was placed inside a set of boxes, which, with the addition of a table top, was transformed into the banqueting table. At the end of the scene, the first witch appeared and stood alone on stage, a voodoo doll raised in the air. Suddenly, the banqueting table flew apart, the boxes at the side flying across the stage and the table top shaking, after which the second and third witches emerged from inside it. This moment, described by one young audience member as 'awesome' (Globe Education, 2011f), was genuinely alarming, successfully creating a sense of tension and fear in a bright outdoor space with no possible recourse to lighting-effects.

The capacity of the productions to generate palpable excitement in their audiences, grabbing their attention through the use of shock tactics and maintaining it through the energetic staging and fast-paced action was one of their most notable features. *Romeo and Juliet* and *Macbeth* started with loud noises that cut over the audience chatter and shocked them into attention; *Romeo and Juliet* with a loud trumpet call followed by vigorous drumming and *Macbeth* with the sound of an electric guitar followed by an explosion after which the soldiers began sliding down ropes, climbing down ladders and abseiling onto the stage accompanied by a soundtrack of an electric guitar, drumming, and explosions. The focus was then maintained by the swift transition of one scene to the next without a break, a necessary feature of a theatre in which there is no possibility of a blackout or lowering of the curtain. In all the productions, as one group of characters were leaving the stage, the next were already entering and speaking, allowing no time for the audience to begin chatting or moving around.

The Playing Shakespeare productions are unique in providing young audiences with full-scale, only slightly cut productions of Shakespeare's plays, which, in crediting young people with the ability to concentrate and engage with a Shakespeare play of nearly 2 hours in length, have succeeded in capturing their imaginations. With the use of the whole theatre as a playing space, audience and actor interaction and direct address, the young audiences have often been caught up in the action of the play to the extent of participating verbally. The productions have clearly sought to appeal both to the demands of the school curriculum and to the lives of the young audiences, the use of contemporary dress, music and semiotics helping to clarify character identities and relationships and allow the audiences to identify with the plight of a character. The productions have also permitted young audiences to experience the plays in a space very close to that for which they were written – a space that encourages imaginative engagement and active response, something all too easily lost in cinematic adaptations of the plays with which young people are most readily familiar.

Online resources

Globe Education's Playing Shakespeare website offers a collection of free online resources, aimed to support the study of the plays. Although the resources were created primarily for the productions' target audiences of Key Stage 3 pupils, Globe Education acknowledges that the resources offered may be 'equally applicable at other levels of study' (2011i). Each of the websites has been clearly designed with young people in mind, with a style that resembles a social networking site, numerous links to explore on each page, and an attractive, visually stimulating design. The sections into which each site is divided replicate the key areas in young people's classroom study of the plays – 'Language', 'Character and Motivation', 'Themes and Issues' and 'The Text in Performance'.

The Language resources are linked closely to the National Curriculum for which, at both GCSE and A-Level level, the highly weighted assessment objective AO2 specifies that candidates should explore the way in which 'language, structure and form contribute to writers' presentation of ideas, themes and settings' (AQA, 2010, p. 1) and in which students are rewarded for their ability to recognize literary devices. Students are able to explore the text for various scenes using tools that draw attention to these devices, providing drop-down lists that identify examples of onomatopoeia, alliteration, feet, rhythm and similes as well as a glossary of highlighted words.

In addition to offering language resources, these sections also include links to interview material with the director or actors, allowing the user some insight into specific choices made in the production about these key scenes and helping to emphasize to students that a play is an entity that is open to interpretation, the choices of actors and directors shaping its meaning on the stage. A similar function is fulfilled by the sections on The Text in Performance that contain links to information about all the key areas of the production.

As the site acknowledges, it is vital that students understand that the plays were written to be performed, and this section helps them to understand the range of elements that comprise the process of taking a play from page to stage. Both sets of resources stress the interpretative nature of performance, helping students to understand that meaning is ultimately constructed through the choices made by different members of the production team, an understanding that ties in with Key Stage 4 requirements that students see more than one production of a play, presumably in order to make them aware of the range of interpretative choices offered by a theatrical text.

The Characters and Motivations section for each play is cleverly designed to emulate Facebook, a format with which most young people are readily familiar. Like most Facebook pages, each character's page allows users to view their status and profile information, including hometown, age, 'also called', 'personal philosophy' or 'motto' and 'views on' sections, all of which make use of quotations from the play. These quotations neatly summarize the information given by Shakespeare about each of the characters and chart their development in the process of the play. Macbeth's 'also called' section, for example, contains the quotes: 'brave Macbeth' (*Mac*.1.2.16); 'O valiant cousin! worthy gentleman!' (*Mac*.1.2.24); 'this fiend of Scotland' (*Mac*.4.3.232); 'Hell-hound' (*Mac*.5.8.3) and 'this dead butcher' (*Mac*.5.9.35), drawing the user's attention to the way in which Macbeth declines in the eyes of others in the process of the play.

Like Facebook profiles, the pages also permit the user to see the character's friends, wall and photos. The wall messages from one character to another are comprised of lines from the play, again providing a simple means of gauging the characters' relationships to one another. Romeo's wall, for example, contains messages from Mercutio – 'You are a lover, borrow Cupid's wings' (*Rom*.1.4.17) and 'A plague on both your houses . . .' (*Rom*.3.1.108); Juliet – 'You kiss by the book' (*Rom*.1.5.109) and 'Art thou gone so? Love, lord, ay husband, friend, / I must hear from thee every day in the hour' (*Rom*.3.5.43–4); the Friar – But come young waverer, come, go with me, / In one respect I'll thy assistant be . . .' (*Rom*.2.3.85–6) and 'thou are wedded to calamity' (*Rom*.3.3.3). These quotes chart key moments in Romeo's story and in his relationship with other characters in a way that is immediately accessible.

The profiles for *Ado* and *Macbeth* also permit the user to send messages to the character. In most cases the messages sent are directed towards the actors, entitled, 'I think your acting is good' (Globe Education, 2011c) or 'you were my fave actor' (2011d) and are only one or two lines in length. However, there are a few notable examples of audience members engaging with the debates of the play and the motivations of the characters. One message vituperates the murderers for their role in Banquo's death, asking them 'Did you know you were manipulated by Macbeth into killing his own best friend? Were you not guilty about what you had done to someone who was innocent?' while also recognizing that their actions were 'understandable when this is a way in which you can earn money for a living' (2011e). Another on Lady Macduff's page demonstrates a recognition of the relevance of the play's issues to contemporary audiences – 'This lady has amazing strength, not only has she just found out that her partner, her husband, the Father of her children has gone than she is faced with the reality of raising her children as a single Mother. How more relevant than this to today's family make-up can you get?' (2011b). While these pages do contain limited responses, and seem to act for the most part as 'fan' sites, they nevertheless provide a forum through which young people can express their views anonymously, without fear of criticism, and encourage them to think about the reasons behind the characters' actions.

A nice metafictional touch is the 'Shakespeare quotes' section on each character's page, an application also available on Facebook. Each of the characters has an appropriate quote from another Shakespeare play, neatly linking characters and themes across the canon. Romeo's quote is – 'And why not death, rather than living torment? / To die is to be banished from myself, / And Silvia is my self. Banished from her / Is self from self, a deadly banishment' from *The Two Gentlemen of Verona* (3.1.170–3). This quote closely resembles Romeo's 'Ha, banishment! be merciful, say "death"; / For exile hath more terror in his look, / Much more than death: do not say "banishment"' (*Rom*. 3.3.12–14) linking the two plays – one a tragedy and the other a comedy. Both lovers, banished from the city in which the woman they love lives, find death preferable to banishment. Ultimately, however, while Valentine and Silvia are united in a 'happy ending', Romeo and Juliet are united only in death, the comparison demonstrating the proximity between elements of the two genres in the Shakespearean canon.

The Themes and Issues pages are interesting for what they tell us about the themes perceived as most significant and relevant to the young audiences. Each site highlights four main themes: *Ado* – Love and Relationships, Public and Private, Appearance and Reality and Reward and Punishment; *Romeo and Juliet* – Love and Lust, Guilt and Blame, Duty and Loyalty and Fate and Chance; and *Macbeth* – Violence, The Witches, Ambition and Tragedy. In each case (excepting 'The Witches') the themes selected are universal, equally applicable to the lives of young people in the twenty-first century as those in the sixteenth or seventeenth. This encourages users of the sites to empathize with the concerns of the characters and to recognize both the similarities and differences between the issues presented in the plays, and those of their own lives.

The pages contain message boards that invite users to contribute responses to questions based on the main themes. Again, this format is one with which young people are familiar, since message boards of this kind appear on a number of social networking sites. The questions are open, inviting a range of responses, for example: 'Romance versus friendship, which is stronger?' (Globe Education, 2011m). This question was particularly popular with many of the varied responses evidencing in-depth consideration of the relationships in *Ado*: 'Benedick and Claudio were soposed [*sic*] to be be [*sic*] very good friends, but when Beatrice asked Benedick to kill Claudio he agreed. He would not have done that if there [*sic*] friendship was stronger than his feelings for Beatrice'; 'Friendships are stronger in, "Much Ado About Nothing", because a couple of the romantic relationships ended up with a couple of people getting hurt throughout the play'; 'Throughout "Much Ado About Nothing" there were many relationships, both romantic and friendly. At times in the story both of which fail and succeed in many ways. As to which ones were stronger; that depends on the individual' (2011m).

The websites also contain links to essays on prevalent 'Issues': the *Ado* website to four essays by Dr Farah Karim-Cooper on Women, Marriage, Bastards and Slander. Again, the themes are quite general, applicable both to the lives of the young users and those of the characters in plays written over 400 years ago. Karim-Cooper's essays invite the young reader to think about the themes in relation both to the play and their own experiences. She begins her essay on Women by asserting: 'you would think that the place of women in Shakespeare's time was very different from today', acknowledging that 'on many levels this is true' (2011). However, she goes on to invite the reader to consider 'examples of prescriptive literature that tells women how to dress, what to eat, how to get a man, how to keep a man, what we should think, when we should get married, the age we should have children, how skinny we should be or how young we should look' (2011), drawing attention to many of the topics commonly covered by magazines read by teenage girls and young women. She also notes that 'today, in many parts of the world, young girls are considered to be wholly responsible for the honour of their families' (2011) as is Hero, raising a subject regularly discussed in the media, and doubtless of direct relevance to some of the young people using these resources. The method of relating the themes of the play to the lives of young people, both by posing questions about the relevance of the play's values today, and by drawing specific parallels between Renaissance life and that of the twenty-first century is one that is undoubtedly effective in encouraging young people to engage with the prominent issues of the play – gender politics, arranged marriage, sexual fidelity and family honour.

The Playing Shakespeare productions and online resources have succeeded in finding ways in which to engage the imagination and interest of young people while fulfilling the requirements of the National Curriculum. The success of the project is evidenced not only in terms of the number of schools who continue to participate in the scheme year after year, but also in the subsequent popularity of the productions as educational resources. The National Strategies commissioned podcasts of the productions of *Ado* and *Romeo and Juliet* for downloading in the classroom, the first of which was downloaded by 'over 17,000 listeners' in its first year (Department for Education, 2009b). Perhaps the greatest indication of the success of the programme, however, has been in the responses from the young audiences themselves that have been, as Fiona Banks reports, 'extraordinary . . . spontaneous and intense' (2008b, p. 164).

Interview with Bill Buckhurst – Benedick in *Much Ado About Nothing* (2007 and 2008) and Director of *Romeo and Juliet* (2009) and *Macbeth* (2010 and 2011) – Conducted on 17 November 2010

HOW DID YOU BECOME INVOLVED IN PLAYING SHAKESPEARE?

I'd never worked at the Globe before but had always wanted to. I went up for the job of Benedick in 2006 and it really appealed to me because it was a great part and a short run, and this sort of thing had never been done before – it was a unique project, where a somewhat edited version of this play was going to be performed specifically to 14-year-olds. I remember going to see Shakespeare when I was 14 and generally being very bored and unengaged, and this was an opportunity to put Shakespeare on the stage for this age group and to try to engage them and make it exciting.

WHY DO YOU THINK THAT IT IS SO VALUABLE FOR YOUNG PEOPLE TO HAVE THEIR OWN PRODUCTION, AS OPPOSED TO BEING TAKEN TO SEE A GLOBE PRODUCTION IN THE MAIN SEASON?

That's a very good question, because as a director of these shows I start by thinking 'what engaged me as a 14-year-old?' and actually those things haven't really changed. I think that often in Shakespeare productions directors feel the need to challenge themselves to do something that no one's done before, and there is no bad thing in that, but our goal is very different to what it might be if we were just doing a normal production of the play.

SO IT BECOMES MORE ABOUT THE CLARITY OF THE STORYTELLING?

Absolutely, and I think that sometimes clarity of storytelling can go out of the window in productions.

WHO CHOSE THE PLAYS, AND WHY THESE PARTICULAR PLAYS?

I'm not involved in that so I can't give a definitive answer. *Much Ado* was on the curriculum, and I think that *Romeo and Juliet* is the play that a lot of young people encounter as their first Shakespeare play. In my work as a practitioner at the Globe I have discovered that on the whole young people of around 14 are familiar with the story of *Romeo and Juliet*. *Macbeth* was chosen because of its cracking story, I suppose. It's not very long, as the plays go; it's a good length, and it's got all the elements that make for a good old story. Certainly when I've met young people in the classroom they respond well to the tale as a whole.

COULD YOU DESCRIBE THE OVERALL CONCEPT OF EACH OF THE PRODUCTIONS AND EXPLAIN A LITTLE BIT ABOUT THESE CHOICES, FOR EXAMPLE, WHY YOU CHOSE TO DO *MACBETH* IN MODERN DRESS (AS WITH *MUCH ADO*) BUT *ROMEO AND JULIET* WITH THIS ANACHRONISTIC FEEL?

On *Romeo and Juliet* I worked with designer Ben Staines and what we were very clear about was that if young people are going to come to the Globe, most of them will be coming for the first time and the one thing that we didn't want was to make it gimmicky and to take away from the architecture of the space. It could be quite tempting to do things with your design that could take away from what is already there, but we wanted young people to come and experience The Globe as well as the play. With *Romeo and Juliet* we also didn't just want to update it for the sake of it. We could have had all the kids on mobiles with baggy trousers, but that wasn't what we wanted to do either. We wanted to take the audience on a magical journey. Shakespeare himself is quite unspecific in that play. OK it's Verona, but it's Verona/England in the 1590s and so we wanted to get that sense of a mix of worlds and styles. So we went for this thing that we called 'Period-Urban'. It mixes Elizabethan costume with something a little bit more modern, which is similar to how it may have been when it was first performed. They may well have mixed a little bit of what they thought Verona might have been like in the 1400s with whatever they could get from the 1590s, so we mixed and matched. The back wall was a kind of Veronese building front but with graffiti on it, but the graffiti was done in such a way that there were no words, but rather patterns. We were able to get a few hoodies in but without saying – 'This is you up here'. I think that a lot of young people's Shakespeare can be in danger of trying to say – 'Look, it's you. We may sound funny but actually we're no different to you.' That's fine, but it's not what we wanted to do.

MACBETH WAS CONTEMPORARY THOUGH, WASN'T IT?

Yes. I've got a real thing about doublet and hose unless it is really good. And having done this a few times now we have learnt a lot and know that there is no point in putting obstacles there that are going to hinder the story. For example, putting codpieces on the actors – we know that that is going to mean at least 15 minutes for the audience to recover from hysteria. I think that with *Macbeth*, one of the conversations that came up with designer, Isla Shaw, was that this is a world that has been ravaged by unrest and war. So it felt right that there should be a military backdrop to this. Even Lady Macbeth's costumes had a slight military cut and look to them. These people are used to violence. Again we went for something that is sort of like our world, but it's not, so we're not being too specific, although we are using the Scottish flag. And, of course, we're living in a world now where young people are seeing so many images of war and so it seemed right to allude to that through modern military dress.

CAN YOU EXPLAIN YOUR CONCEPT FOR THE WITCHES IN THAT PRODUCTION?

We started thinking – 'Who are the witches?' There is so much left unexplained by Shakespeare – who these people are, and what their motives are for what they do, and what they do exactly? We also knew that we didn't want to do cackling old women. There's nothing wrong with that, but we wanted to do something a bit different. One of the things that came out of discussion was that this was a world where young people had been affected – they had been victims of war – and that it might be interesting to go down that road with the witches. So, what we developed in rehearsal was this idea that one of the witches – played by Karen Bryson – was possibly a mother of two kids who had been killed during the war. Now, none of this is explicit in our production but it was something for her to think about. So we then came up with the idea that the other two witches might be school kids – the spirits of her children. Again this is not explained in the production, but she found it useful to think that what she is doing by planting these seeds in Macbeth's mind is an act of revenge: the war is responsible for the death of her kids. As the audience were coming in we had soldiers outside, checking them and asking for their papers, and then when they came in, the two actors playing the witches would be sat on stage dressed as school kids, chatting to them and asking whether the audience had seen their Mum – as if they were trapped in some sort of afterlife. It was great because the kids got to know them and engage with them. And then, through the magic of theatre, they disappeared, and the show started, and then, when they made their appearance in the second scene one of them sat up in the body bag, and then got out of the bag, and the other came out of one of the boxes, and the kids were totally freaked out, because they recognized them but they were different – they had gone backstage and got messed up with blood and a dishevelled uniform.

AND I SUPPOSE THAT BY HAVING THEM SUDDENLY SIT UP AND EMERGE OUT OF A BODY BAG AND THEM HAVING CHANGED FROM WHEN THE KIDS SAW THEM BEFORE, YOU GET THE SENSE OF FEAR AND HORROR AT THE SUPERNATURAL THAT MAYBE WE HAVE LOST. WE NOW TEND TO ASSOCIATE WITCHES WITH HARRY POTTER, WHEREAS MANY OF THE JACOBEANS WOULD HAVE BELIEVED IN WITCHES AND BEEN TERRIFIED BY THEM.

Absolutely. I did a lot of reading about witches at the time and I didn't realize until then the level of fear that people would have had about them. As you say, we have lost all that, so we had to find another way in there. That was important to us, to find another way to create that sense of eeriness. Another thing that worried me about *Macbeth* was that until we did it there had only been one other production at the Globe, and it seemed that it might have been avoided because there have been so many fabulous productions in indoor theatres, where you can have special effects and lighting. And I was wondering about how you create this sense of tension and fear for the audience when you can't turn off the lights.

HOW DO YOU THINK YOUR PRODUCTIONS HAVE MADE A VIRTUE OF THE SPACE AND THE FACT THAT YOU ARE WORKING IN DAYLIGHT? CAN YOU USE THESE ELEMENTS TO ADVANTAGE RATHER THAN SEE THEM AS AN OBSTACLE?

I think that this is the thing about the Globe. Having acted and directed there now, if you use all the perceived obstacles in the space then it is the most liberating, freeing place to work in. The possible obstacles are the roof being open, the pillars and the fact that it is pretty much in the round. So, we found that you have to move it; it has to be active. And we are playing to an audience who are traditionally perceived as not that bothered by Shakespeare and generally used to fast edits in films and playing computer games, so we had to try to use all the resources we could to engage the audience. You have to play to the whole auditorium, not just those in front of the pillars, so we did lots of work about taking the play out to the audience. And when you do, you understand why he wrote the way he did and it becomes more exciting to play and to watch. Again, using the yard really works – bringing actors through the yard makes the audience really feel part of the action. And we took that to another level with *Macbeth* when we had zip wires going across the theatre and ladders. It is often very hard to engage the upper galleries in these shows, so I was really keen to bring them in. We've also had to find ways to control the surges of sound from the audience. So at the top of the show for *Macbeth* we had a loud explosion, which terrified them and we had special permission to have electric guitars, and this came above the noise of the crowd.

IT SEEMS THAT EVEN MORE THAN IN THE GLOBE MAIN SEASON PRODUCTIONS, THE PRACTICE OF TALKING DIRECTLY TO THE AUDIENCE IS A KEY FEATURE OF THE PLAYING SHAKESPEARE PRODUCTIONS. OFTEN THE ACTORS SEEM TO USE IT TO MAKE A NOISY SECTION OF THE AUDIENCE QUIETEN DOWN, OR TO GRAB THEIR ATTENTION. JAMES GARNON DOES THIS PARTICULARLY WELL IN *MACBETH*.

I am glad that you noticed that. James is a brilliant actor and he knows the space very well which really helps, and he gets the fact that this stuff is not internalized – it is shared and debated with an audience. And, if you take a thought directly to one person in the audience it seems to spread through the crowd, and that is a very useful way of engaging them. I found when playing Benedick that if you felt that you were losing the audience, and you really know with a young crowd, then one of the most effective things is to take the time to engage them and to bring them in. After a few shows you really start to find the lines that you can share with the audience, and if I was doing a show in the main season I would also want to find those moments.

THE PRODUCTIONS SEEM QUITE DIVERSE IN THEIR CASTING – ROMEO WITH HIS LONDON ACCENT, MERCUTIO WITH HIS NORTHERN ACCENT, AND THE CAST BEING FROM A RANGE OF DIFFERENT ETHNIC BACKGROUNDS. WAS THIS IMPORTANT IN REFLECTING THE DIVERSITY OF THE AUDIENCE?

That's really interesting. I don't think that it was necessarily a conscious decision. I remember casting Romeo, and there were lots of really beautiful, well-spoken young actors, who were great, but I felt strongly that that wasn't the sort of person that Romeo was. I was really keen to find someone who was more of a young lad about town, because I think he is. He's just a guy who is all over the place, who is going through puberty and discovering himself. James Alexandrou happened to come through the door and he seemed right. He hadn't done much Shakespeare, but I knew he could get there, and I liked what he brought to the character because he wasn't your archetypal Romeo.

THE THING IS THAT YOU THEN BELIEVE IN THE ROMEO WHO ENGAGES IN BAWDY JOKES WITH MERCUTIO AND BENVOLIO WHICH OFTEN SEEMS INCONGRUOUS WITH THE SENSITIVE ROMANTIC.

Absolutely. I have to say though that that casting came with its own problems. I had assumed that because he hadn't been in Eastenders for a couple of years that it wouldn't have been an issue, but it took about 10 minutes for the shouts of 'Martin' (he played Martin Fowler) to die down. To his credit he grabbed their attention and they became completely enthralled by his Romeo.

DID YOU PREPARE THE TEXTS, AND HOW? WHICH EDITION DID YOU START WITH?

I did all the editing. I think that I used the Penguin and cut it down from there. One of the things that I have been very clear about is to keep as many of the words as possible. It is easy to try to tell the story in as few words as possible, but this is not what this project is about. It is about giving young people a full-scale production. However, there are time constraints, and there are these problems of the number of actors available. Some of the more obscure stuff which no one is going to get goes.

I NOTICED THAT YOU CUT A LOT OF THE FINAL SCENE OF *ROMEO AND JULIET*.

It does go on a lot in the tomb. I probably could have kept Paris in that scene, but I didn't think that we missed anything. I thought that we should probably just crack on with the story. Likewise I cut the Friar's speech.

WELL, EVERYONE IN THE AUDIENCE ALREADY KNOWS EVERYTHING THAT THE FRIAR IS GOING TO SAY AND THE AUDIENCE IS READY FOR THE PLAY TO END.

It is really bizarre. Maybe it is one of those 'in case you missed anything' moments. Maybe it is to give the guy who played the Friar more lines. I mean, our Friar, Colin Hurley, would have delivered it beautifully but at that time in the play I think that you just need to get on with it.

IN *ROMEO AND JULIET* IT SEEMED THAT EVERY TIME ANYONE MENTIONED ANYTHING TO DO WITH SEX, THE AUDIENCE ERRUPTED AND DIDN'T QUIETEN DOWN FOR QUITE SOME TIME. I NOTICED THAT IN *MACBETH* YOU CUT LINES LIKE 'COME TO MY WOMAN'S BREAST', WAS THAT BECAUSE YOU HAD LEARNT THAT THIS WOULD PROBABLY JUST CAUSE DISRUPTION?

The Globe gives you a kind of ownership of the play when you are watching in that space. The space seems to be asking for a reaction. The audience feel able to respond, and I love it when they do that; I love it. But, there are moments where it's not helpful in getting the story over. At that point in the play you don't want to lose them. It's a really important bit and so we thought, let's nip it in the bud.

WHEN YOU DID *MUCH ADO ABOUT NOTHING,* DID YOU ANTICIPATE THESE REACTIONS, BECAUSE I HAVE TO SAY THAT I WASN'T EXPECTING THAT 14-YEAR-OLDS WOULD CHEER AND APPLAUD EVERY KISS?

I think it's fair to say that we had no idea whatsoever. We thought we did, but we didn't. We had our first entry as the boys through the yard, so we were waiting outside listening, and at the very beginning of the very first show, Colin Hurley, who played Dogberry, came onstage to ask everyone to turn off their mobile phones, and the place erupted and they wouldn't shut up for him and he stood there for quite a while and then just had to walk off. We were standing outside thinking 'What on earth is going on? This is going to be crazy'. So we got all pumped up and really went for it in terms of contacting these kids as we came through the yard. We were basically saying – 'It's OK, you can join us'. I remember getting on stage and just having to take the biggest breaths in order to get the sound out above them. I think in terms of an acting work-out there's nothing like it.

When we did *Much Ado* the second time around, there was a moment when I put my arm around the actor playing Claudio in a friendly gesture, and the first time I did it the place just went mad and were shouting out 'gay', and I remember looking at them and thinking – 'What on earth?' But because of that reaction we just cut that move because it's not helpful sometimes. It's only useful when it is in tune with the story, for example, it was really touching when the audience went 'aah' when Romeo looked upset, it showed that they were really with his story.

SOME OF THE REACTIONS WERE VERY ODD THOUGH, WEREN'T THEY? THERE WAS THAT MOMENT IN *MACBETH* AFTER MACBETH RECEIVES THE NEWS THAT LADY MACBETH HAS DIED WHEN THE AUDIENCE USED TO LAUGH; AND THEY LAUGHED A LITTLE AT THE DEATHS OF ROMEO AND JULIET ON THE DAY THAT I SAW IT.

I think that the laughs are to do with feeling uncomfortable. They're not quite sure how to react. Sometimes Romeo and Juliet's death they would react with – 'Don't drink it' or 'Don't do it', 'She's alive!' There's something about that play that is really interesting because you are told at the beginning what happens, you know the story and yet you are still willing them at the end to survive. So when they did die there is that uncomfortable feeling and the laughing is a kind of nervous reaction.

WHO DECIDED NOT TO HAVE AN INTERVAL? I WAS AMAZED THAT THE KIDS REMAINED ENGAGED FOR NEARLY TWO HOURS WITHOUT A BREAK, PARTICULARLY WHEN SOME OF THEM WERE STANDING.

It was partly to do with the logistics of manoeuvring the crowd and partly the time issue – they have to be out by a certain time. We've had a number of discussions about whether it is too long, but we've thought that they can deal with it. They are certainly never bored. It is very encouraging to see them all so engaged.

THERE WAS A LOT OF PUBLICITY ABOUT YOU CONSULTING THE POLICE ABOUT THE FIGHT IN *ROMEO AND JULIET*. WHAT EXACTLY HAPPENED?

It's not true. It was an unfortunate lack of communication. I think that there may have been an informal conversation between someone in Globe Education about the young people who were coming but nothing at all like what was reported. It was entirely fabricated. It was extraordinary because it generated radio debates and lots of press articles, but it was based on nothing.

Notes

1 Contemporary references suggest that the Globe theatre held around 3,000 audience members, around twice the number permitted by current health and safety laws in the new theatre. If we suppose that the yard held around double the 700 'groundlings' who are permitted to stand in it today, it would have been extremely crowded. Dessen suggests that 'the high value they placed on costumes would preclude close physical contact with the groundlings' (2008, p. 48) who Thomas Dekker famously dubbed 'stinkards' (1609, p. 2) due to their smell.

2 In the 2007 production Beatrice was similarly clad in the early scenes in dark colours, with a long-sleeved black top, black trousers and a black coat.

3 Kenneth Muir explains that this was 'an old joke' (1984, p.xxii)

4 At the time of the play's publication, 'Father Garnet's equivocation during his trial for complicity in the Gunpowder Plot was still an active and much publicised concern' (Mullaney, 1995, p. 123).

5 Paul Edmondson notes that in Declan Donnellan's 1987 production for Cheek by Jowl 'a female Porter . . . made jokes about stockbrokers and the Minister for Health, while in Gregory Doran's 1999 RSC production, Stephan Noonan was 'an interesting example of an improvised Porter' (2005, p. 129).

Web resources

Department for Children, Schools and Families (2008), 'Shakespeare for all Ages and Stages':
www.education.gov.uk/publications/eOrderingDownload/ShakespearesBooklet.pdf
Department for Education, 'Improving Teaching of Shakespeare':
http://webarchive.nationalarchives.gov.uk/20110809091832/
http://www.teachingandlearningresources.org.uk/secondary/english/improving-teaching-shakespeare
Globe Education, Playing Shakespeare website:
http://playingshakespeare.org/archive/

CHAPTER TWO

Shakespeare on Film: Baz Luhrmann's *William Shakespeare's Romeo + Juliet* (1996), Michael Almereyda's *Hamlet* (2000) and Christine Edzard's *The Children's A Midsummer Night's Dream* (2001)

'The definitive *Romeo and Juliet* for the contemporary teenage audience' (Dixon, 2000, p. 132): so Wheeler W. Dixon describes Baz Luhrmann's *Romeo + Juliet* (1996). Luhrmann's film is that most frequently associated with Shakespeare for young people and has been widely written about; praised and criticized in almost equal measure – for its originality and contemporary relevance and for its dumbing-down of Shakespeare and frantic camera work. The film, 'aggressive[ly] market[ed] toward a teenage audience' (Loehlin, 2000, p. 121) has also been credited with 'initiating the boom in Shakespearean screen adaptations for the teen market' (Friedman, 2008, p. 1). Douglas Lanier views this film as partly responsible for the 'series of youth pop Shakespeares – *10 Things I Hate About You* (1999), *Never Been Kissed* (1999), Almereyda's *Hamlet* (2000), '*O*' (2001), *Get Over It* (2001), *The Glass House* (2001), *Rave Macbeth* (2001), *The Street King* (2002), and *Deliver Us from Eva* (2003)' (2006, p. 182). Luhrmann's *Romeo + Juliet* and Michael Almereyda's *Hamlet* differ from the other films cited by

Lanier in using Shakespeare's text, albeit often rearranged, heavily cut and sometime rewritten. Friedman provides a useful terminology to distinguish between these two types of film describing as 'versions' films that 'primarily use Shakespeare's original language for a particular play and 'adaptations' as those that employ the 'basic plotline, characters, and thematic issues from a particular play' but use, for the most part 'the contemporary vernacular' (2008, p. 3). Chapter 9 explores such 'adaptations', while this chapter concentrates on film 'versions' of Shakespeare that are clearly designed to appeal to young people, focusing on *Romeo + Juliet* and Almereyda's *Hamlet*, alongside Christine Edzard's *The Children's Midsummer Night's Dream* (2001), explicitly aimed at children aged 8–12 with a cast consisting of this age group. It looks at the three films' style and setting, appeal to young audiences, treatment of the text, reception and wider impact on the perception of Shakespeare for children and young adults.

William Shakespeare's Romeo + Juliet

Baz Luhrmann's *William Shakespeare's Romeo + Juliet* has been described as a 'pop version' of the play, its modern rock soundtrack, rapid camera action and swift intercutting of scenes often reminiscent of a music video. Indeed, while Shakespeare's play often requires an audience to concentrate for as much as 15 minutes on a scene set in a single location, Luhrmann's film splits these into a series of short scenes with frequent shifts in location. This is Shakespeare for the cinema generation, where, audiences are unused to watching scenes of long than a couple of minutes. Shakespeare's 1.1, for example, intercut with the title sequence, is divided into over 30 scenes, moving from the 'Gas station' to the 'Minimart', the interior of a 'Chopper', to the 'Prince's Precinct Office' and the inside of 'The Montague limousine' to the 'Beach' (Luhrmann and Pearce, 1996, pp. 3–17). The audience receives constant visual and aural stimulation, arguably to excess, but there is little danger of boredom, a frequent accusation flung at Shakespeare in the classroom.

Luhrmann transfers Shakespeare's play from Renaissance Verona to the contemporary fictional American city of Verona Beach, a 'placeless' (Rothwell, 1999, p. 241) city constructed from multiple 'images and icons of the twentieth century' (Luhrmann, 1996) where the two families are rival leaders of corporate industries and the young gangs of Montagues and Capulets drive fast cars, commit arson, take drugs and engage in gun fights. As Kenneth S. Rothwell remarks, 'there is absolutely nothing new about putting Shakespeare in modern dress but dressing him in the jeans and T-shirts and pierced bodies of the MTV generation ratchets the transgressiveness up a notch' (1999, p. 241). One of the most transgressive sequences is that leading up to the Capulet's ball in which Mercutio's Queen

Mab speech is transformed into a rant about drug addiction. This speech about dreams and fairies is notoriously difficult to interpret, standing, as some have argued, outside the body of the text as a 'set piece' (Cartwright, 1991, p. 54; Kahn, 1981, p. 91; Bloom, 2005, p. 38). Within a contemporary setting Mercutio's musings about the 'fairies' midwife' (1.4.55) who haunts men's dreams are not easy to place; however, Luhrmann finds a contemporary equivalent to Mab – an ecstasy-like drug that distorts perception and alters the mind. The moment in which Romeo takes the white pill before heading off to the Capulet party is typical of many young people's preparation for an evening out and places the young protagonist and his friends firmly in the world of contemporary youth culture.

By updating the play to this contemporary environment Luhrmann is clearly bringing the characters and themes closer to the experiences of his modern teenage audiences; however, he resents the implication that in doing so he has in some way taken the play further away from Shakespeare. Indeed, the director's commentary on the DVD is peppered with assertions about fidelity to Shakespeare's intentions – 'our rule really was to maintain absolutely the language, but to ask the question at all times – if Shakespeare were making a movie, what choice do you think he would make?' (Luhrmann, 1996) – and with comments about Shakespeare's own status in the popular culture of his day. Defending his film against the accusation that by introducing pop music into the play he has in some way 'desecrated Shakespeare', Luhrmann responds that 'one of the things about Shakespeare was that he totally stole popular culture or anything on the street . . . but particularly he took popular music and just put it in his shows because that was a way of engaging his audience in the story telling. Every choice we've made in terms of cinematic devices has been grounded in some reality of the Elizabethan stage' (1996). Certainly evidence suggests that in the Renaissance theatre all productions were costumed predominantly in contemporary clothing irrespective of their historical setting, providing a similar experience for an Elizabethan audience to that created by Luhrmann for a twenty-first-century audience.[1]

The primary motivation behind the modern setting was, according to Luhrmann, to make the often complex and antiquated language of the play accessible to modern audiences not regularly acquainted with Shakespeare's work, by finding 'modern day images and equivalents that could decode the language of Shakespeare' (1996). For example, Luhrmann explains the layers of equivalents in the first scene – the choice of the gas station as a modern-day equivalent to the town square and the allusion to Western films as a means of situating a twentieth-century audience in 'a world where people carried weapons all the time' (1996). He also explains the inclusion of the large Jesus statue in the centre of the fictional city, as a shorthand means of emphasizing the centrality of religion in the lives of Shakespeare's characters. Religious imagery abounds in this film, bound up with all the major characters, and helps to provide a framework of Catholicism within which the dominant concerns of the play – the necessary marriage of the two young characters prior to their sexual liaison, patriarchal dominance, the central role of the Friar and the union of the protagonists in death, can operate within a twentieth-century setting.

Although Luhrmann's film was not exclusively made for a teenage audience, it has become synonymous with Shakespeare for young people. James N. Loehlin argues that the depiction of the central characters, at war with the older generation, 'links it to a whole series of teen films from the 1950s onwards', films that portray teenagers as 'misunderstood adolescents' (2000, p. 122). Luhrmann played on this association by casting young actors readily associated with teen films. His decision to cast Leonardo DiCaprio as Romeo was influenced by his view that this actor 'does seem to symbolize his generation' – the generation for whom the director sought to 'reveal these eternal characters anew' (Luhrmann and Pearce, 1996, 'A Note from Baz Luhrmann'). All too often in the theatre the protagonists are played by actors in their late twenties or early thirties, this being the stage in most actors' careers at which they are sufficiently experienced to play such a major role. But frequently these actors lack the youthfulness, vulnerability and awkwardness of teenagers and are unlikely to resonate with audiences of actual 13-year-olds. Following in the tradition of Franco Zeffirelli's 1968 film version of the play that featured 15-year-old Olivia Hussey and 17-year-old Leonard Whiting as the lovers, Luhrmann's film emphasizes the youth of the protagonists with the young-looking 16-year-old Claire Danes as Juliet and 21-year-old DiCaprio as Romeo.

Jennifer L. Martin suggests, however, that Luhrmann's 'depiction of adolescence through these two characters is more worldly' that of Zeffirelli's film (2002, 41), undoubtedly partly a result of the film's contemporary setting. When we first meet Romeo he is the archetypal rebel – a James Dean figure, smoking a cigarette; 'a troubled adolescent youth' to whom a young, contemporary audience can relate (Luhrmann, 1996). Juliet, although often dressed in white (most notably as an angel at the ball), is not characterized by fragility and innocence but by intelligence, knowingness and emotional maturity. She darts withering looks at her mother, laughs at Paris in the ball scene, pushes Romeo back into the elevator for a second kiss and delivers the line 'nor any other part / Belonging to a man' (2.1.83–4) with a knowing smile. Her isolation from the other characters, which Luhrmann identifies as key to our understanding of Juliet – 'she lives in this ivory castle and it is very difficult to get at her, or for her to get out' (1996) – also serves to make her appear independent. She has no connection with her selfish and neurotic mother or her abusive and overbearing father, and unlike Romeo with his gang of friends, we never see her contemporaries. Although her connection with the Nurse is one of affection – 'the trusted, loved nanny' of Juliet (Luhrmann, 1996) – we see little intimacy between the pair.

Luhrmann comments that his casting of Danes was partly due to her 'unmissable characteristic' of being 'a sixteen-year-old girl with the maturity of a thirty-year-old', well suited to the character of Juliet whom he describes as 'a very smart, active character' who 'really drives the piece' (Luhrmann and Pearce, 1996, 'A Note from Baz Luhrmann'). However, Michael Anderegg argues in opposition; that Luhrmann's cuts to Juliet's role diminish Shakespeare's character – 'quite capable of dissimulation and irony as well as anger and fierce determination', turning her into 'an ideal Victorian Juliet . . . neither a contemporary teenager nor a Shakespearean heroine' (Anderegg, 2003, p. 62). It is true that in Luhrmann's film Juliet loses some of her more intricate and deceptive wordplay – 'Indeed I never shall be satisfied / With Romeo until I behold him, dead, / Is my poor heart . . .' (3.5.93–5). Nevertheless, Danes' Juliet does not come across as a submissive figure. She 'cries out impatiently' (Luhrmann and Pearce, 1996, p. 89) to the Nurse in the equivalent of 2.4, delivering the line 'I would thou hadst my bones and I thy news' (2.4.27) 'under her breath' (p. 89) in evident frustration; snaps at her mother – 'Now, by Saint Peter's Church, and Peter too,/ He shall not make me there a joyful bride' (3.5.116–17) and screams 'Proud can I never be of what I hate' (3.5.147) at her father in aggressive defiance.

The relationship between Romeo and Juliet is central to the play's story; however, as Deborah Cartmell notes, at times the love between the central pair is 'overshadowed by the more colourful world of violence which surrounds them' (2000, p. 46). Luhrmann creates a world of vivid brutality with teenage gang culture at its centre – a multicultural world of 'guns, drugs, conspicuous consumption and civic breakdown' (Loehlin, 2000, p. 121). This is a highly contemporary world, which brings to the fore some of the most pervasive and worrying aspects of modern youth culture – casual violence, recreational drug-taking and the consistent influence and intervention of the media – albeit often taken to aesthetic extremes.

The fight scenes in 1.1 and 3.1, although substantially reduced in terms of dialogue, are drawn out with a series of violent bouts. In the first scene, following a handful of lines, mostly reassigned and rearranged, interspersed with a series of taunting noises and laughter, a gun fight of around 2 minutes ensues prior to the Prince's order to 'Throw your mistempered weapons to the ground' (1.1.84). The elaborate fight choreography is 'highly reminiscent of films directed by Sergio Leone or John Woo' (Hatchuel, 2004, p. 28) and does much to establish the film's credentials as an action as well as a romantic movie. Similarly in 3.1, the fight scene in expanded to take in a series of fighting styles and a number of locations, from the beachfront where the arrival of the Capulets references 'a gun fight scene from a Western' (Luhrmann, 1996) to the wrecked theatre of the Sycamore Grove where Mercutio is stabbed with a shard of glass. Following Mercutio's demise the fight then moves from the beach to the streets with a car chase ending in a slow-motion crash after which Romeo fires three shots at Tybalt, sending him flying back into the water at the base of the Christ monument. These high-energy violent sequences clearly appealed to the young audiences who saw the films. Peter Newman, writing about their responses, quotes a young boy who remarked: 'I thought it was going to be a girly film, but there was a lot of killing – that was cool' (1997, p. 37). Although Loehlin argues that this response and others that likened the film to an 'MTV video' are 'somewhat depressing' (2000, pp. 131–2), the very fact that teenagers were responding positively towards Shakespeare, able to understand and become involved in the plot, to listen to Shakespeare's language without commenting negatively on its intelligibility or archaic words must be seen as a positive outcome. Indeed, that young people themselves were relating the film to contemporary genres seems to bear out Luhrmann's assertion that his film is putting Shakespeare's work back at the centre of popular culture.

Luhrmann's film is intimately related to popular culture from the outset through its use of the media as a framing and highlighting device. The film opens with a television screen from which a newscaster delivers the prologue as a news item, and ends with the same voice, taking the Prince's lines – 'A glooming peace this morning with it brings . . .' (5.3.304), as footage is shown of the lovers' bodies being removed from the tomb. The tone of the film's ending is, however, difficult to discern. The death of the young lovers is almost glorified with the tomb glowing with the light of hundreds of candles and the soundtrack of Wagner's 'Liebestod' ('love-death') from *Tristan und Isolde* linking them to other romantic literary pairs whose relationships are seen to be consummated in death. The sentimental montage of their love affair that follows Juliet's suicide seems to enhance this notion of their love coming to fruition in this final moment. However, the film does not end on this note of heightened romantic tragedy. Luhrmann cuts the exchange between Montague and Capulet in which Montague pledges to 'raise her [Juliet's] statue in pure gold' (5.3.298) and Capulet to reciprocate. Instead the film ends with television images of the bodies of the lovers being taken from the tomb in body-bags, the unglamorous reality of their fate brought to the fore in the suddenly unsaturated and grainy images. This final media intrusion denies the lovers their private, romantic union – as Loehlin comments, 'their idyll is interrupted, reduced, commodified, turned into televised spectacle' (2000, p. 130).

The tone of the ending is, as Samuel Crowl remarks, an issue of 'lively critical debate about how ironically (or pessimistically) we are meant to read' it (2003, p. 134). Luhrmann himself seems to argue for a straightforward, sentimental reading of the ending, contrasting it with the energetic, metafilmic, comic opening sequence: 'as the vortex moves towards death we strip away the heightenedness, we strip away the comedy, we strip away the artifice, until finally the boy goes to the girl' (1996). Co-screenwriter Craig Pearce further confirms the intended seriousness of the film's final moments: 'It was very important for us . . . to really feel the tragedy of loss of these two young lives. You have all the running around and fighting and glamour at the beginning, but you've got to actually, really feel the loss at the end' (1996).

The film ends with the track – 'Exit Song for a Movie' – written specially by Radiohead once they had viewed pieces of the film and 'talked about the feel of it' (Luhrmann, 1996). With its lines – 'we hope your rules and wisdom choke you' – the song highlights the culpability of the intergenerational conflict in the tragedy, apparently laying at least some of the blame for events at the feet of the Montague and Capulet parents. Anderegg quotes one of the film's producers who asserts that 'the moral of the story . . . is that if you teach hatred to your children you lose them' (2003, p. 80). However, as he goes on to argue, it is less the parents than the younger generation who are seen to 'maintain the deadly feud' (p. 63) in Shakespeare's play. Certainly in Luhrmann's film the images seared on the viewer's eye at the end are those of the violent and indulgent actions of the young Montagues and Capulets – a terrifying picture of the tragic loss of young lives generated through gang warfare, which is as much a feature of contemporary society as of Shakespeare's Verona.

Although Luhrmann's film substantially pares down the Shakespearean text, it opens with the prologue repeated twice – first as a news report, delivered from within a television screen, and then, as the film expands from televisual to cinematic space, as a voiceover akin to a cinema trailer, the lines intercut with titles for the central characters, newspaper headlines and images of Verona. Luhrmann explains that this duplication of the prologue was designed 'to give the audience a chance to acclimatize . . . their ear to the language' (1996). Both the repetition of this essential background information and the series of visual images with which the film begins ease the viewer into the Shakespearean text, situating them in the world of the film and its central characters before they are required to engage with substantial passages of dialogue.

Even the substantial passages of dialogue are much reduced from the full text, Luhrmann replacing some of the play's language with visual imagery. This is an inevitable consequence of transferring a text written for a theatre in which plays were performed in broad daylight with no lighting effects, limited scenery and, often compromised sight-lines which, Warren D. Smith argues, required essential pieces of action to be described to those unable to see them (1975, p. 14) to the naturalistic medium of film. Lines of explanation or description such as 'The grey-eyed morn smiles on the frowning night' (2.2.1) become unnecessary when it is possible to show the arrival of 'the beautiful morning' (Luhrmann and Pearce, 1996, p. 73). However, Luhrmann's film goes further than merely translating such descriptions of setting into visual realities. The visual image of water is, for example, used to highlight a series of themes in the play – purity, sexuality and, as Luhrmann explains, the need to 'escape' (1996), a desire expressed by Romeo in Shakespeare's play through the image of baptismal waters – 'Call me but love, and I'll be new baptized; / Henceforth I never will be Romeo' (2.1.92–3). When we first see Juliet, her 'serene' features are submerged in the bath as she enjoys a moment of peace from the frantic screaming of the Nurse and Lady Capulet. The young lovers' first meeting is then conducted in silence through an aquarium, while the waters of the swimming pool provide a sanctuary from surveillance. These silent moments, charged with sexual tension, are some of the most powerful in the film – more so, one might argue, than the gabbled exchanges of heavily edited dialogue – and suggest, as Courtney Lehmann notes, 'a symbolic return to a prelinguistic economy of representation, wherein image is anterior and, indeed, preferable to language' (2001, p. 210).

While many of the cuts function to make the story flow with greater speed and clarity and little is lost in terms of essential content, the main criticism that can be levelled at Luhrmann's cutting is that it appears to show little regard for the play's verse, a lack of concern reflected in the frequent presentation in the Screenplay of lines of verse as prose. The verse exchanges between Romeo and Tybalt, for example, in 3.1 are pared down such that the lines consistently lapse out of the verse form:

Tybalt   Boy, this shall not excuse the injuries
   That thou hast done me!
   He smashes Romeo across the face; Romeo crashes into the roadway

Tybalt   (yelling) Turn and draw.
   A cut has opened in the side of Romeo's mouth. He . . . speaks through bloodied teeth.

Romeo   I never injured thee,
   And so, good Capulet, which name I tender
   As dearly as mine own . . . (Luhrmann and Pearce, 1996, p. 100)

Presumably partly with his target audience in mind, Luhrmann also cuts much of the play's rhetoric and complex wordplay, meaning that viewers are rarely faced with lengthy monologues or dialogue that does not relate directly to the story. Punning exchanges such as those between Sampson and Gregory at the beginning of the first scene are cut, as are the Nurse's comic digressions about Juliet's age in 1.3 (lines 18–59). In terms of monologues, Friar Laurence's speech in 2.2 (lines 1–30), cut from 30 lines to 14, becomes a science lesson to a pair of altar boys, Romeo's speech at the beginning of 5.1 (lines 1–11), reduced from 11 to 7 lines, becomes a diary entry and Juliet's three monologues are severely cut, 'The clock struck nine' (2.4.1–17) speech being entirely absent, 'Gallop apace' (3.2.1–33) reduced from 33 lines to 12 and her 'potion' speech (4.3.14–57) pared down from 43 lines to 3. This is undoubtedly partly because monologues are difficult to sustain within the naturalistic framework of a film such as this, where characters rarely break the fourth wall. While films such as Richard Loncraine's *Richard III* and Oliver Parker's *Othello* feature asides or soliloquies spoken directly to the camera, a more common filmic device is to render such speeches internal monologues with the lines relayed in voiceover, as if the audience has access to the character's thoughts, a technique which Luhrmann uses only for Romeo's 'And all this day an unaccustomed spirit . . .' (5.1.4) diary entry.

One of the most extreme cuts – which, in fact, mirrors that of Bill Buckhurst in the Globe's 'Playing Shakespeare' production of the play is that of Paris and Friar Laurence from the final scene. Following a high-octane chase sequence in which Romeo runs towards the church, evading police patrol cars and the marksman on the Prince's chopper, he enters Juliet's tomb alone – 'once you enter the world of the tomb . . . it's all about Romeo and Juliet' (Luhrmann, 1996). This focus on the two young lovers simplifies the final scene, removing the friar's inherently undramatic repetition of events to which the audience have already been privy, and places Romeo and Juliet firmly at the centre of the tragedy – a story of young lives destroyed.

Reviews of Luhrmann's film were mixed. The directorial inventiveness was not in question; however, while some critics found that his constant innovation made the film fresh and accessible – 'a stylish and stylised reworking of a timeless story rendered palatable for a broad audience' (Film 4, 1996) – for others it obscured the story – 'Why' asked Janet Maslin in the *New York Times*, 'bury *Romeo and Juliet* amid all this creative ferment?' (1996). Justified criticism was also made of the naturalistic, rushed delivery of the young actors in whose mouths Shakespeare's language is barely recognizable as verse and its rhetorical and poetic richness almost entirely obliterated. Shakespeare's language – its sounds, wordplay and rhythm – is the victim of this film, consistently cut, mumbled or swamped by the insistent soundtrack.

Lanier takes on many of the criticisms levelled at the film, asking a series of questions – 'Did such adaptation lead to dumbed-down accessibility or travesty? Was Shakespeare's oppositional potential being blunted, his cultural authority appropriated by an omnivorous pop culture industry? Was pop adaptation merely a matter of dressing up traditional Shakespeare in a glossy pop veneer?' He suggests that Luhrmann's film is more sophisticated than many of its critics infer, anticipating these types of criticism by using the device of 'cinematic self-parody' to take the film to 'comic extremes' and create a 'knowing distance from the act of contemporizing Shakespeare' (2006, p. 183). Certainly Luhrmann's film contains a series of witty postmodern references to Shakespeare's other works, an intertextuality that seem designed to appeal more to Shakespeare aficionados than teenagers encountering Shakespeare's work for the first time – the theatre in town is called 'The Globe', the beach store 'The Merchant of Verona Beach', and the cleaners 'Out, Out Damn Spot Cleaners'. The film's use of self-conscious cinematic and televisual devices – the newscaster who delivers the prologue as a television broadcast and the allusions to the genres of pop-video, gangster movie and Western – may also be seen as contemporary equivalents of the metatheatre central to Shakespeare's plays; 'a surrogation of the playful feel of Shakespeare's theatre' (Worthen, 1998, p. 1103) and thus part of Luhrmann's professed aim of recapturing the essence of Shakespeare's play for a contemporary audience.

What became clear, however, was that irrespective of the critics' views, the film found its audience in the teen market. When the *New York Times* asked the question 'Where is the audience willing to watch a classic play thrown in the path of a subway train?' (Maslin, 1996), the answer was, as Crowl remarks, 'in cineplexes across the country and the world: in the secondary schools' (2003, p. 120). The film grossed $11,133 million (Hindle, 2007, p. 244) in its opening weekend, ranking number one at the box office. Crowl notes that when he attended the film on its opening night, the cinema was 'packed with high school kids' who erupted into 'squeals' at the first sighting of DiCaprio (2003, p. 130).

Peter Newman's survey of students between the ages of 14 and 17 indicates that their responses to the film were largely 'enthusiastic' (1997, p. 36). Although some of the remarks indicate that the main attraction for many young people was the film's stars ('The previews looked good, I also like the two starring actors' (K. B., 16); 'Orlando [*sic*] Decaprio [*sic*] is hot!' (D. P., 15)), many of the young people's comments suggest that their viewing of the film enhanced their understanding and appreciation of the play: 'After reading the "book", the film helped me to *see* what I was reading' (J. P., 17); 'some parts of the book that I didn't understand, when I saw the movie, I understood better' (D. P., 14); 'I hated reading the story, but I loved the movie' (P. L., 16) (Newman, 1997, p. 37). Perhaps Luhrmann's greatest achievement has been to sell William Shakespeare's *Romeo and Juliet* to young people who were formerly averse to the author and his work, opening their eyes to the potential of Shakespeare's plays to come alive in performance and to seem contemporary, relevant and intelligible: 'Although Shakespeare's name is attached to the title, viewers might forget and think that they are watching an Elizabethan-language gangsta rap' (J. M., 15); 'When Romeo goes to the party, they give him drugs and he meets Juliet. Kids are always falling in love left and right, and drugs are a part of society' (K. L., 16); 'Shakespeare's swordfights and men in tights do not compare with the violent gun wars between these two tattooed, gun-toting clashing clans' (K. S., 17) (Newman, 1997, pp. 36–7).

Hamlet

If Luhrmann's film was 'Shakespeare for the MTV generation' (King, 2002, p. 252), Almereyda's was '*Hamlet* for the information age' (Kipp, 2003). In this version of the play, Claudius is the CEO of the 'Denmark Corporation', contained within the 'Elsinore Hotel' in Manhattan, a location awash with

CCTV cameras, television screens, phones, intercoms and computers. Hamlet is an amateur film-maker, his soliloquies frequently taking the form of video diaries, while Ophelia is a photographer, recording details of her life on a Polaroid camera. These elements are not, however, used merely superficially, to evoke the contemporary setting. For Almereyda the play's themes of 'innocence and corruption, identity and fate, love and death, the division between thought and action' may be 'heightened, even clarified, when colliding with the spectacle of contemporary media-saturated technology' (2000, p.x). Certainly the play's prominent theme of surveillance is enhanced by the constant presence of equipment designed to observe, scrutinize and record:

> A lot of the play is about people spying on each other and being watched and playing parts and being aware of themselves playing parts. And that corresponds to contemporary reality where cameras are on the present and images within images are on the present, at least in the city. So that seemed like a natural way of mirroring things that were going on in Shakespeare's text. (Almereyda, quoted by Fuchs, 2000)

The ghost is first captured on the security monitor, Ophelia is wired up for her encounter with Hamlet in 3.1 and Hamlet's conversation with Polonius ('To be honest [as this world goes], is to be one man picked out of ten thousand' (2.2.180–1)) is captured on a surveillance camera.

The inability of characters to communicate effectively with one another is a further theme highlighted by the film's use of technology – the ubiquitous telephones and answering machines that place much of the dialogue at a remove. All of Claudius' dealings with Rosencrantz and Guildenstern are conducted over the telephone, Hamlet's utterances at the end of the nunnery scene (3.1.135–44) are left as two messages on Ophelia's answerphone and the second half of Hamlet's exchange with his mother in 3.4 is conducted by phone from the hotel basement. This lack of direct communication – a common feature of contemporary society – adds to the sense of Hamlet's isolation from other characters – his inability to get through to them literally and figuratively. It also serves to suggest Gertrude and Claudius' lack of concern for Hamlet when, prior to the Mousetrap, they are rolling around together on a bed while receiving Rosencrantz and Guildenstern's report on speakerphone. As Almereyda states, this is 'unmistakably a *Hamlet* of its time' (Kipp, 2003), as much an exploration of the anxieties of twenty-first-century America as of Shakespeare's drama.

However, throughout his commentary on the film, Almereyda, like Luhrmann, consistently asserts his desire to stay faithful to Shakespeare's text while updating it – 'An ideal *Hamlet* would be the one most true to Shakespeare and most modern at the same time'; 'The chief thing was to balance respect for the play with respect for contemporary reality' (2000, pp.viii, ix). The difficulty of being faithful to Shakespeare's *Hamlet* is, of course, compounded by the fact that the play exists in three quite different texts, all of which seem to represent the play at a different stage of its theatrical development. There is no such thing as 'Shakespeare's *Hamlet*'. However, Almereyda's fidelity to Shakespeare manifests itself both in his adherence to Shakespearean dialogue (albeit in a dramatically condensed form) and, in a similar fashion to Luhrmann, in his anxiety to use the genre of film to enhance rather than reduce Shakespeare's language – to find 'a parallel visual language that might hold a candle to Shakespeare's poetry' (Almereyda, 2000, p.x). Like Luhrmann, Almereyda makes substantial use of water imagery, particularly in relation to Ophelia, foreshadowing her eventual death by drowning. However, unlike in *Romeo + Juliet,* water seems less associated with purity and intimacy than with reflection and distortion. In addition to being subject to constant observation, the characters in Almereyda's film are consistently confronted with images of themselves, in a series of reflective surfaces – the glass walls of the Elsinore Hotel, the mirrored doors of Gertrude's bedroom and the various watery surfaces into which Ophelia gazes. These 'reflections and refractions' suggest, as Maurice Hindle observes, 'the devious, sinister, evasive and oblique nature of much of the reality of the Manhattan Hamlet world' (2007, p. 202). They also highlight moments of self-scrutiny – Hamlet's 'How all occasions do inform against me' monologue (4.4.31–65, Thompson and Taylor, 2006) delivered into the toilet mirror on the plane to England and Claudius' 'O my offense is rank' (3.3.36–72) soliloquy spoken into the shattered mirror of Gertrude's bedroom, which returns a distorted image, emphasizing the King's inability to see clearly into his soul.

In Hindle's view, 'perhaps the principal device used to invest the movie with the essential dramatic energies and meanings of Shakespeare's play is that of presenting two radically contrasting visual worlds and viewpoints' (2007, p. 199) – the film's main colour visual, shot on super 16mm and Hamlet's amateur movies, displayed in heavily pixelated black and white. This contrast effectively distances Hamlet from Claudius' saturated corporate world and permits the audience a glimpse of events from his troubled and bleak perspective, a perspective devoid of colour and 'mirth' (2.2.298).

Almereyda's film is less visually spectacular than that of Luhrmann, shot on mobile 16mm cameras, and influenced not by the action films that inspired Luhrmann but by the work of Orson Welles – the landscapes 'shot from an odd camera angle' (Crowl, 2003, p. 188). However, although perhaps less obvious than Luhrmann's, this film also had a clear appeal to the youth market, not least in Almereyda's decisions about casting.

Key to Almereyda's conception of the film was the portrayal of Hamlet as a young man. Like Luhrmann's film, Almereyda's *Hamlet* features protagonists younger than is often the case in productions or films of the play (as Almereyda notes, no film of *Hamlet* features a protagonist under 30 (2000, p.viii)). Ethan Hawke, 27 at the time of filming, plays Hamlet as

a 20-something graduate student, while Julia Stiles, who was only 17 when
cast as Ophelia (Crowl, 2003, p. 196), straddles the boundary between
childhood and womanhood. Almereyda comments – 'I was struck by the
fact that no film of *Hamlet* features a truly young man . . . The character
takes on a different cast when seen more clearly as an abandoned son,
a defiant brat, a narcissist, a poet/film-maker/perpetual grad student – a
radiantly promising young man who doesn't quite know who he is' (2000,
p.viii). Of course, the question of Hamlet's age is complicated by the play's
variant texts. Depending on which of the texts one consults, Hamlet is
either 18 or 31.[2] It may be that such a dichotomy resulted from the altering
of the lines to fit the age of the leading actor in various productions on the
Renaissance stage. While Hamlet could conceivably be a student at 30,
other elements of the text – his often petulant behaviour, the election of
Claudius as his father's immediate successor and the constant references to
him as 'young Hamlet' (1.1.151; 5.1.144) – seem to reinforce the sense of
Hamlet as a young man.

Hawke's Hamlet is certainly recognizable as an adolescent – moody and
obtuse, slouching around with 'unkempt' hair and dark glasses, even indoors
(Almereyda, 2000, p. 9). His choice of clothing contrasts with that of the
'adults' in the corporation, who wear suits and ties while Hamlet wears a
knitted bobble hat. As Cartmell notes, this Hamlet seems so unsuited to the
corporate world, so 'childish' beside the 'debonair, well-groomed Claudius'
that Almereyda eventually 'decided to drop the line about Claudius popping
"in between th' election and my hopes" (5.2.65) due to the absurdity of
Hamlet succeeding his father' (2004, p. 82). While Kyle McLaughlin's
Claudius is a 'confident', 'focused' corporate business-man (Almereyda,
2000, p. 10), Hamlet seems to represent a mixture of adolescent grubbiness
and self-conscious rebellion. Throughout the film he is identified with a
series of anti-capitalist revolutionaries – pictures of Che Guevara and
Malcolm X adorning his walls.

Almereyda asserts that he always kept in mind the play's 'adolescence-
primed impact and meaning for me – the rampant parallels between
the melancholy Dane and my many doomed and damaged heroes and
imaginary friends: James Agee, Holden Caulfield, James Dean, Egon
Schiele, Robert Johnson, Vladimir Mayakovsky, Jean Vigo' (2000, p.viii)
many of whom contributed in some way to the creation of the film's
protagonist. Images of James Dean, 'suffering beautifully in *East of Eden*'
(Almereyda, 2000, p. 57) prompt Hamlet's 'O what a rogue and peasant
slave am I' (2.2.552–607) soliloquy in the absence of the players, the
association of the protagonist with this archetypal teenage rebel further
enhancing the impression of his defiant adolescence. Hawke asserts,
similarly to Almereyda, that for him Hamlet has always been 'more like
Kurt Cobain or Holden Caulfield than Laurence Olivier' (Almereyda,
2000, p.xiv), invoking two more tortured souls whose influence is evident
in Hawke's grunge-style, angst and permanently depressive state. Indeed,

Judith Buchanan argues that 'the sheer number of character parallels in the play makes of this Hamlet's malaise almost that of an era rather than merely that of a solitary individual at odds with his generation' (2005, p. 239). It is largely this sense of Hamlet as an archetypal contemporary youth, which helps to give this film its evident teen appeal.

The danger, however, of this interpretation of the character is that it lacks nuance. Hawke's Hamlet seems constantly sullen and temperamental, his performance missing much of the protagonist's potential humour, so evident in David Tennant's recent performance (directed for television by Gregory Doran (2009). If Tennant brought to the role some of the manic energy that characterized his performance as Doctor Who, Hawke's interpretation is haunted by some of his previous roles as teenage loners – a 'self-pitying "slacker" in *Reality Bites* (1994) and introspective student in *Before Sunrise* (1995)' (Rosenthal, 2008, p. 48).

Hawke was not the only actor in the cast associated with films for the teenage market. For Crowl, Stiles similarly brought the ghosts of some of her previous roles to her portrayal of Ophelia – in particular the 'independence and stubbornness' of Kat in Gil Junger's *10 Things I Hate About You* (2003, p. 196). Like Danes' Juliet, Stiles' Ophelia has the spirit of a feisty contemporary teenager, often missing in portrayals of the character that stress her fragility and obedience. Although her Ophelia is infantilized by Polonius, who buys her balloons and insists on tying her shoelaces for her, she is equally capable of showing her resistance to and resentment of both her father and brother – standing 'irked, only half listening' (Almereyda, 2000, p. 25) when Laertes offers her advice, reacting 'sternly, as if to challenge' (p. 36) Polonius' assertions about her relationship with Hamlet and attempting to snatch back Hamlet's letter to her when Polonius shows it to Claudius and Gertrude. Her lines of acquiescence to Laertes, Polonius and Gertrude – ''Tis in my memory locked / And you your self shall keep the key of it' (1.3.85–6), 'I shall obey, my lord' (1.3.136) and 'Madam, I wish it may' (3.1.44) are all cut, further emphasizing her resistance.

Robert Dominguez, writing in the *Daily News,* suggests that the casting of Hawkes, Stiles and Liev Schreiber (Laertes), then at the height of his *Scream* fame, seemed 'an obvious attempt at attracting a young audience' (2000). Whether or not this was the case, their casting certainly serves to link the film to the genre of the teen movie, leading critics (such as Lanier) to write about it in the same breath as other 'youth pop Shakespeares' (Lanier, 2006, p. 182).

Also potentially appealing to a young audience is Almereyda's decision to cut the play radically to only 111 minutes in length. With the removal of '60 percent of the text' (Crowl, 2003, p. 192) the film is 'energised' (Almereyda, 2000, p.ix) not only by the contemporary setting but also by the pace of the action. Almereyda's cuts to the text remove lines that sit at odds with the contemporary setting and pare down instances of complex rhetoric and wordplay. However, unlike Luhrmann, Almereyda leaves many of the characters' long speeches largely intact, including Hamlet's 'To be or not to be' (3.1.58–92) and 'How all occasions do inform against me' (4.4.31–65, Thompson and Taylor, 2006), both of which are shot simply, tracking Hamlet, in the first case, through the video-store aisle, and the second through the gangway of the aeroplane. Almereyda's preference seems rather to be to cut whole scenes or episodes – 1.1, the dialogue between Polonius and Reynaldo (2.1.1–74) all the exchanges involving or relating to the players, and the gravediggers (5.1) – largely reducing the play to a domestic tragedy focusing on Hamlet.

Similar to Luhrmann, Almereyda felt the need to ease the audience into the Shakespearean text, resulting in the complete cutting of 1.1 (although a short excerpt is introduced as a flashback in 2.2). As he explains, having shot this opening scene in the lobby and basement, 'it became apparent that the Elizabethan language, coming thick and fast at the outset, confused our early audiences' (2000, p. 135). Almereyda, therefore, begins the film with a series of titles that provide the background to the story in clear, simple terms and help to situate the ensuing action, followed by a montage of shots of New York that establish the key locations – the Denmark Corporation and Hotel Elsinore. This is followed by a sequence in which Hamlet delivers a few pared-down lines from his 2.2 speech 'What a piece of work is a man' (2.2.305–12) interspersed with television footage from Bosnia, introducing the protagonist and his eclectic film-making, and attuning the audience's ear to Shakespeare's language without immediately bombarding them with essential plot information. This decision acknowledges the film's potential audience as that of non-Shakespeare specialists for whom the play's language might be off-putting, and finds a necessary means of engaging them in the opening scenes. It also places Hamlet (and as importantly, Ethan Hawke) at the centre of the film from the outset, simplifying the play by cutting down on the subtext and political content in a way that makes it highly accessible, but arguably less rich and varied in tone.

Despite the disastrous reception of the film at its preview screenings, Almereyda's *Hamlet* became, as Crowl notes, 'a surprise success' (2003, p. 18). Although the film had a limited release, showing, at its peak, at only 93 screens in the United States, the gross per screen was higher than some of the biggest grossing Shakespeare movies of the 1990s: Zeffirelli's *Hamlet*, Michael Hoffman's *A Midsummer Night's Dream* and Luhrmann's *Romeo + Juliet* (Hindle, 2007, p. 244).

Although it is difficult to assess the degree to which the film has proved a success with the teenage market, largely because most young people are likely to have encountered the film on DVD rather than at the cinema, many of the reviews and criticism attest to its obvious youth appeal. Kevin Thomas writing in the *LA Times* praised Almereyda for making 'Shakespeare come alive for contemporary audiences of all ages, especially young people' (2001) and Maurice Hindle asserts that it is 'a movie that speaks "with most miraculous organ" to the youthful audience who are the prime target for Shakespeare film-makers of the new millennium' (2007, p. 205).

Certainly, the marketing of the film seemed aimed at teenagers, the film's trailer using a rock soundtrack quite different to that of the film itself, and a limited amount of the Shakespearean text. As Emma French elucidates, it 'resembles the trailer for Luhrmann's *Shakespeare's Romeo + Juliet* in its insistent homage to the rapid editing and narrative style of music videos and in both its visual and aural style', its soundtrack apparently 'created to situate the film in the successful teen filmed Shakespeare adaptation genre' (2006, pp. 54–5).

Almereyda himself has commented that some of his favourite comments on the film have been 'from young people who hadn't read *Hamlet* before or hadn't felt so charged up about it' (Fuchs, 2000). As an introduction to the play, the film is clear, engaging and accessible, holding a mirror up to contemporary American youth who are likely to identify more readily with this awkward, morose hero than with Olivier's dulcet tones or Branagh's witty and accomplished prince. However, one would hope that those young people who 'hadn't read *Hamlet* before' would take this film as inspiration for reading the play in its entirety, an experience for which the film is no substitute.

A Midsummer Night's Dream

Unlike both Luhrmann and Almereyda's films that, while clearly designed to appeal to a teenage audience with their casting, style and setting, were not exclusively aimed at young people, Christine Edzard's *The Children's Midsummer Night's Dream* was aimed specifically at an audience of children, more particularly those of primary school age. The title of Edzard's film, however, refers not only to the intended audience, but also to the film's cast who were aged between 8 and 12 years, a casting choice that singles the film out in the history of Shakespeare in the cinema. Children have, of course, regularly been used in film and television versions of the play in the roles of the fairies, but never have Titania, Oberon, the lovers and the mechanicals been played by pre-teen youngsters on screen.

The film begins with a group of primary-aged children watching a puppet-show version of *A Midsummer Night's Dream* in an Elizabethan-style theatre, a performance given theatrical authority by the voices of Derek Jacobi and Samantha Bond, leading British Shakespearean actors. The puppet show is highly traditional and static and many of the young audience fidget and look bored. However, rather than the actors eventually winning their young audience over to their way of presenting Shakespeare, the children usurp the roles of the puppets in order to make the play their own. The resonant actorly voices associated with professional performances of Shakespeare are replaced by the voices of contemporary London youth.

The children's usurpation of the play is not only a matter of contestation over performance style; it is also an appropriation of the themes and debates of the play. As Jacobi's Theseus delivers the lines – 'wanting your father's voice / The other must be held the worthier' (1.1.54–5) to the puppet Hermia, one of the young audience members (Jamie Peachey) rejoinders with heartfelt outrage – 'I would my father looked but with my eyes' (1.1.56), simultaneously resisting the authority of the actor and that of the Duke. From this moment the young audience become more engaged in the action, applauding Hermia's refusal to 'give sovereignty' (1.1.82) to Demetrius. Gradually other spectators begin to assume the roles of the lovers, first Demetrius, then Lysander and Helena, until the curtain closes on the puppets, and the scene continues in the increasingly empty theatre and then in the children's houses.

The opening, as Lanier writes, 'suggests the need to move Shakespeare from heritage culture mired in staid decorum and reverence for the past to an active engagement with the multicultural, urban British present and the new generation that occupies it' (2006, p. 167). However, it is difficult to make sense of this initial section of the film as a 'modern dress' interpretation of the play since the discussion of marriage, virginity and lovemaking sit awkwardly in the mouths of the prepubescent youngsters dressed in their school uniforms, in particular the boys who seem too young to be capable of serious relationships. Mentions of Hermia's 'virgin patent' (1.1.80) and Demetrius having 'made love' (1.1.107) to Helena are greeted with the inevitable wolf-whistles and giggles from their peers, serving to emphasize the distance rather than the proximity between the experiences of the characters and those of the young audience.

As the film moves increasingly into the forest and into Elizabethan dress, with the arrival of the fairies at the beginning of Act 2, it becomes more palatable – if akin to the experience of watching an often rather wooden school play. With the children moving into adult attire it becomes easier to view the romantic traumas and professions of love as those of Shakespeare's characters as opposed to young schoolchildren. However, the fact that the roles are played by children has clearly informed many of the directorial decisions, and the production lacks any acknowledgement of the play's darker elements – the threats of death, forced sexual encounters and potential dangers of the wood.

Producer Olivier Stockman's discussion of the film betrays a rather simplistic and naive view of the play as one of simplicity and innocence. He asserts that for Edzard, 'the play is fundamentally much simpler than people make out it is' (Hatchuel and Vienne-Guerrin, 2004, p. 117). However, it is dangerous to assume that because the play has, at its centre, young lovers and fairies it lacks complexity. Stockman discusses the three groups of characters portrayed by the children – the lovers, the fairies and the mechanicals – suggesting that each has an innocence close to that of the young people; however, his discussion further exemplifies his failure to acknowledge the play's sexual and political overtones and its often bawdy language. Twice in his discussion he refers to the absence of sexual intimacy in the play: 'the lovers are young people; they talk about love but they haven't done it, they haven't kissed, they're just very excited about it. That's relevant to young children in the same way as it is relevant to the characters in the play'; 'It is not actually in the play. There are lots of words and teasing, but the characters don't actually do it' (pp. 116, 122–3). While it may be true that there are no explicit stage directions for the lovers to kiss, Lysander's claim in the first scene that Demetrius has 'made love' to Helena, though not necessarily a reference to sexual intercourse, implies that there has been some form of intimate contact between the pair, and the text very clearly indicates that Titania, at the very least, embraces Bottom in a sexually intimate manner:

> Sleep thou, and I will wind thee in my arms.
> Fairies, begone, and be all ways away.
> So doth the woodbine the sweet honeysuckle
> Gently entwist; the female ivy so
> Enrings the barky fingers of the elm.
> O, how I love thee! how I dote on thee!   (4.1.39–44)

In Edzard's production there is no physical contact between the pair at this point, Titania lying down at a distance from Bottom.

Stockman goes on to describe the fairy characters as 'really the ideal of what the children love to play at . . . being magical . . . being able to fly, being able to transform themselves', claiming that an 8–12-year-old does not have to 'make a complicated effort to act Titania, whereas a 20-year-old actress may find it difficult' (Hatchuel and Vienne-Guerrin, 2004, p. 116). However, the fairies – Titania in particular – are far more complex than this. Their 'magical' quality is only one element of their characterization, which, for Titania also revolves around issues of jealousy, power, love and sexuality – all of which are surely more likely to have a greater proximity to the experiences of a 20-year-old than to a child. Stockman may be closer to the truth in drawing parallels between the mechanicals and the young cast – 'they are inexperienced with their ambition of being actors and the children are exactly like the mechanicals; they are genuinely the mechanicals, they're not pretending to be stupid, they are not pretending not to be able to articulate or to understand their lines, they just are' (p. 116). However, this lack of distinction does not necessarily serve Shakespeare's play. The proximity in acting styles between most of the child actors and the mechanicals means that there is no real distinction between the quality of the mechanicals' play in Act 5 and that of the rest of the film. The humour of the play-within-a-play is, therefore, lost, and one feels uneasy about laughing at the efforts of Quince and his colleagues since it is not apparent whether one is laughing at the poor, inarticulate delivery of the mechanicals or the poor, inarticulate delivery of the children.

This is a chaste, innocent and unsophisticated representation of the play and its relationships, a style of presentation enhanced by the set and costume designs – the forest, flowers, pools and picturesque fairies alluding to Victorian and Edwardian illustrations for children's editions of Shakespeare, such as those of Arthur Rackham and W. Heath Robinson. This lack of sophistication and simplicity of style is similarly evident in the film's use of special effects. The use of abrupt jump-cuts, which resemble those of Peter Hall's 1968 film of the play, in order to suggest the magical appearance and disappearance of the fairies and the obvious bursts of dry-ice are in danger of looking merely amateurish. However, the lack of technical sophistication is, in Lanier's view, part and parcel of the deliberate intention to return 'Shakespeare and Shakespearean performance to an earlier golden age of cultural "innocence", a time before Shakespeare became invested with directorial preoccupations and prejudices and highbrow standards of "proper performance"' (2006, p. 162). It thus becomes, in Lanier's view, as much a political statement as an artistic one – an implicit criticism of the directorial sophistication and imposition of 'concepts' that has dominated Shakespeare production since the 1960s.[3]

The message of the film is clearly that young people can own Shakespeare for themselves – that it is not merely the domain of trained adult actors. To an extent it succeeds in conveying this message – giving the children the opportunity to perform the play, and showing, at points, how a childlike vision of the play can be both innocently refreshing and illuminating. As Crowl notes, the play 'isn't just child-friendly – it is child inspired' abounding 'in references to children' (2003, p. 168) that are highlighted when delivered by the young cast. However, on another level, the film fails to convey this message of accessibility and universality, since the children are clearly not capable of making sense of much of the text, delivering the lines, with a few exceptions, in a dead-pan, often stilted manner that betrays a lack of understanding and suggests little relishing of the words or characters and reinforces the notion that Shakespeare is safest in the hands of trained professionals. Crowl rightly observes that 'what the film misses . . . is the experience of watching a child be captured and absorbed by what he or she is saying' (p. 165). Indeed those who seem to be gaining most enjoyment from their involvement are the children cast as fairies, who pop up around the forest, grinning cheekily and often giggling but rarely burdened with delivering more than a couple of lines.

Nevertheless, irrespective of whether they understood the text in its entirety, it is difficult to underestimate the degrees of pleasure, satisfaction, self-esteem and knowledge that the children taking part must have gained from this project. Stockman describes how the 364 children who participated 'were also involved in preparing the costumes, the sets, all the forest . . . not just acting but also doing clapper boards and things like that' (Hatchuel and Vienne-Guerrin, 2004, p. 118), gaining an intimate knowledge of the process film-making as well as of Shakespeare's play and working closely as part of a large collaborative experience.

Less obvious, however, is the gain for the young viewer. The children's delivery, the lack of action, limited use of special effects and the rather bland, if pretty, design provide little stimulus, and although the onscreen audience might appear to enjoy watching their friends stuttering their way through the lines, it would seem more beneficial to those studying the play to watch a more visually stimulating, clearly spoken film version such as Hoffman's or Adrian Noble's. Stockman asserts that the schools' audiences to which the film has been shown, while not understanding everything, 'get mesmerized by seeing children like themselves doing it' (Hatchuel and Vienne-Guerrin, 2004, p. 124). While it may be true that there is a fascination and a sense of ownership inherent in seeing children of your own age performing Shakespeare, surely the issue of understanding would be helped by seeing performers who themselves understand what they are saying.

Edzard's is a full-length version of the play, its running time of 113 minutes being comparable to that of adult film versions such as Max Reinhardt's (117 minutes), Hoffman's (116 minutes) and Noble's (99 minutes). The text is present almost in its entirety, with the only discernible cut, up until the awakening of the lovers and the return to the puppet theatre, being the rude punning on the subject of French beards in 1.2 ('Why what you will . . . bare-faced' (1.2.85–91)), which is presumably cut due both to the complex wordplay and the undesirability of having to explain the joke to the young cast. Lines that often fall victim to the red pen in professional productions due to their verbosity or complex rhetoric are retained, the children being given credit for an ability to tackle the whole of Shakespeare's play. Only lines attributed to the puppets are cut – a number of Theseus and Hippolyta's lines on discovering the lovers asleep in 4.1, for the obvious reason that the puppet 'actors' cannot appear in the wood, and some of Theseus and Philostrate's and the noble audience's dialogue in 5.1 – retaining the focus of the film on the child actors, as opposed to the puppets, in this final scene. Indeed, although we return to the puppet theatre at the beginning of 5.1, the camera is more often focused on the mechanicals getting ready backstage and on the audience of school children arriving in the theatre than on the adult-voiced puppets. While the puppets remain on stage, they are sidelined by the fact that the auditorium is reconfigured into a square focused around a central playing space on the floor where the mechanicals perform. They are also shown up by the audience of school children in a reversal of traditional perceptions of audience behaviour. As the puppets comment rudely on the mechanicals' low quality but well-intentioned production, the children sit attentively, casting disapproving glances and even verbally hushing their adult counterparts.

The film did come in for some criticism over the quality of the performances – Richard Burt, for example, asserting that 'as the film goes on . . . the puppets are more human than the children, who start to look more puppet-like and more wooden' (Hatchuel and Vienne-Guerrin, 2004, p. 121). However, others praised it for its efforts to 'reorient the ways in which the Shakespearean corpus is transmitted and appreciated' (Thornton Burnett, 2002, p. 167), placing children at the centre of the interpretative process and making a virtue of the lack of polished performances by providing a sense of spontaneity, discovery and 'play' (Edzard, quoted by Thornton Burnett, 2002, p. 169).

Conclusion

Although Luhrmann and Almereyda's films were not aimed exclusively at young people, both seem to have a youth appeal that exceeds Edzard's film, aimed at the youth market. While Edzard's may be a visually pretty production, it lacks the contemporaneity of Luhrmann and Almereyda's films, which, with their modern dress, music and pop culture references, bring Shakespeare's plays firmly into the late twentieth/twenty-first century and the experiences of their young protagonists closer to those of young audience members. Also, while Luhrmann and Almereyda cast young protagonists with previous form in teen movies, and obvious sex appeal, Edzard's cast of prepubescents, while endearing, are less likely to attract other young people to the film.

Edzard's film also suffers from its rigorous adherence to the text. Rather than finding, as do Almereyda and Luhrmann, appealing and often witty means of translating Shakespeare's language into visual imagery, Edzard's production features long passages of text, delivered with little visual variation, which are surely liable to lose the attention of young audience members. While a relatively full text in the hands of experienced Shakespearean actors, as in Kenneth Branagh's *Hamlet,* has the potential to engage an audience, in Edzard's film, the text is spoken for the most part in such a stilted manner that it is often tedious and sometimes barely intelligible. Luhrmann's film similarly suffers, though not to the same degree, in terms of the delivery of the lines, and while the visual energy and imagery may be seen to provide some compensation, the language and particularly the verse fall casualty to the actors' lack of experience in speaking Shakespeare. The verse-speaking of Almereyda's film is the most accomplished, no doubt partly because, although his Hamlet and Ophelia are both young, his actors had, for the most part, some experience of performing Shakespeare. While Edzard's film may be accused of cutting too little however, Luhrmann and Almereyda might be accused of cutting too much, Luhrmann in his chopping of the lines with little regard for the verse form, and removal of all of the play's soliloquies, and Almereyda in the elimination of much of *Hamlet's* humour, as embodied not only in Hamlet's own dialogue, but also in the characters of Osric and the Gravediggers.

Each of these films has its own merits, and the box-office figures for Luhrmann and Almereyda's films (although the latter received only a limited cinema release) are testament to their success. While Edzard's film may not have done well at the box-office and seems to have little appeal for audiences, young or old, there can be no doubt that its great achievement was in the process rather than the result.

Notes

1 The Peachum drawing of *Titus Andronicus*, apparently depicting the play in performance in the Elizabethan period, shows, despite the play's setting in Ancient Rome, the characters dressed predominantly in Elizabethan clothing with some concessions towards Romanesque costume. Similarly, Cleopatra's demand in *Antony and Cleopatra* that Charmian 'cut my lace' indicates the original costuming of the character in a Renaissance bodice in an Ancient Egyptian setting (1.3.71) (see Rokison, 2010a, p. 83).

2 Kathleen O. Irace, *The First Quarto of Hamlet* (Cambridge: Cambridge University Press, 1999), p. 15.

3 See Robert Smallwood, 'Directors' Shakespeare' (1996).

Web resources

Dominguez, Robert (2000), 'A Renaissance Man Tackles Shakespeare'. *Daily News*:
    http://articles.nydailynews.com/2000–05–11/entertainment/18140524_1
    _Ethan-hawke-hamlet-gattaca
Film 4 (1996), 'Romeo + Juliet: Review':
    www.film4.com/reviews/1996/william-shakespeares-romeo-juliet
Fuchs, Cynthia (2000), 'Interview with Michael Almereyda'. *Pop Matters*:
    www.popmatters.com/pm/interviews/almereyda-michael.shtml
Kipp, Jeremiah (2003), 'Michael Almereyda'. *Senses of Cinema*:
    www.sensesofcinema.com/2003/great-directors/almereyda/

PART TWO

Short Shakespeare: Cut-Down Versions for Children and Young People

CHAPTER THREE

'Shakespeare's Stories': Prose Narratives and Picture Books

Lamb's *Tales from Shakespeare*

In 1807, Charles and Mary Lamb published *Tales from Shakespeare*, 'Designed for the use of young persons', as an 'introduction to the study of Shakespeare' (Lamb and Lamb, 1807, vol. 1, p.iii). The Lambs published 20 of the plays, omitting all the Histories and Roman plays, presumably deeming these less suitable for the 'young ladies' for whom it was their 'intention chiefly to write' (p.vi). In the Preface to their *Tales*, the Lambs set out their aims – 'to make these *Tales* easy reading for very young children' and to give them 'a few hints and little foretastes of the great pleasure which awaits them in their elder years' when they encounter the plays for themselves (p.v). However, they did, they admit, struggle to retain the simplicity of the *Tales*, since 'the subjects of most of them made this a very difficult task' (p.vi). This is a point all too easily glossed over, and indeed the Lambs do not dwell on the matter; however, it seems pertinent to ask at this point, in relation both to the Lambs' text and subsequent prose versions of Shakespeare for young people, whether the subject matter of many of the plays is simply unsuitable for 'very young children'. This is an issue to which I will continue to return in discussing the ways in which the plays are adapted and presented for children, not only in narrative form, but also in the cut-down versions of the plays for primary school audiences discussed in Chapter 5 and the Animated Tales, discussed in Chapter 6.

Shakespeare's plays are rife with sexual and violent content, and one does not need to look far to find rape, attempted rape, sexual infidelity, prostitution, incest, adultery, murder and mutilation, all of which subjects seem less than suited to a young audience. The Lambs deal with this 'unsuitable' material, largely by excising it, or presenting it in euphemistic language not easily intelligible to their young readers. In *All's Well That Ends Well*, Bertram's statement in his letter to Helena is curtailed – 'When you can get the ring from my finger, which never shall come off, then call me husband, but in such a Then I write a Never' (Lamb and Lamb, 1807, vol. 2, p. 12). There is no mention of the other condition – the 'child begotten of thy body that I am father to' (*AWW* 3.2.58–9) – either here or later in the story when Helena declares herself to have fulfilled the conditions. Helena and Bertram's 'secret meeting' thus remains platonic, with Helena seeking only to beg 'the ring from off his finger as a token of his regard', while Bertram offers her nothing more than 'flattering compliments and love discourse' (Lamb and Lamb, 1807, vol. 2, pp. 17–18). Likewise, in *Pericles* the subject of incest is entirely glossed over, with Antiochus described simply as having done 'a shocking deed . . . in secret' (p. 231). Even the mention of breasts is apparently considered too much for the young readership to cope with, the Lambs preserving Imogen's modesty in *Cymbeline* by moving her mole from her 'left breast' (*Cym.* 2.2.37) to her 'neck' (Lamb and Lamb, 1807, vol. 1, p. 169). Given these significant changes and evasions, the Lambs' comment that young people, when finally encountering the plays themselves 'will discover in such of them as are here abridged . . . many surprising events and turns of fortune' (pp.viii–ix) seems something of an understatement. It might well prove 'surprising' to a reader of *Pericles*, given to understand that Marina was sold as 'a slave', making her master rich by teaching 'music, dancing, and fine needle-works' (p. 248), to discover that she is in fact sold as a prostitute and her virginity routinely threatened by her 'master', a bawd.

In addition to glossing over the more 'unsuitable' aspects of Shakespeare's plays for their young readers, the Lambs go out of their way to assert the moral value of the stories, and indeed the plays, for the young reader. The plays, they assert, are able 'to teach courtesy, benignity, generosity, [and] humanity' (vol. 1, p.ix). The assertion of the didactic value of drama is, of course, not a phenomenon peculiar to the Lambs, or indeed to Shakespeare, the capacity of drama to 'instruct' as well as 'delight' being a feature of dramatic criticism from Horace's *Ars Poetica* (c. 18 BC) to Brecht's 'The Modern Theatre Is the Epic Theatre' (1930). However, the Lambs are extreme in their praise for Shakespeare's ability to inspire virtue and honour in the reader, expressing their wish that the *Tales* 'may prove enrichers of the fancy, strengtheners of virtue, a withdrawing from all selfish and mercenary thoughts, a lesson of all sweet and honourable thoughts and actions' (p.ix), quite a task for plays, in which, as Robert A. Logan notes, 'Shakespeare does not allow us a quick and easy resolution in assessing the characters' moral worth or their underlying motivations' (2007, p. 232).

Despite the Lambs' efforts to stress the moral benefits of their stories for young readers, the negative criticism of the *Tales* on their publication centred around concerns that 'morals' had failed to be 'deduced' (*Literary Panorama*), and that the stories were not 'very proper studies for female children' (*Anti-Jacobin Review*) (Wells, 1993, p. 189). The *Tales* have continued over the years to come in for criticism, although less associated with their moral content than with their style and form, Lord David Cecil bemoaning their 'undramatic manner, unlikely . . . to excite children', Robertson Davies complaining that 'rob[bed] of his poetry' they reduce Shakespeare to 'tedious stuff' and Andrew Lang arguing that young children 'are best introduced to Shakespeare by Shakespeare himself' (all cited by Wells, 1993, pp. 190, 193). These are, of course, arguments which continue to rage in relation to both the Lambs' *Tales* and more recent prose versions of Shakespeare. Alison H. Prindle, writing in 2002, argues that versions following 'in the footsteps of the Lambs, attempting to mediate between children and Shakespeare by presenting the play in narrative form . . . create an observer's role for the child', depriving them of the 'collaborative, interactive role offered by the original genre, the drama' (p. 138), a point which I take up later in this chapter.

The Lambs themselves were themselves regretful about the loss of Shakespeare's poetry – although less for its dramatic quality than for its 'beauty' and use of 'excellent words' (vol. 1, p.v). Indeed, this is the other major 'apology' of their Preface. Perhaps rather overemphatically, given their choice of task, they bemoan the status of their work as 'small and valueless coins' and 'faint and imperfect stamps' (p.v) of Shakespeare. They have, they assert, made an effort to use Shakespeare's own words 'whenever it seemed possible' (p.iii), and this is done relatively seamlessly, with the authors incorporating brief phrases from the plays into their text, both in the dialogue and in the narration. However, in places where a clarification of the lines or inclusion of a description of physical action might involve having to explain something that the authors would rather avoid, they present the text largely unedited, with little elucidation, such that one wonders whether young readers are likely to find their text any easier to read than the originals. Clearly the Lambs do not wish to be explicit about Angelo's desire to have sex with Isabella in 2.4 *Measure for Measure*, but it seems hard to believe that any young child would be able to comprehend much of the following passage, which reproduces almost word for word the dialogue from the original text:

> Isabel, angered to the heart to hear him use the word Honour to express such dishonourable purposes, said: 'Ha! little honour to be much believed; and most pernicious purpose. I will proclaim thee, Angelo, look for it! Sign me a present pardon for my brother, or I will tell the world aloud what man thou art!' 'Who will believe you, Isabel?' said Angelo: 'my unsoiled name, the austereness of my life, my word vouched against yours, will outweigh your accusation. Redeem your brother by yielding to my will, or he shall die to-morrow. As for you, say what you

can, my false will overweigh your true story. Answer me to-morrow'. (Lamb and Lamb, 1807, vol. 2, p. 80)

In such instances the assertion that their aim has been 'to make these *Tales* easy reading for very young children' must be called into question, and along with it, the purpose of such an exercise in relation to a morally complex play like *Measure for Measure*.

Pre-war narrative versions

In his British Academy lecture, 'Tales from Shakespeare' (1987), Stanley Wells provides a comprehensive outline of the various editions of Lamb's *Tales*, and of other narrative versions published between 1893 and 1914 – 'the period during which the Lambs' *Tales* were at the height of their popularity' (1993, p. 204): *Tales of the Drama* by Elizabeth Wright Macauley (1822), *The Juvenile Shakespeare* by Caroline Maxwell (1828), a series of tales retold by Joseph Graves for Duncombe's Miniature Library (c.1840), *Shakespeare's Stories Simply Told* by Mary Seymour (1880), *Phoebe's Shakespeare* by Adelaide C. Gordon Sim (1894), E. Nesbit's *The Children's Shakespeare* (1897), Arthur Quiller-Couch's *Historical Tales from Shakespeare* (1899), Mary MacLeod's *Shakespeare Story-Book* (1902), Thomas Carter's *Stories from Shakespeare* (1910) and *Shakespeare's Stories of the English Kings* (1612) and Alice Spencer Hoffman's *The Children's Shakespeare* (1911).

The aims and methods emphasized by the Lambs in the Preface to their *Tales* – to provide a clear and simple introduction to Shakespeare for young readers in the hope of encouraging them to tackle the plays when older, and to protect their young minds from elements of immorality in the original texts – are common to many of the prose versions cited above, as is the promotion of Shakespeare as a source of moral guidance and expresser of universal truths and virtues. Indeed, Shakespeare's plays are put into the service of providing everything from 'beautiful stories' for little girls (Sim, 1894, p. iii) to 'a handbook to patriotism' for English boys (Quiller-Couch, 1899, p. vi), remaining all the while 'subservient to the best purposes of morality' (Macaulay, 1822, p.vii) (all quoted by Wells, 1993, pp. 198–201). Caroline Maxwell goes so far as to claim that in creating her text, 'on no occasion has the fair purity of the youthful mind been for one moment forgot' (1828, p.iv). As Wells wittily comments, 'presumably Caroline Maxwell, like Macbeth, had no children' (1993, p. 199). As publications such as Roald Dahl's enormously popular *Revolting Rhymes* (1982) make apparent, young children relish scatological and sexual jokes just as they relish rhyme and rhythm, both of which they are deprived of in these early narrative versions.

Narrative versions 1930–85

Wells identifies a 'major shift in moral values' (1993, p. 204) around the time of the anonymous publication of *Shakespeare Tales for Boys and Girls* (c.1930), a shift which runs through G. B. Harrison's *New Tales* (1938), Marchette Chute's *Stories from Shakespeare* (1960), Irene Buckman's *Twenty Tales from Shakespeare* (1963), Roger Lancelyn Green's *Tales from Shakespeare* (1964), Ian Serraillier's *The Enchanted Island: Stories from Shakespeare* (1964), Bernard Miles' *Favourite Tales from Shakespeare* (1976) and *Well-Loved Tales from Shakespeare* (1986) and Leon Garfield's *Shakespeare Stories* (1985), all of which Wells discusses. Gone are the sententious character judgements, such as Sim's moralizing assessment of Romeo that if only he 'had been a little more patient and less selfish, and had remembered that he had no right to kill himself just because he was unhappy . . . everything might have been right' (1894, pp. 145–6).

Buckman's *Tales* are particularly remarkable for their willingness to preserve the ambiguities of Shakespeare's text and refrain from offering judgement on the characters. Her conclusion to *The Taming of the Shrew* is quite different from the Lambs', for example, in its openness and avoidance of misogynistic sentiment:

> And to the wonder of all present, the reformed shrewish lady spoke as eloquently in praise of the wife-like duty of obedience, as she had practised it implicitly in a ready submission to Petruchio's will. And Katharine once more became famous in Padua, not as heretofore, as Katharine the Shrew, but as Katharine the most obedient and duteous wife in Padua. (Lamb and Lamb, 1807, vol. 2, pp. 42–3)

> And the reformed Katherine, to show how thoroughly she had changed, delivered a long sermon on the duty of an obedient, submissive wife to her lord and master. Whether she said it with her tongue in her cheek, we do not know, but all the company listened in silence . . . (Buckman, 1963, p. 29)

However, the tendency of adapters to censor the texts for their young readership is still apparent, even if not to the same extent as in the work of the Lambs and their peers. In most of the prose versions of *Hamlet*, for example, the authors remove almost all suggestions of Hamlet's obsession with Gertrude's sexuality, evident in Shakespeare's play almost to a greater degree than his concern with Claudius' guilt as a murderer. In the 'closet scene', the overt references to Gertrude's sexuality – the 'enseamed bed' and the act of 'honeying and making love' (3.4.82–3) – are excised by Chute, Buckman, Lancelyn Green, Miles and Serraillier. Only Garfield does not shy away from some of the more sexually charged moments in the story, describing Hamlet in the queen's closet as laying bare 'his mother's easy lust and the shameless corruption of her bed' (1985, p. 193).

Despite the tendency of these texts to censor elements of the stories, there is a notable difference in the forms of justification for adaption set forward in their prefaces and introductions. Far less emphasis is placed on the plays' morally didactic benefits and the focus shifts to discussions of what narrative form is able to offer the young reader that dramatic form cannot. Chute explains that because Shakespeare was writing plays he 'never stopped to explain anything. If he had been telling his stories in the form of a novel he would have let his readers know what his characters looked like, what clothes they wore, what kind of houses they lived in and what they were thinking about. But since he was a playwright he put his people on-stage without any explanations' (1960, p. 13). Miles makes similar assertions: 'the plays only give you what people *say* to each other. They don't tell you what they look like or how they dress or what kind of house they live in. We don't know how they get from place to place or what has been happening to them between the time you saw them last and the next time they appear' (1976, p. 8).

The implication is that Chute and Miles's own narratives can fill in these gaps and thus create a less demanding reading experience. What their assertions fail to acknowledge, of course, is that characters' clothing and the specifics of location are rarely of interest in Shakespeare's work. When such details are of significance, such as Hamlet's 'suits of solemn black' (1.2.78) or the fact that the Capulet house is surrounded by an 'orchard' whose 'walls are high and hard to climb' (2.1.105) then Shakespeare's characters vocalize them. As Paul Menzer asserts, 'Shakespeare's plays take pains to identify locale *when it serves the play*' (my italics) (2006, p. 16). However, as Bernard Beckerman notes, of the 345 scenes in Shakespeare plays written for the Globe, more than 200 are unlocated (1962, p. 235) – presumably because their setting is of no import – and since the plays would have been performed on the largely unadorned Globe stage, the setting of such scenes would have been no more apparent to the Early Modern playgoer than it is to the reader. As for knowing how a character has got from one place to another or what they have been doing since we last saw them, if this information is essential to the plot then it is conveyed, and if it is not conveyed, this is usually because it is irrelevant. Indeed, if one spent too much time thinking about how characters got from Egypt to Rome and vice versa in *Antony and Cleopatra*, one would soon discover the implausibility of their rapid movement from one country to the other. The point is that the swift transition from one location to the next serves the action of the play and the practicalities of the journeys are best ignored.

Although these texts differ from the pre-1914 texts discussed by Wells in their lack of emphasis on the morality of the tales, they resemble them in continuing to stress their value as introductions to Shakespeare, pointing the reader thereafter to the originals. Chute expresses her hope that her book 'may open a door that to some people is closed and give a glimpse, however, slight, of what lies beyond' (1960, p. 14) and Miles that his stories 'will lead you to love Shakespeare and all the wonderful characters he created for the rest of your lives' (1976, p. 9). How, or when, such a transition to the originals might be made is not enlarged upon. Chute and Miles also continue, in the mode of the Lambs and their successors, to declare Shakespeare's status as a genius, whose work transcends time and offers insight into universal aspects of human nature. Chute describes Shakespeare as 'not only one of the greatest of poets and storytellers, but . . . also one of the greatest playwrights' who 'understood so well the demands of the theatre that time has not aged or weakened his plays and they still leap to life on any stage', adding that 'something of this can be explained by the fact that he was a genius' (1960, p. 12). Miles similarly describes Shakespeare as 'the greatest play-writer the world has ever seen' and though slightly less effusive in his bardolatry, points out the transcendent nature of the plays in asserting that they are 'full of interesting people doing very much the sort of thing people do today' (1976, pp. 8–9).

A new aspect is also apparent in the Prefaces of Chute and Miles – an emphasis on the theatrical status of the plays – as pieces written to be performed. Both authors include details of the Elizabethan stage – its structure, demands, audiences and performers, Chute describing Shakespeare as 'a man of the theatre', continuing, again in hyperbolic terms, to claim that 'there was never any writer who knew as much about stagecraft as William Shakespeare' (1960, pp. 12, 17). However, despite Chute's emphasis on Shakespeare's work as material written for the theatre, there is little evidence in her own text of any attempt to convey such theatricality to the reader, except possibly in the use of the present tense which alone fails to provide an imaginative immediacy. Miles' achievement is somewhat different, possibly because he too was a 'man of the theatre'. His book includes large, full-colour illustrations by Victor Ambrus, which, Miles expresses in his introduction, he hopes will make 'the stories will come alive as vividly as if you were watching them being performed by live actors in a real theatre' (1976, p. 9). Although they do not resemble theatrical scenarios, the pictures are certainly striking, and often depict the characters in dramatic action poses – Macbeth holding out his bloody hands in horror after the murder of Duncan, grasping with outstretched arms at the empty chair on which he sees Banquo's ghost and Macduff holding aloft the head of Macbeth (pp. 24–5, 28, 32). However, it is Miles' writing which also helps to bring the stories to life. Although lacking in dialogue (Miles explains that he found it too difficult to turn Shakespeare's words into 'everyday English' (p. 9)), Miles' narrative conjures some vivid images – 'suddenly there came a flash of lightning and there were three witches right in their path, their ugly faces lit by the glow from their magic fire' (p. 15). He also uses interpretation, much as might a theatre or film director, in imagining some of the play's episodes, for example, in making the dagger which ushers Macbeth to Duncan a creation of the witches – 'it was really one of the witches who had hung the dagger in the air, masking her face with her ragged sleeve as she offered Macbeth the handle' (p. 20).

Wells praises Miles' text for its 'free, idiosyncratic' take on the plays, but it is in the work of Leon Garfield that, in Wells' view, the reader is really treated to the experience 'not of reading the twelve plays that he includes, but of seeing them performed' (1993, p. 208). Wells compliments, in particular, Garfield's ability to visualize action 'that could be used as stage business' (p. 208). Instances of this can be seen in Garfield's version of *Macbeth* in detailed descriptions of characters' movements or expressions. Following Lady Macbeth's cry 'But screw you courage to the sticking place and we'll not fail', Garfield writes of Macbeth that 'He stared at her, and she at him. He bowed his head'; hearing the knocking on the gate following the murder of Duncan, that Macbeth 'shook and trembled and stared down at his murderer's hands'; and when informed of Lady Macbeth's death that 'he shrugged his shoulders' and 'sighed' (1985, pp. 276, 278, 287). Each of these descriptions is reminiscent of the sort of action that one might expect to see on stage, and provides insight into Macbeth's thoughts and feelings.

Garfield also uses dialogue far more regularly than Miles, and rather than attempting to turn it into 'everyday English' (Miles, 1976, p. 9), draws all his dialogue directly from the plays, exposing his readers not only to the stories, but also to Shakespeare's language with its inherent theatricality. However, despite Garfield's use of substantial passages of Shakespearean dialogue, the lines, and in particular the verses, are frequently edited, or broken up by the narrative in such a way that little of the rhythm, mood or pace of the Shakespearean text is captured. For example, the witches' opening lines are narrated:

> 'When shall we three met again?' howled one, above the shrieking of the wind. 'In thunder, lightning or in rain?'
>
> 'When the hurly-burly's done!' came the answer, lank hair whipping and half muffling the words. 'When the battle's lost and won!' (1985, p. 271)

Although the words are unaltered, their fragmentation, albeit with highly evocative narrative description, obscures the iambic tetrameter and rhyme scheme of the lines, and hence the incantatory nature of this exchange. The problems inherent in the presentation of verse lines as prose is something to which I will return in both this chapter and in Chapter 4 when looking at graphic novel editions of the plays. Although elements such as Shakespeare's imagery and symbolism, alliteration and assonance may be retained when dialogue is presented as prose rather than as verse, elements such as rhyme and metre and the fundamental distinction between verse and prose, all significant features of characterization, and transmitters of meaning, are lost.

Post-1990 narrative versions

Since Garfield's *Shakespeare Stories*, there has been little if any cessation in the publication of narrative versions of Shakespeare for young people. The 1990s and 2000s have seen a wealth of visually engaging storybook versions of the plays, including Lois Burdett's *Shakespeare Can Be Fun!* series, which seeks to introduce children as young as 7 to Shakespeare's plays, Marcia Williams' *Mr William Shakespeare's Plays* (1998) and *Bravo Mr William Shakespeare!* (2000), Andrew Matthews' *Orchard Book of Shakespeare Stories* (2001)[1] and the *Usborne Illustrated Stories from Shakespeare* (Dickins et al., 2010), all aimed at the younger end of the primary market, Anna Claybourne's *Usborne Stories from Shakespeare* (2004), Beverley Birch's *Shakespeare's Stories* (1997)[2] and *Shakespeare's Tales* (2002), Bruce Coville's retellings for Dial, *The Shakespeare Collection* series published by Hodder Wayland, Geraldine McCaughrean's *Stories from Shakespeare* (1997) and Adam McKeown's *The Young Reader's Shakespeare* series all aimed, like Garfield's retellings, at slightly older students.

These versions tend, as did many of their predecessors, to err towards the more popular, and often perceived as child-friendly plays, the most common choices being *Hamlet*, *Macbeth*, *A Midsummer Night's Dream*, *Romeo and Juliet*, *The Tempest* and *Twelfth Night*, while the darker *Pericles*, *Measure for Measure* and *All's Well That Ends Well* do not make an appearance in any of the publications. Noticeably different from the Lambs, however, is the inclusion of Roman and History plays – in particular *Julius Caesar*, which is one of the plays chosen by Williams, Matthews, Birch, McCaughrean and McKeown, presumably due to the emphasis in education on cross-curricular study, and the capacity of this play to be used in History as well as English lessons.

The texts published since 1990 seem no less concerned than their predecessors with promoting the figure of Shakespeare as 'the repository of Western culture and aesthetic value' (Marchitello, 2002, p. 185), almost all asserting the longevity of his work and its universal appeal. Geraldine McCaughrean's adulation of Shakespeare extends not only to the plays, which she describes in hyperbolic terms as 'so remarkable, so complete, and of such universal appeal that four hundred years later the whole world is still enthralled', but also to Shakespeare's personality, about which she makes some untenable and unfounded comments, describing him as 'a man without arrogance or pretensions' who, were he to time-travel to the present day, would not relish the 'glossy fame and adulation' he has achieved, but be more concerned with the way in which he 'bought immortality with his extraordinary wealth of words' (1997, pp. 6–7). The *Usborne Illustrated Stories from Shakespeare* goes one step further, including a 'Life and Times of William Shakespeare' as an appendix to the plays, an account no less sanitized and idealized than their versions of his plays. Shakespeare's career in theatre is presented as one of unceasing and increasing success, with his plays drawing 'huge crowds' (Dickins et al., 2010, p. 404) and his fellow actors praising him as the company's 'best comedian' (p. 403), something about which Will Kempe and Robert Armin might have had something to say. He is even credited with having the idea for one of the company's most successful actions – the moving of the Theatre to Southwark (p. 409). Only Bruce Coville redresses some of the balance, actually bemoaning the adulation of Shakespeare as a curse rather than a blessing, stating that 'possibly more than any other writer, the Bard bears the curse of greatness – a reputation that leads many people to an ill-founded fear that the writing is "too hard"' (1997, 'Author's Note'). Certainly there is an air of awe surrounding Shakespeare, which is exacerbated by sycophantic accounts of his genius.

Despite their continuing reverence towards Shakespeare, these recent retellings display far less concern than their earlier counterparts with justifying their work, those which contain introductions, prefaces or appendatory material bearing no mention of the moral or didactic elements of Shakespeare's work, nor any assertion of the strengths of narrative over dramatic form. The former tendency may reflect a desire to emphasize, as Burdett's titles suggest, the 'fun' elements of Shakespeare, and not to be seen to condescend to children, despite, as will be seen, the continuing tendency of these editions to censor the stories. The latter tendency may be the result of recent critical discussion stressing the merits of teaching Shakespeare in the classroom through performance.[3] Indeed, in these editions the emphasis on the plays as pieces written for the theatre extends beyond the inclusion of details of the Renaissance stage and its audiences to attempts to bring elements of the playhouse experience alive.

Matthews and McCaughrean both include details about the theatre for which Shakespeare wrote, and make assertions in their introductions that the plays are best experienced in performance – 'there is no substitute for seeing the play, nor for reading the glorious language of the poet himself' (McCaughrean, 1997, p. 7); 'Shakespeare did not intend people to sit down and read his plays – they were meant to be acted in the theatre in front of an audience; only their can their magic truly happen' (Matthews, 2001, 'Foreword'). Like Miles' *Favourite Tales*, however, although the inside cover of Matthews' *Shakespeare Stories* invites the reader to 'step into a truly theatrical experience' (2001), neither Angela Barrett's illustrations nor Matthews' writing style are particularly dramatic, the former being, as Barrett herself describes, largely based on real landscapes – 'woodland photos . . . from a holiday in France', 'the garden at the Villa Rufalo' and 'the Scottish landscape', rather than theatrical sets (pp. 122–3) and the latter being presented on the page as a straightforward prose narrative, albeit with substantial use of dialogue. Burdett's texts also stress their theatrical dimension, claiming on the back cover that they can be used for 'staging as class plays as well as reading aloud'; however, while like most narratives it is possible to dramatize the books by having some pupils read aloud the narrative and others perform the dialogue, Burdett's text seems no more immediately suitable for such an exercise than other storybook versions. Surely if teachers wish to stage elements of a Shakespeare play they are best pointed towards the theatrical texts themselves, or to cut-down play versions by authors such as Carl Heap, discussed in Chapter 5.

Alison H. Prindle praises Marcia Williams' books as the only storybook versions that 'attempt to preserve their dramatic character visually' (2002, p. 144). Arguing that most contemporary narrative versions follow their predecessors in presenting the plays as 'story', she applauds Williams's books for making 'clear' that the play 'is a play' (pp. 138, 144). Certainly Williams' books come closest to giving young readers some notion of the plays as performance pieces with the narrative text accompanied by depictions of the actors and audience members in the Globe Theatre – the actors speaking lines of dialogue from the Shakespearean text, albeit in heavily edited form, and the audience members commenting, often wittily or ironically on the action: 'I don't think this is quite suitable for children' (*Macbeth*) (Williams, 1998, n.p.). The preface of *Mr William Shakespeare's Plays* is even addressed to 'Dear Play-Goer' and asks the reader to imagine that they 'have been transported to the England of William Shakespeare's time', to the Globe Theatre 'where all the plays in this book are to be performed' ('Dear Play-Goer').

It is evident that some aspects of narrative versions of the plays for children have changed in recent years; however, Stephanie Gearhart, writing about storybook versions of *Hamlet* for young people, remarks that although 'by the end of the twentieth and the beginning of the twenty-first centuries, children's Hamlets begin to look quite different from their predecessors', 'some of the same troubling aspects of nineteenth- and early twentieth-century Hamlets for children persist in contemporary adaptations of the play' (2007, p. 55). These 'troubling aspects' are in Gearhart's view the tendency of writers to both censor the text for children, and also to 'interpret' it – making plain assertions about areas of the plays that Shakespeare leaves deliberately ambiguous. Ophelia's death, for example, the nature of which, in *Hamlet*, remains uncertain, Gertrude describing it as an accident (4.7.135–55), while the gravediggers suggest that she may have having 'wilfully [sought] her own salvation' (5.1.1–2), is presented in straightforward terms by many of the authors. Burdett, Birch, Williams, Anthony Masters (*Shakespeare Collection* (2000)) and McCaughrean remove any reference to her 'doubtful' death, presenting her drowning as a simple accident. Conversely, Matthews and the authors of the *Usborne Illustrated Shakespeare Stories* present it as suicide, telling us that Ophelia 'drowned herself' (Matthews, 2001, p. 101; Dickins et al., 2010, p. 375). With various versions presenting such moments in different but equally unambiguous terms, as Gearhart asserts, the only way in which children will 'discover . . . some of the puzzles in the play' is by reading 'a number of adaptations of *Hamlet* for children' (2007, p. 60). Without doing so children are in danger of gaining a misleading impression of some moments in the plays, an impression which may distort their judgement when eventually encountering the original text.

Although contemporary authors are perhaps less moralizing and prudish than those writing in the nineteenth century, they still, as Janet Bottoms notes, 'find it difficult to leave children to judge for themselves the characters, acts and relationships Shakespeare dramatizes' (1999, p. 21), and are still inclined to censor the texts according to what they consider suitable for the young reader. Gearhart points out, for example, that 'Burdett, like the Lambs and Nesbit, glosses over the sexual aspects of the [closet] scene by avoiding any suggestion of Hamlet's desire for attention from his mother and by including some lines that suggest that Gertrude ignore Claudius in the most benign way' (2007, p. 57). Whether or not Hamlet's 'desire for attention from his mother' is 'sexual' is a matter of debate. Nevertheless, Burdett avoids any explicit mentions of Gertrude's sexual relationship with Claudius, much as did her predecessors. She is, of course, not the only one of these writers to 'gloss over' the 'sexual aspects' of the story; indeed, if one compares the post-1990 storybook versions of *Hamlet* with those of the mid-twentieth century, one finds a similar tendency to obscure references to Gertrude's sexuality, and indeed to remove any hint of sexual content in the bawdy lyrics of Ophelia's songs which are decorously removed by all the adaptors and misleadingly described by McCaughrean as 'doleful' (1997, p. 58) and Coville as 'strange and mournful' (2004, n.p.).

The issue of censorship of texts for young people returns us to the question with which this chapter began – are Shakespeare's plays unsuitable for adaptation for very young children? If the plays require, in the eyes of their adaptors, extensive editing of sexual, bawdy and violent content in order to make them appropriate reading material for children as young as 7, then might it not be better to wait until children are older before introducing them to the plays? After all, a film like Baz Luhrmann's *Romeo + Juliet*, aimed at an older age group and replete with sexual and violent images, has proved a popular means of enthusing young people about Shakespeare's work without needing to censor it. Indeed, as the discussion in Chapter 2 suggested, for many young audience members it was precisely these aspects – the sexualization of the young leads and the high octane violence – which most appealed to them.

In writing about contemporary storybook versions of *Hamlet*, Gearhart raises a further issue with Burdett's work – its form. Although she acknowledges that Burdett attempts 'to preserve Shakespeare's language . . . often including much more of the original language than do the Lambs or Nesbit' (Gearhart, 2007, p. 55), her concern lies with Burdett's use of her own rhyming verse as the medium for its transmission. Although Burdett's texts do include elements of Shakespeare's language, they are written in rhyming couplets throughout – couplets composed by Burdett in rather stilted verse form based around a four-stress line. As Gearhart comments, as a result the 'readers lose the poetic verse of Shakespeare' and receive lines which may 'carry them along, but simultaneously distort the graceful iambic pentameter of the original' (2007, p. 56).

One might argue that since the loss of the iambic pentameter is common to all of the narrative storybook versions, even in cases, as with Garfield, where entire lines of Shakespeare' dialogue are incorporated into the text, Burdett's writing is no more guilty of deforming Shakespeare's poetry than that of her colleagues in the genre. Gearhart's assertion that the lack of distinction 'between characters in terms of the way they speak' – in particular in the distinction between verse and prose – is a criticism that might be equally levelled at the prose versions discussed here.[4] However, Gearhart raises an important concern in relation to Burdett's work, arguing that the rhyming couplet structure is particularly distorting since couplets are 'attractive to children and often easy for them to commit to memory', and hence, Burdett's work may encourage young people to memorize 'what are, in essence, the wrong words', an issue which may have 'profound ramifications on children's knowledge of Shakespeare' (2007, p. 5). In Burdett's text of *Twelfth Night*, 'If music be the food of love, play on' (1.1.1) becomes 'If music be the food of love, / Play like the angels from above' (1994, p. 11); Hamlet's 'Speak the speech, I pray you, as I pronounced it to you – trippingly on the tongue' (*Ham*. 3.2.1–2) becomes, 'Speak the speech, but don't overact. Perform the play, with my new words intact' (2000, p. 35) and Claudius' 'When sorrows come they come not single spies, / But in battalions' (*Ham*. 4.5.76–7), 'He turned to his wife who was looking glum, / "Sorrows appear not singly, but in battalions come"' (2000, p. 49). Not only are these verses unbearably stilted and nursery-rhyme like, but they distort some of the most famous lines in the Shakespearean canon, surely a perverse exercise when endeavouring to inspire an ongoing fascination with and knowledge of his work.

In her article 'All the Colours of the Wind' (2003), in which she explains and defends her books as ideal texts with which to introduce Shakespeare to children, Burdett herself enters into the long-running debate about when to introduce young people to Shakespeare's language, and indeed whether there is any value in introducing them to the story without the words, asserting that she does not see the 'narrative story or the language' debate as 'an either/or proposition' but believes that 'both Shakespeare's narrative and language can be introduced simultaneously and the children's understanding will again flow naturally through these various stages' (2003, p. 47). However, although Burdett's work with her own students may involve the introduction of passages of Shakespeare's text, her books themselves do not introduce Shakespeare's 'narrative and language' simultaneously. They tell Shakespeare's stories in couplets which, while they may contain words or phrases from the original, are NOT Shakespeare's lines. There is little doubt that Burdett's work with her own students is exceptional, and the improvements in her pupils' work remarkable. However, this work goes far beyond the texts contained in her books, which provide only a starting point, a point beyond which pupils using the books with less creative and imaginative teachers may not advance.

Apart from Marcia Williams' books which, as discussed, are poly-vocal, the remainder of the post-1990 texts are written as prose narratives, incorporating, to a greater or lesser extent, elements of the Shakespearean text. The *Usborne Illustrated Stories* uses a similar technique to Williams by including occasional Shakespearean lines emanating from the mouths of its characters; however, these quotations are extremely sparse, with one or two lines appearing every few pages, and there is little sense of theatricality inherent in the illustrations. McCaughrean's *Stories* also resemble these books in their combination of modernized prose narrative and brief Shakespearean phrases. However, although the back cover of the book asserts that the use of quotations is 'ingenious', in the absence of illustrated characters into whose mouths the lines can be placed, they are presented in a potentially, rather off-putting academic reference style – indented from the main text and supplied with Act and Scene numbers.

While more extensive and detailed in its narrative than the *Usborne Illustrated* edition, which is clearly aimed at a younger age market, the *Usborne Stories from Shakespeare* contains very little of the Shakespearean text. Apart from a single quotation prefacing each story, the dialogue is entirely modernized. Even elements such as Orlando's poems in *As You Like It* or the casket riddles in *The Merchant of Venice*, which are presented separately from the text, designed to look like hand-written verses, are rewritten by Claybourne. This seems an unnecessary procedure, and one which, like Burdett's rhyming verse, has the potential to mislead. In addition, the four line rhymes with which Claybourne replaces the casket verses sound rather glib in comparison to the Shakespearean originals:

> You did not choose the prettiest views,
> But used your brains, your courage too.
> Well done, for you have chosen true,
> And now the prize belongs to you. (Claybourne, 2004, p. 146)

Beverley Birch's rewriting of the dialogue in her *Shakespeare's Stories* is similarly bemusing, and potentially distorting, being neither Shakespearean dialogue like Garfield's text, nor modernized colloquial speech like Claybourne's and Matthews', but merely a slight translation. In *Romeo and Juliet*, for example, the famous lines 'What's in a name? That which we call a rose / By any other word would smell as sweet' (*Rom.* 2.1.85–6) are rewritten as 'What's in a name! If we call a rose by any other name it would smell as sweet' (Birch, 1997, p. 13), an unnecessary clarification which is less rhythmical and less fluid than the original.

Matthews is perhaps the prose adaptor whose work moves furthest away from the Shakespearean text, taking on an imaginative life of its own in terms of both language and structure. His *A Midsummer Night's Dream*, for example, begins not with an adapted version of 1.1 but with an intimate conversation between Hermia and Helena, not present in the play. As a result Matthews is liberated from attempting to provide a modern 'translation' of Shakespeare's dialogue, inventing his own lines and presenting them in colloquial English – 'His stupid pride's been hurt, that's all – he doesn't love me a bit' (Matthews, 2001, p. 14). His *Hamlet*, *Antony and Cleopatra*, *Richard III* and *Macbeth* are all narrated in the first person, by Hamlet, Servius a centurion, Richard and Macbeth respectively. The decision to use the protagonists as narrators for *Hamlet* and *Richard III* seems appropriate, since they are two of Shakespeare's characters who speak most often directly to the audience, sharing with them their thoughts and feelings. However, the technique is ultimately undramatic, since the multiplicity of voices integral to drama are lost, subsumed into the single subjective voice.

In addition to the text and its layout, the other element of storybook adaptations that has a significant impact on their reception is the illustrations. Illustrators take on an interpretative role in choosing how to depict the characters, their environment and their actions, and the decisions which they make have the potential to affect the reader's engagement with the story. Possibly nowhere is such a decision more significant than in the depiction of Caliban in *The Tempest*. Although Caliban is described by Prospero as 'A freckled whelp hag-born, not honour'd with / A human shape' (1.2.284–5), this is a subjective description, and one borne of his disgust for Caliban's uncivilized nature. Since the late eighteenth century a number of critics have sought to revise this perception of Caliban as a monstrous figure and stress his status as a 'noble savage'. However, as Gerald Graff and James Phelan suggest,

> indeterminacy is an essential feature of his character. He crosses several boundaries: half-human, half-devil, or perhaps half-human, half-fish; abnormal mentally and physically; savage, 'strange beast', and 'moon-calf'. As 'wild man', he is also a composite, possessing qualities of the 'noble savage' as well as the 'monster'. (2000, p. 265)

He is thus an extremely difficult character to depict, and has 'in various eras been seen as a tortoise, a giant fish, a grotesque monster, a primitive everyman, an anthropoid missing link, and – especially nowadays – an American Indian or Caribbean slave of African or mestizo ancestry' (Alden T. and Virginia Mason Vaughan, 1991, p.xiv).

Given this recent trend towards the humanization of Caliban, it is perhaps surprising to discover that he is presented in many of the contemporary adaptations, particularly those for young children as a monster. Marcia Williams, for example, having described him as 'the monster Caliban', presents him as a fantastical creature – part man, part animal, part dragon, with Dalmatian-like spots and a tail, small dragon's wings and pointed, devil-like ears; Tony Ross, undoubtedly influenced by Matthews' description of him as 'a strange creature . . . shaped like a man', its skin 'covered with glistening green scales' and its eyes 'yellow as a lizard's' (2003, p. 15), depicts him as a scaly monster in the individual Orchard Shakespeare publications; and Tony Morris, picking up on Chris Powling's description of his as 'the witch's lazy monster of a son' (2000, p. 16) illustrates him as a hairy beast with slanting eyes and sharp nails. The illustrations for Burdett's books are all produced by her pupils, as part of their work on the plays, and show a similar universal perception of the character as a monster – a green alien, a red man-like creature with webbed hands and feet, and a green monster with a dragon-like tail and claws (Burdett, 1999, pp. 23, 35, 39, 43, 53). While the text merely describes Caliban as 'more ugly beast than man' (p. 21), these drawings encourage other readers to view Caliban as a fantastical, inhuman creature, a perception which has significant ramifications for their interpretation of the story and its power dynamics. At the other end of the scale we find the straightforward illustration of Caliban in the *Usborne Illustrated Stories from Shakespeare* as a man, barely differentiated from the other characters, in accordance with his simple description as 'Prospero's servant' (Dickins et al., 2010, p. 136). Only Angela Barrett in *The Orchard Book of Shakespeare Stories* seems to capture the composite of noble savage and monster, presenting Caliban as shaped like a man – akin to a native African – with a bare chest, short skirt made of skin and necklace of sharks' teeth, but with scaly skin, browny-green in colour.

Although these illustrators are doing essentially what theatre designers do in deciding how to depict the various characters, as Bottoms argues, these books, which often constitute young people's first encounters with the plays, are in danger of 'robbing children of the right to ask their own questions and form their own judgements' (1999, p. 23). Picking up on the presentation of Caliban, she argues that we do not need 'to present Caliban as either a comic grotesque or wronged colonized native if we let children encounter [him] through [his] own words and actions' (p. 23). In her view, the best encounter with Shakespeare is one in which children can 'wrestle with the characters and their dilemmas, as actors do in the rehearsal process' (p. 23) – a practical encounter which encourages exploration and speculation rather than presenting children with facts and explanations. This is, of course, precisely the form of encounter which is recommended in the National Strategies 'Shakespeare for All Ages and Stages' and QCDA 'Active Shakespeare' initiative discussed in Chapter 1, both of which draw on rehearsal room exercises recommended by the Shakespeare's Globe and the Royal Shakespeare Company in order to encourage an active, experimental approach to the study of the plays.

This is not to say that these illustrated narrative texts do not have some role in children's encounters with Shakespeare. They can usefully be read to a child, much like a plot synopsis in a theatre programme, prior to going to see the play, aiding their understanding of what happens on stage. They may also serve to enthuse young people about Shakespeare's stories, and help to dispel ideas that his work is either boring or difficult. However, as has been explored, there are several elements of these storybook Shakespeares, from their earliest incarnations to their present forms, which are problematic in serving as introductions to the plays – the censorship and editing of apparently 'unsuitable' elements of the texts, which may prove misleading; the narrative form of the books, which deprives young people of an encounter with Shakespeare's language and leaves them with what Marchitello rightly describes as 'the least part of Shakespeare' – the stories (2002, p. 182); and their non-dramatic form, which, as both Bottoms and Prindle assert, provides children with a solitary reading experience, rather than with a collaborative and active viewing or performing one – an experience for which, after all, the plays were originally written.

Notes

1 Published both as *The Orchard Book of Shakespeare Stories*, illustrated by Angela Barrett and as individual texts, illustrated by Tony Ross.
2 Later published by Wayland in individual editions as *Shakespeare's Tales*.
3 See Chapter 1.
4 See Abigail Rokison (2010b).

CHAPTER FOUR

Shakespeare and the Graphic Novel

As Stephen Weiner explains, in the early 1980s, 'several complementary elements gelled at the same time, bringing graphic novels to the forefront of popular culture' (2004, p. 114). In the twenty-first century, the continuing popularity of this genre has had a noticeable impact on the publication of Shakespeare texts for young people in both Britain and the United States, with Simon Greaves beginning publication of the *Shakespeare Comic Books* series in 1999, two British series – *Manga Shakespeare* and *Classical Comics* – launching in 2007, and 2008 seeing the introduction of Wiley's *Manga Edition* and the addition by SparkNotes of graphic novel editions to their already highly popular *No Fear Shakespeare* series. In addition to these new texts, in 2006, Can of Worms Press acquired the rights to the Oval Projects *Cartoon Shakespeare* series, originally published in the 1980s, reproducing the original four editions.[1]

Comic book Shakespeare is, of course, not a new phenomenon. In 1941, Albert Kanter launched Gilberton publishing's *Classics Illustrated*, a series of graphic versions of literary classics including five Shakespeare titles, published in the 1950s – *Julius Caesar, A Midsummer Night's Dream, Hamlet, Macbeth* and *Romeo and Juliet*. These publications, which contained an edited version of the Shakespearean text, were designed 'to encourage youth to read the classics' (Wetmore, Jr, 2006, p. 175), in other words, intended, much as were many of the narrative Shakespeares discussed in the previous chapter, as introductions to Shakespeare after which students could and should experience, according to the final page of each edition, 'the enjoyment of the original' (p. 175). However, as Kevin J. Wetmore, Jr, observes, often these texts became substitutes for the originals rather than guides towards them (pp. 175–6), something which some critics found concerning, and which, as we will see, is an ongoing concern regarding the use of graphic novels in the classroom.

Although these texts subsequently went out of print, the resurgence in popularity of graphic texts in the 1980s led to the production of new versions of *Classics Illustrated* with new illustrations for a new readership. Only one Shakespeare text – *Hamlet* – was published in 1990, but in 1997 digest-size versions of the original *Classics Illustrated* versions of Shakespeare were reproduced by Acclaim Comics, again with an emphasis on their introductory nature. Marketed as 'study guides', the tagline for the series was 'Your doorway to the classics' (Wetmore, Jr, 2006, p. 194). Outlining this reemergence of graphic novel Shakespeare, Wetmore, Jr, notes a decline in the comic industry since the early 1990s, but asserts that 'the form will continue to exist for the foreseeable future' and that 'it would not be unusual for new Shakespeare-influenced and inspired graphic novels to appear in the future' (p. 195). This statement prefigures the surge of popularity in the genre, with the advent of the *Cartoon Shakespeare, Manga Shakespeare, Classical Comics*, Wiley *Manga Edition* and *No Fear Shakespeare Graphic Novels* editions over the subsequent three years. This chapter will explore these editions, focusing on *Macbeth*, a text, which, as will be discussed, lends itself particularly well to the genre of Manga.

Although the name 'graphic *novel*', commonly given to cartoon and Manga versions of Shakespeare and other classics, suggests a narrative form, similar to those texts discussed in Chapter 3, the Shakespeare graphic novels actually contain very little narrative description, this being confined to brief scene-settings at the start of an episode. Thus, while, like the illustrated storybook versions, they combine elements of the verbal and visual, bringing the characters to life on the page, they do so in a form much closer to that of theatre and film productions, with the text, in dialogue form, emanating from the mouths of the characters.

Indeed, the texts of many of these graphic editions, particularly those that use an unexpurgated version of the Shakespearean text, are closer to editions of the plays traditionally used in school. However, the illustrations provide an added dimension, enabling the reader to see clearly who is speaking, to whom, and in what setting, as well as aiding them in visualizing the physical action accompanying a particular sequence of dialogue. Rosie Blau, writing in the *Financial Times*, suggests that 'a cartoon version of Shakespeare is in some ways truer to the original than reading the text alone' since 'the visual element was always supposed to be part of the experience' (2007), while Adam Sexton goes one stage further, arguing that graphic novels might be '*more* visual than a stage production of one of the plays of Shakespeare' since 'unbound by the physical realities of the theatre, the graphic novel can depict any situation, no matter how fantastical or violent, that are able to pencil, ink and shade' (2008, p. 2). For Sexton graphic novels are the ideal vehicle for depicting Shakespeare's work, since they are both visual and 'potentially no less verbal' (p. 3) than Shakespeare's plays. In addition to providing the reader with the visual benefits characteristic of theatre or film production, they allow the reader to see the words on the page, and to 'linger over speeches' or reread difficult sections (p. 3).

Graphic novels are not, however, perhaps as universally accessible as these commentators would seem to suggest. In the latter half of the twentieth century, notions of literacy have changed, with visual literacy becoming an essential skill. Although most young readers are familiar with interpreting the proliferation of visual images which resonate throughout our culture, the visual literacy required to interpret a graphic novel is a particular skill, which is likely to be acquired mainly through familiarity, 'the learning curve for building coherent meaning' being 'one of the common hurdles for new readers' of graphic texts (Brenner, 2007, p. 66).

Brenner outlines a series of features of the layout of Manga texts which, once recognized by the reader, help to clarify the storytelling – including devices designed to indicate who is speaking and to distinguish flashback from the main narrative. However, these devices – the use of 'different edge designs' to speech bubbles for different speakers and a shift in background colour for flashbacks in order to 'indicate that panels are not taking place in the same timeline' (2007, p. 68) – are by no means universal to the graphic novel editions of *Macbeth*. The *Manga Shakespeare: Macbeth* (Appignanesi and Deas, 2008) seems particularly difficult to follow, even, one assumes, for the most seasoned Manga reader. While some lines are placed in speech bubbles clearly emanating from particular characters, others are placed in unconnected speech bubbles which are not distinguished by colour or outline, often making it difficult to discern who is speaking. In the equivalent of 1.2 *Macbeth*, for example, the dying Sergeant's lines 'So from that spring . . . fresh assault' (1.2.27–33) are placed in unconnected speech bubbles overlaying a picture of 'The Norweyan Lord' beginning his 'fresh assault' – a flashback to the action being described, but one which here retains the same background colour as the main narrative (p. 7). Duncan's subsequent question 'Dismayed not this our captains Macbeth and Banquo?' (1.2.34) is placed on the following page, accompanying a picture of Macbeth and Banquo – again a flashback (p. 18). While the device of flashback is one readily recognizable from film, where conversations are often overlaid with images depicting what is being described, in the case of film it is still possible to discern who is speaking from their voice. In the *Manga Shakespeare* text, with the absence of the aural dimension, it is easy to lose the sense of to whom lines belong, and hence the overall coherence of the dialogue.

The *No Fear Shakespeare Graphic Novels* (SparkNotes and Hoshine, 2008), *Classical Comics* (McDonald and Hayward, 2008a) and *Graphic Shakespeare* (formerly known as *Cartoon Shakespeare*) (Von, 1982) editions of *Macbeth* make more use of the devices described by Brenner to clarify the nature of various speeches, particularly in the variations in 'edge designs' for speech bubbles. All place characters' soliloquies and asides in cloud-like thought bubbles to distinguish them from the dialogue; *No Fear* and *Classical Comics* use dotted lines to indicate lines which are whispered; *Classical Comics* and *Graphic Shakespeare* use jagged outlines for speech bubbles containing shouted lines or exclamations and *Classical Comics* and the Wiley *Manga Edition* (Sexton et al., 2008) use uneven outlines for the witches' speech bubbles. The Wiley *Manga Edition* also makes some distinction between soliloquies and asides and the remainder of the dialogue, printing them in white on a black background, as opposed to black on white. These devices, even if not immediately recognizable to the reader, are easy to pick up, and, in some cases, help to provide some indication of the tone of the lines, another feature of these texts comparable with theatrical and film productions. The 'aural' dimension to the text, provided by the indications of shifts in volume and mood, is further enhanced in the *Classical Comics*, *No Fear*, Wiley *Manga* and *Manga Shakespeare* editions by the use of 'sound effects' which appear in large letters across some illustrations to indicate various diegetic sounds – the drum which ushers in Macbeth (1.3); the tolling of the bell (2.1) and the knocking at the castle gates (2.3) as well as the occasional non-diegetic atmospheric noise, such as the 'Kraka-boom' which ushers in each of the apparitions in the *Manga Shakespeare* edition. The use of visual indicators to provide a soundscape for the play is another aspect of its presentation which helps to bring the text to life for readers, giving it a multidimensional quality.

Despite the many positive reviews of the graphic Shakespeare texts, which stress their theatricality, visual appeal and ability to clarify the action of the plays, from the early *Classics Illustrated* versions to those published in the last decade, questions have been raised about the suitability of the genre as a means of introducing young people to Shakespeare. In the 1950s, Delmore Schwartz complained about the unpoetic nature of the *Classics Illustrated* texts (1952, rep. 2004, p. 55) and Frederic Wertham argued that the violent style of some of the illustrations resulted in the corruption of both 'Shakespeare and the child' (1954, p. 143). The question which was constantly asked in relation to these texts was 'whether Shakespeare elevates comics or if comics debase Shakespeare' (Wetmore, Jr, 2006, p. 174). This is a question which continues to be asked of the new generation of graphic texts. In May 2007, having recognized the recent resurgence in the popularity of comic book Shakespeare, BBC Education editor Gary Eason asked, 'is this a valid way of introducing the Bard to new readers?' (2007). Eason does not arrive at a definite answer to this question, perhaps because it cannot be answered with a simple 'yes' or 'no'. The validity of graphic novels as an introduction to Shakespeare's work depends on which texts are being used, at what point in a student's school career, and for what purpose.

Classical Comics produce three different editions of each play – 'Original Text', 'Plain Text' and 'Quick Text'. The Original Text, like the *Graphic Shakespeare* versions, provides an unexpurgated text, placed in speech and thought bubbles. As such, it provides readers with access to the whole play in a form more immediately accessible and visually appealing than the standard edited texts generally used in the classroom. The illustration of each verbal exchange, as discussed above, has a theatrical or filmic dimension, which helps to bring the text alive on the page. However, like theatrical and indeed film productions, these texts are necessarily interpretative. As Wetmore, Jr, comments, 'the artists creating a graphic novel . . . must make the same choices as the design team of a theatre company', deciding where and when to 'set' the play and must 'cast' the characters by deciding how to represent them physically (2006, p. 172). In addition to taking on the function of the designer, they must also assume the roles of both director and actor – making interpretative decisions about how characters relate to one another, what actions accompany their lines and what mood they are in. This is an element of graphic novels which could be seen to limit young people's imaginative engagement with the text, closing their eyes to the range of possible nuances and interpretations.

The illustrations in the *Classical Comics: Macbeth* Original Text edition which accompany the dialogue between Macbeth and Lady Macbeth in 2.2 (1–48), for example, show Lady Macbeth drinking from a horn of wine, smashing a flagon of wine to the floor in rage, pushing Macbeth to the ground and viciously slapping him when asking why he failed to leave the daggers with the grooms (McDonald and Hayward, 2008a, pp. 34–6). While this is one possible interpretation of the exchange, it is quite an extreme version, which seems to play against the respectful term of address, 'worthy thane' (2.2.42) which Lady Macbeth uses towards her husband. This is, one might argue, no more problematic in terms of young people's encounter with the Shakespearean text than their experiencing of the play in the theatre or cinema, where interpretative decisions are necessarily made. Indeed, it may raise interesting and provocative discussion on ways of reading or playing a scene. However, theatre and film productions are generally viewed *alongside* the study of the text. There is perhaps a danger that if these editions are used as the sole texts of the plays in the classroom, young people may view them as providing a definitive reading of a scene rather than one of many possible interpretations.

In my view, the main problem with the use of the *Classical Comics* and *Graphic Shakespeare* texts, as classroom editions,[2] is that raised by Schwartz in relation to the *Classics Illustrated* texts – the setting of all the lines as prose. While I do not subscribe to Schwartz's concern that this representation of the text is likely to have the effect of alienating the 'juvenile reader' so that when he does 'at some later date encounter poetry printed as poetry he is likely to be annoyed, if not irritated to the point where he refuses to read whatever is printed as poetry at all' (1952, rep. 2004, p. 55), I would argue that the basic distinction between verse and prose, obscured by these editions, is an important part of the study of the plays, in particular in assessing character status, tone and mood. The failure to distinguish one medium from another is the failure to recognize Hamlet's method of assuming an 'antic disposition' (*Ham.* 1.5.173), Lear's verbal as well as physical descent into madness, and the difference in the linguistic registers of the lovers and the mechanicals in *A Midsummer Night's Dream*.

The first issue at stake – the interpretative nature of comic-style illustrations – is applicable to all the graphic texts discussed here, perhaps more so in the case of *Manga Shakespeare*, for while the illustrations for the other editions discussed here all present a pseudo-Medieval world, not unlike that of Roman Polanski's film version of the play (1971), the *Manga Shakespeare* edition transfers the story to 'a future post-nuclear world of mutants' (Appignanesi and Deas, 2008, back cover) peopled by samurai warriors, a world away from the setting of Shakespeare's *Macbeth*. The witches are alien-like monsters, with green claws and piercing yellow eyes; Duncan is less the 'gracious' (3.1.67) king bearing his faculties 'so meek' (1.7.17) than a broad-shouldered aggressive-looking warlord; Banquo is depicted with an eye patch and a cigar hanging from his lips, blowing smoke into the face of one of the witches as he demands to know his fate, and Macduff (clearly not 'of woman born') is a huge mutant with four arms. Some have argued that this is one of the strengths of the *Manga Shakespeare* – its translation of the plays from one culture into another – 'high culture into pop-culture' (Grande, 2010, p. 1); Western culture into Japanese 'exotic otherness' (p. 15) to which Blau argues Shakespearean tragedy is 'perfectly suited' with its 'abiding concerns' of sex and violence (2007). Douglas Lanier suggests that in straddling these different realms, the texts provide 'an important means by which notions about Shakespeare's cultural significance is created, extended, debated, revised, and renewed' (2002, pp. 19–20) while Troni Grande praises the texts for working 'effectively to inject a revivifying contemporaneity into Shakespeare' (2010, p. 14). In the case of the *Manga Shakespeare Macbeth* the elements are less contemporary than futuristic, but, in injecting *Macbeth* with elements of science fiction, they draw on visual images more immediately recognizable and accessible to young readers than those of Medieval Scotland. Macbeth, for example, delivers his order 'Bring me no more reports' (5.3.1), through a speaker phone built into the arm of his throne, as he sits, surrounded by television screens all displaying Malcolm's face (Appignanesi and Deas, 2008, p. 164) – a clear visual manifestation of his obsession with the witches' prophesy: 'What's the boy Malcolm? / Was he not born of woman?' (5.3.3–4). The image echoes an earlier point in this text in which Duncan's crowning of Malcolm as 'Prince of Cumberland' is made to the television cameras, Macbeth subsequently re-viewing the image on a huge screen as he mulls it over (p. 43) – 'That is a step on which I must fall down, or else overleap' (1.4.48).

Praising the *Manga Shakespeare*: *Macbeth* for its 'translation of a work from one culture into another', *The Scotsman* draws comparison between this text and Akira Kurosawa's highly successful *Throne of Blood* (1957), arguing that the Manga version has 'some of the same strengths, while staying truer to the text' (*The Scotsman*, 2008). *Throne of Blood* has been widely praised for the fact that 'Kurosawa and his co-writers . . . miraculously transplant *Macbeth* in such a way that it retains deep roots in Shakespeare and in Japanese history (feuding warlords) and theatre (Noh)' (Rosenthal, 2007, p. 105). One of the reasons for this seamless transposition of the play from Medieval Scotland to Japan was, as Maurice Hindle explains, because Shakespeare's play has a 'social, political and military setting which does obviously parallel the structure of the samurai warrior society' (2007, p. 100). Although the samurai warrior culture presented in the *Manga Shakespeare* edition is a futuristic rather than a medieval one, it may be argued that similar notion of power structures, 'swordplay and revenge' (p. 100), continue resonate.

It is also unarguably true that the *Manga Shakespeare* editions, which adhere for the most part to Shakespeare's language, provide a 'truer' rendition of Shakespeare's *Macbeth* than Kurosawa's film, which is only loosely based on the play, with key characters altered or removed, back stories added and the moral centre of the play shifted. However, although the *Manga Shakespeare* website asserts the 'educational quality' of the texts, stressing the academic credentials of the editorial team, the text used in the *Manga Shakespeare: Macbeth* is heavily edited. Much of the imagery, for example, is cut, prioritizing the transmission of the story over its style of delivery. Also, some cuts, while allowing the basic sense of a speech to be conveyed, severely affect its overall meaning. The start of Macbeth's speech 'If it were done . . .' (1.7.1–10), for example, is reduced to

> If it were done, then it were well done quickly. If the assassination could catch success, this blow might be the be-all and the end-all here. We but teach bloody instructions, which, being taught, return to plague the inventor. (Appignanesi and Deas, 2008, pp. 58–9)

The alteration of the first sentence from 'If it were done when 'tis done, then 'twere well / It were done quickly' (1.7.1–2), obscures, from the outset, Macbeth's concern with the possible repercussions of his action which haunt this speech. The subsequent removal of 'trammel up the consequence', 'that but' and 'But here . . . life to come' (1.7.3, 4 and 6–7) alters the sense from that of Macbeth declaring his preparedness to sacrifice an afterlife if he could be sure of present success on earth, to a basic statement of cause and effect – 'If the assassination could catch success, this blow might be the be-all and the end-all here' (Appignanesi and Deas, 2008, p. 58). Thus, while the reader is made aware that Macbeth is contemplating the outcome of his intended murder of Duncan, his mode of thinking is obscured by the cuts.

Wetmore, Jr, might be justified in asking of the impulse to cut the text in these graphic novels – 'How is this any different . . . from a stage production that, in order to have the audience out by 11.00pm, cuts . . . some of the longer scenes?' (2006, p. 174). Certainly, although the cuts considerably exceed those common to most theatre productions, they resemble in volume the cuts made to theatrical versions of Shakespeare for young people, discussed in Chapter 5, which attempt to reduce the text to around an hour in length. However, unlike most of these theatrical texts, the structure of the verse is compromised in the *Manga Shakespeare: Macbeth*. Not only are the lines, as in the *Classical Comics* Original Text and *Graphic Shakespeare* editions, laid out as prose, but the cuts are made with little regard for the metre, rhythm or rhyme scheme of the original, the editor cutting odd words from lines and piecing together new sentences which lack fluidity. Rhyming couplets which mark significant aphorisms are frequently obscured by cuts which disrupt the pentameter,[3] and the distinctive iambic tetrameter rhythm of the witches in their chanting is undistinguishable from the more common pentameter of the other characters, or indeed from prose.

The text of the Wiley *Manga Edition: Macbeth*, although also cut down and set out as prose, is far less extreme in its method of editing than the *Manga Shakespeare*, the editors tending to remove complete lines of dialogue, retaining the basic structure, rather than, as in the case of the *Manga Shakespeare*, effectively rewriting Shakespeare's dialogue. Although some of the cuts disrupt the pentameter, for the most part the rhythm and rhyme schemes of the text are preserved, in particular in the witches' scenes, where although a number of lines are cut, the basic iambic tetrameter is retained. The most noticeable editorial intervention in the Wiley *Manga Edition*, apart from the removal of the Hecate scene (3.5), a scene regularly cut in performance, comes in the reordering of certain sequences of lines – the moving of Lady Macbeth's opening soliloquy of 1.5: 'They met me in the day of success . . . crown'd withal' (1.5.1–29) to before 1.4, and the reordering of the text in 3.1 to intersperse Macbeth and Banquo's dialogue with their thoughts (Sexton et al., 2008, p. 87). The reasoning behind these changes is not immediately apparent, but they might be compared to the sorts of editorial choices made by film directors of Shakespeare, to break up long scenes or aid clarity of storytelling.

These Manga texts, with their filmic elements, are probably best compared in their style and treatment of the text to Baz Luhrmann's *Romeo + Juliet*, which, as discussed in Chapter 2, showed little regard for the verse form in both the layout of the screenplay and the cutting of the text, but found a series of vivid images from popular contemporary youth culture, served up with a good measure of violence, and visually appealing characters with which to make the story appealing and immediate. Indeed, the *Independent on Sunday* makes just such a comparison in writing about the *Manga Shakespeare* series, declaring that it 'does in book form what film director Baz Luhrmann did on screen – make Shakespeare cool and accessible to a younger generation' (SelfMadeHero, 2011c).

These elements of explicitly depicted violence and sexually heightened presentation of characters are features of the *Manga Shakespeare*: *Macbeth* in which Lady Macbeth is depicted in a tight corset, short skirt and suspenders while most of the male warriors are shown with bare, athletic chests. Grande's suggestion that the age-old motives of censorship may be behind some of the cuts made to the *Manga Shakespeare* texts seems, therefore, surprising, given the apparent lack of censorship inherent in the illustrations. Writing about the *Manga Shakespeare*: *Romeo and Juliet* and *A Midsummer Night's Dream*, Grande remarks on the 'many cuts pertaining to the sexual imagery in both plays' (2010, p. 13), in particular to Mercutio's 'bawdy banter' in 1.4 and 2.4 *Romeo and Juliet*, suggesting that these are motivated by the 'impulse to preserve what Henry Giroux has called the "myth of childhood innocence"' (p. 14), an impulse which, as discussed in Chapter 3, can be seen throughout the history of narrative retellings of Shakespeare for children. This impulse is less obvious in the *Manga Shakespeare: Macbeth*, partly because, as Eric Partridge notes, '*Macbeth* is the "purest" of the tragedies, and except for the Porter Scene, pure by any criterion' (1947, p. 57). The Porter scene is entirely expunged from the *Manga Shakespeare: Macbeth*, but whether this is motivated by censorship or simply due to its lack of contribution to the story is difficult to discern. With a semiclad Lady Macbeth, her top falling from her shoulder to reveal an ample bosom as she cries 'Come to my woman's breasts' (Appignanesi and Deas, 2008, p. 51) and a shirtless Malcolm declaring 'But your wives, your daughters, could not fill up the cistern of my lust' (p. 143), the impression is not of a desire to shelter readers from the play's sexual content.

The *Shakespeare Comic Books* editions, although similar in their treatment of the text to the Wiley *Manga Edition*, are quite different from these editions in terms of style, and, significantly, layout of the text. What is immediately clear on opening one of these *Comic Book* editions is that the text has been prioritized over the illustrations. While illustrations accompany most exchanges, these are, in the *Macbeth* edition (Greaves, 2003a), simple black-and-white line drawings, and cede space on the page to the written text which appears, uniquely in the graphic editions discussed here, in both the original language and in a modern 'translation', which appears below each section of the text. Despite the assertion from writer Naomi Alderman which appears on the company's website – 'Amazing! It's really like a staging of Shakespeare' (Shakespeare Comics, 2011) – these editions are less theatrical or filmic than the other texts discussed in this chapter. One feels slightly that this publisher has attempted to do too much – to incorporate too many ideas – so that the edition falls between a number of stools. It is not visually exciting enough to engage a reluctant reader, who is faced with mass of words, due to the dual-text approach;

equally, the clarity of the text is somewhat obscured by the layout, with the translation below the original text disrupting the flow of the reading experience. However, the *Shakespeare Comic Books* edition does have one positive distinctive feature in its layout, it being the only graphic version that, while making cuts to the text, retains the verse form in the layout. Although in some cases the lines are divided in order to fit into speech bubbles, each verse line begins with a capital letter, and words running over into the next line of text are indented. Thus the rhyming scheme of the witches' lines is made perfectly apparent, as are rhyming couplets and the distinction between verse and prose.

Before discussing the nature of the parallel translated text provided by the *Shakespeare Comic Books* editions, we move to graphic novels editions which solely employ a translation of the plays into modern English, in order to enable some comparison of the styles of translation. Both the Plain Text versions of the *Classical Comics* and the *No Fear Shakespeare Graphic Novels* texts are comprised of line-by-line conversions of the original text, with the aim, according to Barnes and Noble, of making the plays 'easier to read' (n.d.) for those students who may struggle with the Shakespearean text. *Classical Comics* equally suggest that such texts may have a place in the classroom for readers who might be 'deter[ed]' by Shakespeare's language (*Classical Comics*, n.d., 'Education'). These editions of the play may take some of the fear out of studying Shakespeare; however, director of the National Association for the Teaching of English, Ian McNeilly, finds the use of such texts in the classroom worrying. While the graphic novels containing Shakespearean dialogue provide, in McNeilly's view, a welcome aid to teachers 'in making the plays accessible and enjoyable', his reaction to these modernized texts is that 'if you are just telling the plot, what's the point?' (quoted by Eason, 2007). Indeed, the claim by *Classical Comics* that their Plain Text editions retain 'the full essence of the play' (*Classical Comics*, n.d., 'Text Versions') is easily dismissed, when one considers that so much of the 'essence' of Shakespeare's plays reside in his language. Equally, as Jennifer Hulbert, Kevin J. Wetmore, Jr, and Robert L. York point out, the translation of Shakespeare's lines 'is almost always reductivist and falls into self-parody' (2006, p. 20). They give as an example Hamlet's line to Ophelia – 'Get thee to a nunnery. Why wouldst thou be a breeder of sinners?' (3.1, 123–4) which is translated by the *No Fear Shakespeare: Hamlet* parallel text edition as 'Get yourself to a convent at once. Why would you want to give birth to more sinners' (SparkNotes, 2003a, p. 143) – asserting 'Something is lost in translation, literally' (p. 21). One of the major issues with trying to simplify this line is that the double meaning inherent in the word 'nunnery' – possibly alluding to either a convent or a brothel, or simultaneously to both – is lost. Puns revolving around homophones, synonyms or double meanings, particularly those which have fallen out of common parlance, are inevitably difficult to retain when attempting to translate a text into 'plain' English.

Lady Macbeth and Macbeth indulge in wordplay from the outset, indicating their deceptive natures. As Mireille Ravassat asserts in her discussion of 'translating the ambiguities of wordplay' in *Macbeth* into French – 'more than ever in *Macbeth*, Shakespeare probes into the perils of verbal duplication and duplicity, puns becoming fatal' (2007). As Ravassat goes on to discuss, the translation of such puns into another language is rife with problems of equivalency, which frequently result in the obfuscation of the double meanings. Ravassat identifies three examples in Lady Macbeth's dialogue in 1.5 of ambiguous meanings obscured by translation – 'That I may pour my spirits in thine ear' (1.5.25), 'spirits' here having multiple meanings – 'immaterial qualities', 'courage' and 'distilled poison' (Brooke, 1998, p. 112); Lady Macbeth's invocation to the spirits to 'fill me from the crown to the toe top-full / Of direst cruelty' (1.5.41–2), 'crown' having the obvious meaning of head, but concealing a reference to Lady Macbeth's ambition for the royal crown; and her assertion that Duncan 'must be provided for' (1.5.66) which plays 'intentionally and sardonically on her double role as hostess and accomplice in regicide' (Ravassat, 2007). There are, in fact, many more ambiguities in Lady Macbeth's lines in this scene, her speech 'The raven himself is hoarse . . .' (1.5.37–53) having 'a density of language and imagery that makes commentary extremely difficult' (Brooke, 1998, p. 112), let alone, one imagines, the production of a simplified, modernized translation. The phrase 'sightless substances' (1.5.48), for example, encompasses the sense of blindness, invisibility and unsightliness (p. 113), 'pall' (1.5.50) brings together the meanings of to 'cover' and to 'appal' or 'become appalling' (p. 113), and 'keen' (1.5.51) the meanings of 'sharp' and 'eager' (p. 113).

These instances of wordplay, which can be made evident to students through commentary or footnotes, are almost all obscured in the *Classical Comics* Plain Text and the *No Fear Shakespeare Graphic Novel*. 'Fill me from the crown to the toe' becomes simply 'fill me from head to toe' in both texts (McDonald and Hayward, 2008b, p. 21; SparkNotes and Hoshine, 2008, p. 31), removing any reference to royalty; 'must be provided for' becomes 'Has to be wined and dined' (McDonald and Hayward, 2008b, p. 22) and 'has to be cared for' (SparkNotes and Hoshine, 2008, p. 33) obscuring the ominous threat; 'sightless substances' become 'invisible agents' (McDonald and Hayward, 2008b, p. 21) or demons who 'wait invisibly' (SparkNotes and Hoshine, 2008, p. 31) removing two of the possible meanings; 'pall' becomes merely 'shroud' in both texts (McDonald and Hayward, 2008b, p. 21; SparkNotes and Hoshine, 2008, p. 31) obscuring the potential sense of horror; and 'keen knife' becomes simply 'sharp knife' (McDonald and Hayward, 2008b, p. 21) or 'razor-like knife' (SparkNotes and Hoshine, 2008, p. 31), the alternative meaning of readiness lost. Lady Macbeth's speech is thus reduced in complexity and ambiguity, and her duplicitous nature made less apparent.

Although in the *Shakespeare Comic Books* editions, the translated text does not stand alone, but rather seems intended to provide a full exegesis of the parallel Shakespearean text, the inclusion of a translation of the lines as opposed to footnotes, which are capable of pointing the reader towards a range of possible interpretations, has, as Hulbert, Wetmore, Jr, and York assert of the *No Fear Shakespeare* parallel texts, the capacity to be reductive. In the case of the examples cited above from Lady Macbeth's speech, 'crown to toe' is translated as 'top to bottom' (Greaves, 2003a, p. 9), 'sightless substances' are 'evil creatures' (p. 10), and 'pall' is 'wrap' (p. 10), all similarly simplistic to the solely translated texts. In the case of the *Shakespeare Comic Books* edition, the translations are also often rather bizarre, ranging from the painstakingly literal and frankly redundant, to the strangely interpretative. In the first scene, for example, 'Upon the heath' (1.1.6) is unnecessarily translated as 'On the heath' (p. 1), while 'Hover through the fog and filthy air' (1.1.11) – the meaning surely quite clear – is given the oddly creative translation 'Fly on through a sick and dark world' (p. 1). Similarly Duncan's line 'O valiant cousin, worthy gentleman!' (1.2.24), also easily comprehended, is translated unnecessarily and somewhat inaccurately as 'There's no one better than Macbeth' (p. 2).

The issue of translating every line, even when the meaning is perfectly clear from the original, is another issue raised by Hulbert, Wetmore, Jr, and York in relation to the *No Fear Shakespeare* texts. They quote the opening lines from Macbeth, followed by the *No Fear Shakespeare* parallel text translation, asking the pertinent question – 'What is the clarification for students achieved by changing "There to meet with Macbeth" to "We'll meet Macbeth there"?' (2006, p. 22). The answer is clearly 'none' and the same question could be asked of the alteration of the first line – 'When shall we three meet again?' (1.1.1) to 'When should the three of us meet again?' (SparkNotes, 2003b, p. 3) – in particular the changing of 'shall' to 'should' which actually results in a slight alteration of meaning. It is, however, worth noting that although the *No Fear Shakespeare Graphic Novels: Macbeth* is purportedly based on this translated text of the *No Fear Shakespeare* parallel texts edition, the graphic text retains more of Shakespeare's phrases, not changing lines for which no clarification is required. Hence, in the passage cited above, the lines 'There to meet with Macbeth' and 'When shall we three meet again' are both left in their original form.

The *Classical Comics* Plain Text edition is even more judicious in its translation of the scene, altering only one word – 'ere' to 'before' (McDonald and Hayward, 2008b, p. 8) in this passage, and hence retaining the rhythm and flow of the dialogue, even if the metrical scheme is somewhat obscured by the layout. Indeed this text makes significant effort to replicate the rhythmical and rhyming quality of the witches' lines in all of their scenes, keeping the incantatory spirit of their dialogue. Unlike the *No Fear Shakespeare Graphic Novels* edition, it changes very little of the cauldron charm in 4.1, altering only individual words, such as 'hedge-pig' to 'hedgehog' and 'blind-worm' to 'slow worm' (p. 78), with no effect on the metre. These scenes gain significantly from the prioritizing of rhyme over plainness of meaning, for, though a young reader may not know what a 'brindled' cat is, or a 'fenny' snake, the retention of the ritualistic quality of the spell contributes not only to the characterization of the witches, but also to the enjoyment of the reading experience, an enjoyment which is not present in the *No Fear Shakespeare Graphic Novels* version.

Despite their frequent inability to capture duality of meaning, and the often clunky nature of their dialogue, these translated texts undoubtedly make the plots of the plays more immediately intelligible to young readers, and may well be beneficial as an early introduction to Shakespeare's stories, much like many of the narrative versions discussed in the previous chapter. However, the issue of their function within the study of Shakespeare in the classroom merits further interrogation. Eason summarizes publisher Karen Wenborn on the 'rationale behind' the *Classical Comics* series, stating that 'focus groups involving teachers had produced "incredibly enthusiastic" responses', expanding on this by adding that 'the different layers of text meant they could use them across a class with children of differing abilities reading at the same time' (2009) – a suggestion which is also made on the *Classical Comics* website – 'Our three text versions allow a single class of mixed abilities to work with the same story' (*Classical Comics*, n.d., 'Education'). The positive response from teachers is clear evidence that there is a school market for the *Classical Comics* editions; however, the idea that a student, of whatever ability, might study a Shakespeare play using solely a Plain Text edition of the play, or worse still a Quick Text version is cause for concern. Perhaps a better indicator of how the three different texts can be made to function in the classroom is a testimonial on the *Classical Comics* website from Mrs Breeze 'a teacher in Northamptonshire' who asserts that her sixth formers 'particularly liked the plain text because they could read it quickly and then found it easier to go on to the original' (*Classical Comics*, n.d., 'Testimonials') – using the modernized text as an introduction to the complete play – a means of familiarizing themselves with the story before tackling Shakespeare's language.

The *No Fear Shakespeare Graphic Novels* editions presumably also function best either as introductions to the complete texts or as texts to be read in parallel with the originals, as is made possible by the original *No Fear Shakespeare* parallel text editions. These parallel text editions are regularly used in schools in favour of editions with explanatory footnotes, which require students to work harder to understand the texts. However, as has been seen in the examples cited above, in giving young people a simple translation, with no accompanying footnotes or endnotes, these texts are in danger of reducing down the possible range of meanings and obscuring Shakespeare's wordplay.

The final *Classical Comics* version to come under discussion is the Quick Text edition of *Macbeth*, described on its back cover as providing '"The

Scottish Play" in as few words as possible, while keeping the essence of the story' (McDonald and Hayward, 2008c). Although this edition pares down the dialogue, it does not edit out any sections of the text, as might a stage or film version. Indeed, the reading experience might not be as 'Quick' as its title would suggest, since, in using exactly the same illustrations as both the Original Text and Plain Text editions, this edition still runs to 128 pages, and provides the reader with as full a visual experience as the longer texts. The text is indeed cut down to its bare bones; however, the editors have done a remarkable job of keeping the overall sense, and some of the key sentiments expressed in the play. For example, although Macbeth's famous speech 'She should have died hereafter' (5.5.16–27) is reduced to a mere 34 words which cannot possibly capture the complex biblical references and multiple meanings, nevertheless manages to incorporate a sense that Lady Macbeth's death has come too soon, and of the meaninglessness of life and its fragility, while retaining something of a self-conscious metafictional element in the line 'Life is just a shadow. It's a story told by a fool' (p. 118). Equally, although the witches' dialogue is severely cut down from the version contained in the Plain Text edition, the editors have still made some effort to retain its incantatory nature, building in a more compact rhythm and rhyme scheme into the texts:

First Witch   When shall we meet again?
                   In thunder or in rain?

Second Witch   When the battle's lost and won.

Third Witch   Before the setting of the sun. (p. 8)

Clearly this edition is no substitute for the original as a classroom text; nor is it sufficiently full in its translation to be read alongside the Shakespearean text as a glossary. However, for a young reader, au fait with the genre of the graphic novel, it provides as vivid and detailed an introduction as one might hope to find, with its energetic visual rendition of all the scenes, sufficient lines of dialogue and brief narrative descriptions – 'At Macbeth's castle in Inverness, Lady Macbeth receives news from her husband' (p. 20) – to make the whole story readily intelligible. It compares favourably to the storybook editions which purport to serve an introductory purpose in its more obviously dramatic form, and may have a greater appeal to young boys for whom comics have traditionally been a popular format.

According to the publishers, the Quick Text versions of the *Classical Comics* were designed primarily to engage 'younger and reluctant readers' and to aid students 'where English is not the first language (*Classical Comics*, n.d., 'Text versions'), 'breaking the play down into manageable chunks in order to build confidence' (Bryant, 2011). The graphic texts are also recommended for use across the curriculum, where, as a study carried out by Mel Gibson, lecturer in Childhood Studies at the University of Northumbria, suggests, they can be used to stimulate a variety of creativity and citizenship activities including drawing your own comics, designing masks and acting out graphic scenes and to encourage debate in the classroom on subjects ranging from cultural diversity (comparing Manga to other graphic forms), 'gender and representation' and 'identity' (Gibson, n.d.).

Alongside their published texts, *Classical Comics* issue a Teaching Resource Pack for each title, with a selection of worksheets and suggestions for a range of activities that link with the text. The packs include worksheets and exercises on Background, Character, Language, Plot and Themes, as well as suggestions for Performance and Art activities, aimed at Key Stage 3 and 4. The resources are, the publishers stress, 'independent from the graphic novels' (Bryant, 2011), able to be used as stand-alone resources for study of the play in the classroom. Importantly they are also strongly geared to encouraging an engagement with Shakespeare's language, and thus, as chairman of the company Clive Bryant explains, 'assume the use of the original text' (2011). The resource pack provided for *Macbeth* is extremely comprehensive. However, I would argue, perhaps too much so, making it difficult for teachers to work out what is appropriate for study of the play at what level and to weed out key discussions, such as that of the structure of the Globe theatre (Wenborn, 2009, pp. 16–17) and History of the play (pp. 19–21), from rather unnecessary diversions, such as a discussion of actress Zoe Wanamaker's television and film career and the casting of the Dr Who episode 'The Shakespeare Code' (p. 15).

Perhaps inevitably with such a wide target audience (ages 10–17) (p. 6) the information and exercises provided also vary significantly in terms of the level of challenge and relevance, ranging from rather basic picking of facts out of an article (pp. 9–10), word search (pp. 56–7) and colouring pages (pp. 77–81) which seem to have little educational value, to the far more sophisticated discussion points and tasks relating to the various characters (pp. 38–41), work on iambic pentameter (pp. 46–7), role-play of 'The Trial of Lady Macbeth' (p. 70) and encouragement of creative writing through the development of a sequel to *Macbeth* (pp. 73–6). In the hands of a good teacher, aware of their class's capabilities and with a clear lesson plan in place, some of these resources could prove invaluable in engaging students with the play in a variety of creative and interesting ways. However, in the hands of a less capable teacher there is a danger of students wasting time on unnecessary activities at the expense of studying the text itself.

Shakespeare Comic Books, SparkNotes (publishers of *No Fear Shakespeare*) and *Manga Shakespeare* also provide a range of resources for young readers, ranging from classroom exercises to straightforward information designed to aid individual study or revision of the plays. The resources published by *Shakespeare Comic Books* are similar to those of *Classical Comics*, containing a series of worksheets that can be used in the classroom to enhance children's understanding of the plays. Aimed at either Key Stage 2 or 3, depending on the play, these books contain sections on Background, Character, Language, Structure and the play on stage, each divided into the categories of 'Talking Points', 'In Performance' and 'On Paper or Computer'. In the case of 'Character' study in *Macbeth*, for example, the 'Talking Points' section provides a number of questions beginning with 'When does Macbeth become a monster?' and ending with 'What sorts of things are people today ambitious for? Would anything turn you bad? What would stop you turning bad?' (Greaves, 2003b, p. 8). The 'In Performance' section then expands on this notion, suggesting that students act out a scene 'in which Macbeth is torn between good and bad', one student representing Macbeth, another his '"good" side', calling out reasons why he should 'remain true to Duncan' and the third his '"bad" side', calling out 'reasons why he should murder Duncan' (p. 8). These exercises encourage students not only to engage with the play in a variety of ways, but also to relate it to contemporary society and to their own lives. In the final 'On Paper or Computer' section students are asked to use the descriptions given of the battle by the Captain and Ross in 1.2 to write their own account, requiring them to undertake a close reading of the text and to engage their imaginations in expanding on the sights, sounds and feelings of the battle field (p. 8). These resources, which are again not directly connected to the graphic texts, fulfil many of the criteria set out in the QCDA 'Active Shakespeare' project (2010) and seem particularly well structured in providing suggestions for discovering the plays through a range of different approaches – individual study, group discussion and practical drama activities.

SparkNotes provide resources for all plays in the *No Fear Shakespeare* parallel text series, available online, in print, as an e-book and as an i-phone application. However, unlike the other resources discussed here, these resources are intended for independent study as opposed to classroom teaching, providing information rather than exploratory exercises. The SparkNotes resources are not linked specifically to the *No Fear Shakespeare* parallel text editions, or indeed to the graphic novels, but designed for general study of the plays, with analysis of plot, scenes, characters, themes, motifs and symbols, as well as brief details about Shakespeare and his times. In addition, the guides provide a multiple choice quiz for students to test their knowledge of the play and a series of suggested essay topics and study questions with suggested answers. SparkNotes study guides have come under some criticism in the past, with concerns being raised about students' tendency to use the character and scene summaries in place of reading the whole play, and to use the online guides to cut and paste material from the 'suggested answers' into their own work (Milner and Milner, 2007, p. 53). SparkNotes is, of course, by no means the only resource providing students with access to online study materials, and research shows that the use of electronic media for writing essays, often leading to intentional or unintentional plagiarism, is common across the student population (Jones et al., 2005). The SparkNotes (2011) website has attempted to combat some of these issues, making it clear that their 'literature guides are meant to be read along with the books they analyse. They are not intended to be copied on tests or papers (aka plagiarized)'. However, it is perhaps inevitable that some students given the choice of reading a difficult play for homework, or reading a concise summary of the sort provided by SparkNotes will opt for the latter. One feels that there is a danger that a student, armed with the *No Fear Shakespeare Graphic Novels* edition, and with access to notes on each scene, could get through an examination on a Shakespeare play without ever having read the original text.

SelfMadeHero, publishers of *Manga Shakespeare*, provide some basic online resources to aid students in their understanding of the plays – a short biography of Shakespeare, plot synopses for each of the plays and free glossaries, providing 'straightforward definitions and clarifications of Shakespeare's words' (SelfMadeHero, 2011a). The plot synopses are so brief (running to only one page each), however, that there is little danger of them being used as substitutes for reading the plays; indeed, they function most like the sort of brief summary provided in a theatre programme, to aid audience members in their understanding of the story of the play. The glossary is linked directly to the *Manga Shakespeare* text, providing page references and Manga images of the characters alongside the translations of some words and lines, although act and scene references from the original are also provided. These definitions are, one imagines, pretty essential for most students aiming to understand the text, albeit in its cut-down form, and it seems surprising that they are not contained in the published text itself. Although they are often basic, rarely entertaining the possibility of multiple meaning or ambiguity – 'crown' being translated merely as 'top of the head' and 'keen' as 'sharp' (SelfMadeHero, 2011b, p. 4), for example – there are some occasions where the editors expand to provide more detailed explanations, including pointing up important themes or image strands – 'Banquo's simile ("strange garments") is one Shakespeare uses throughout the play' (p. 4). Although the website asserts that the editors have also 'noted where the language relates to the play in performance' (2011a), however, there is little evidence of this in the *Macbeth* commentary, and indeed no explicit mention of the play on stage.

In addition to these basic resources, SelfMadeHero has, in the words of Troni Grande, 'cashed in on Shakespeare and on manga, offering . . . a growing array of resources for educators of Shakespeare' (2010, p. 6). These include a *Manga Shakespeare* social network which features blogs about the books, and a new project with Promethean Planet, providing interactive whiteboard resources for teaching Shakespeare through Manga. Most significantly, SelfMadeHero are the only Shakespeare graphic novel publishers that offer practical workshops in schools, extending the Manga Shakespeare experience beyond the remote and digitally interactive to the hands-on and actively practical. The workshops, aimed at Key Stage 3 and 4, are either artist or actor-led, the artist-led sessions involving the examination of character, plot and staging through the use of interactive whiteboards, followed by a practical workshop in which students are helped to design their own Manga characters, while the actor-led sessions look at the play in performance using the Manga text, followed by workshop focusing on the performance of a scene from the play. The final workshop entails an actor-led revision lecture for Key Stage 3, using the images from the *Manga Shakespeare* alongside 'Promethean interactive and voting technology' (SelfMadeHero).

As this profusion of resources indicates, graphic novel Shakespeare has become an entire industry. In the case of *Classical Comics* and *Shakespeare Comic Books*, the available resources take the study of the text beyond the published graphic editions, encouraging a full engagement with and interrogation of the original, suggesting that the graphic editions provide, in the eyes of the publishers, a jumping-off point for the study of the plays, much as was advocated by Kanter for his *Classics Illustrated* versions. Since both sets of resources are aimed for use by students from Key Stage 3 onwards, this suggests that the publishers envisage students engaging with the full text well before beginning GCSE study of the plays. While the target age groups for SparkNotes and *Manga Shakespeare* resources is similar – Key Stage 3 or 4 (although SparkNotes are notoriously used by Undergraduate University students) unlike the *Classical Comics* and *Shakespeare Comic Books* teachers' packs – these resources do not actively encourage students to engage with the original text, the *Manga Shakespeare* glossary providing a glossary not of the full Shakespeare text, but of the text as contained in the *Manga Shakespeare: Macbeth*, while SparkNotes seem to spoon-feed students with information rather than challenging them to seek it out for themselves by consulting the primary material. There is very little analysis in the SparkNotes notes of language, emphasis being placed rather on plot, character and themes, all possible to discuss and write about without recourse to the original text, which, as trends for studying set scenes as opposed to the whole play at Key Stage 3 demonstrate, is an all too common occurrence among school students.

Notes

1 Some of these texts are published by Can of Worms as *Cartoon Shakespeare* and some as *Graphic Shakespeare*. They are published in the United States by Black Dog and Leventhal as *Graphic Shakespeare*.

2 The *Classical Comics* 'Original Text' editions claim on the back cover to meet 'UK curriculum requirements' (McDonald and Hayward, 2008) while the *Graphic Shakespeare* series are slightly more circumspect in their recommendation of their texts for use at GCSE and A Level, describing them

as 'an additional teaching resource' and 'stimulating learning resource' (Can of Worms, n.d.).

3   Examples occur at 'Might have been mine! only I have left to say, / More is thy due than more than all can pay' (*Mac.* 1.4.20–1); 'The eye wink at the hand; yet let that be, / Which the eye fears, when it is done, to see' (1.4.52–3); 'Macbeth: We will speak further. Lady Macbeth: Only look up clear; / To alter favour ever is to fear' (1.5.70–1).

Web resources

Barnes and Noble, '*No Fear Shakespeare Graphic Novels: Macbeth*':
   http://search.barnesandnoble.com/Macbeth/SparkNotes-Editors/e/9781411498716/?itm=2&USRI=no+fear+macbeth
Can of Worms Shakespeare:
   www.canofwormspress.co.uk/cartoonshakespeare1.html
Classical Comics:
   www.classicalcomics.com/
Manga Shakespeare:
   www.mangashakespeare.com/

CHAPTER FIVE

Cut-Down Stage Versions for Young Children

In recent years there has been a rapid profusion of abridged Shakespeare productions aimed at primary-school-aged children. 2009 saw the first Young People's Shakespeare (YPS) production at the Royal Shakespeare Company (RSC) – *The Comedy of Errors* – and the launch of Edward Hall's all-male Shakespeare company Propeller's 'Pocket Propeller' with *Pocket Dream* – a heavily condensed version of the company's production of *A Midsummer Night's Dream*. These initiatives from the RSC and Propeller follow in the footsteps of two other leading Shakespeare-producing houses in Britain – the National Theatre (NT) and Regent's Park Open Air Theatre, both of which have, alongside their main repertoire, staged a series of successful shortened Shakespeares aimed particularly at children. The NT has produced *Pericles* (2006), *Romeo and Juliet* (2007), *A Midsummer Night's Dream* (2008), *Macbeth* (2009) and *Twelfth Night* (2010) in versions by Carl Heap as part of its 'Discover' programme for Primary and Early Years, while Regent's Park has staged *A Midsummer Night's Dream* (2008), *The Tempest* (2009) and *Macbeth* (2010) 'Re-imagined for everyone aged six and over', but geared predominantly towards those at the lower end of this age bracket.

In addition to productions such as these, linked to theatre companies with a long history of producing Shakespeare, there are two leading companies whose focus is the production of cut-down versions of Shakespeare for young people – The Young Shakespeare Company (YSC) and Shakespeare 4 Kidz (S4K), the former of which has been running since 1988 and the latter since 1997. Quite different in their approaches, YSC tours primary schools with its simply staged, interactive versions of the plays while S4K tours to large national and international theatres with its elaborately staged musical versions.

This chapter will explore the work of these various companies, focusing in particular on Propeller and YSC's productions of *A Midsummer Night's Dream (MND)* – the nature of their productions, approaches to the text, accompanying workshops and educational materials. *MND* is the play most frequently cited as suitable for introducing Shakespeare to young people and is, as Peter Holland notes, 'so often the way children first encounter Shakespeare' (1998, p.i). When, in 1993, Barrie Wade and John Sheppard surveyed the plays used at various stages of the curriculum by a cross-section of English teachers in the United Kingdom, they found that in Year 7 (aged 11–12), the earliest year surveyed, *MND* was by far the most popular text (1993, p. 270). The play is thus similarly a popular choice with companies producing work aimed at young people, despite Jan Kott's acknowledgement of the intense 'brutality' and 'eroticism' (1964, p. 73) which belie its perception as a 'tale of magic and mischief' (Regent's Park).[1]

Regent's Park has mounted *MND* 21 times in the past 30 years, the play becoming almost synonymous with the theatre. Its regular place in the company's repertoire is undoubtedly partly because it lends itself so well to the open air setting, but mainly because the theatre acknowledges its status as a place where many people experience Shakespeare for the first time.[2] The play was thus a natural choice for the company's first foray into productions 're-imagined for everyone aged six and over' performed throughout the summer season. The reimagining of *MND* in Dominic Leclerc's production involved the cutting of the play to around seventy minutes, the inclusion of a 'prologue' in which the key elements of the story were clearly introduced in non-Shakespearean language, the employment of Bottom as a narrator figure explaining certain points of action, and the use of audience participation encouraging an active engagement with the production. These elements were undoubtedly influenced by the work of YSC, whose co-artistic director Sarah Gordon composed the production's prologue and, along with fellow co-artistic director Christopher Geelan, devised the workshops that ran alongside it. Most reviews praised the narrative and interactive elements of the production and their ability to capture the attention of the young audiences 'from the beginning' (Connor, 2008) and these features have been subsequently employed in other of the reimagined productions.

Rachel Canning's design was also clearly intended to appeal to the younger members of the audience, the production being set in a large Victorian nursery, featuring a huge toy box out of which the characters emerged – Demetrius and Lysander as toy soldiers, Hermia as a music-box ballerina and Helena as a rag-doll – all with rosy-painted cheeks which reinforced their doll-like nature. Emma Catty comments on the other aspects of the productions – 'fairy lights, balloons and bubble machine' – with which 'the theatre work[ed] hard to delight the many children in attendance' (2008), clearly attempting to evoke the magic of the play in a child-friendly way.

However, like many of the productions discussed in this chapter, the production used a cast of only 6 actors to perform the play's 21 roles. Although doubling was undoubtedly a feature of the Elizabethan playhouse, and is frequently used in full-scale professional productions of Shakespeare's work, Sheila Connor, reviewing the play, comments that for her 'young guests aged nine and ten . . . following the plot was not made easy with only six characters constantly doubling up on parts' (2008). Indeed, it seems ironic (but inevitable given funding for children's theatre) that in most productions aimed at the very audiences who need most help in distinguishing between characters, doubling is used to an extent that would be confusing even for most adults.

While most reviews of the production were positive, applauding the theatre's attempts to encourage young people to engage with Shakespeare's writing, one might, as did most of the reviewers, question the suitability of both the play and the production for children as young as 6. Although the play features fairies, it also features threats of death, drug-induced sexual activity and some bawdy exchanges in the Mechanicals' scenes. Also, while young children may be capable of grasping elements of the play, 70 minutes is perhaps too long for most children under 10, and Catty reports that 'by the end of the play, the noise of children fidgeting and beginning to get bored was starting to distract from the action' (2008).

One of the most negative reactions to the production came from *The Observer*'s Lyn Gardner who questioned the motives behind a reimagining of the play in what she felt was a 'patronizing' manner, claiming that 'Shakespeare doesn't require simplification; he simply requires exquisite clarity of execution' (2008). While Gardner may be right that 'given a first-class production of the Dream . . . children will respond with open hearts and minds' (2008), young people of primary school age surely benefit from some form of explanation of the plot in order to fully appreciate or engage with a full-scale production. Also, although Gardner's claim may be true of children at the upper end of the primary school age range, it is not perhaps true of children aged 6 and 7. The question of whether any production of the play, however simply reimagined, is really suitable for, or readily intelligible to this age group, is something which this chapter will continue to explore.

That Regent's Park Theatre has continued to produce productions reimagined for young people as part of its annual repertoire suggests that the strategy has been deemed a success. Although the theatre's next choice of play, *The Tempest*, was 'less immediately child friendly' than *MND* (Finlayson, 2010, p. 292), J. Caitlin Finlayson describes how director Liam Steel 'successfully re-imagined the play for a young audience, without becoming reductive or diminishing the play's poetry, by combining audience involvement with a prologue, child-oriented embellishments such as puppets, and the physically expressive performances of the roles of Caliban and Ariel' (p. 292). Also, although *The Tempest* may seem less obviously suited to a young audience than *MND*, like the theatre's next choice, *Macbeth*, it has a relatively simple storyline with no subplots. In 2011, the theatre's reimagining is extending to Shakespeare's more complex dark romance, *Pericles*. While it is undoubtedly possible, as with Steel's *Tempest*, to emphasize the 'comic features of the play over its more somber, tragic notes', playing up the 'fairytale' elements of the plot (p. 292), a strategy suggested by the theatre's advertisement of the key themes of the play as being 'Magical fairytale, Adventure, Self Discovery, Family and Growing up and growing old' (Regent's Park Theatre, 2003–10b), it is difficult to escape the fact that the themes of incest and prostitution are also central to its story, and difficult to avoid in making the plot clearly intelligible.

It seems surprising, therefore, that *Pericles* should have been the NT's first choice of play for their Primary Classics programme aimed at Key Stage 2 (aged 7–11). Beginning in 2006, Primary Classics has mounted an annual abridged production of a Shakespeare play, touring to a range of London schools with small-scale performances at the NT (in 2009 and 2010 in the Cottesloe Theatre) and supported by a range of workshops and teacher training days. The play texts, adapted by Carl Heap, have been subsequently published with introductory notes aimed at helping teachers or other theatre practitioners to mount their own productions.

Heap's *Pericles* was advertised, much like Regent's Park's production, as 'an exciting tale of shipwrecks and magic, villains and heroes, and a child's fight for survival in a foreign land' (2009b, back cover). While these elements are undoubted features of Shakespeare's play, this description glosses over its darker themes, and makes it sound more like a children's fairytale than 'a world of pimps, bawds and brothels' with 'an unsettling undercurrent' (Kiernan, 2006, p. 196). However, the NT report on the production states that 'Pericles was carefully chosen, as the play raises complex questions about identity, culture and justice, with themes that can deepen children's understanding of their world and the human experience', and that teachers found ways of using the play across the curriculum, investigating the story of *Pericles* 'within topics of study that focus on the more serious themes such as immigration, children's rights and their own lives as well as global issues such as war, famine, family separation and travel' (NT Education, 2006, p. 6).

Although 'there were concerns from some schools about Marina's capture and sale into proposed prostitution' some teachers feeling that the scene was 'too graphically portrayed', other schools felt that 'the scene opened out questions of children's rights, slavery and trafficking in a bold and challenging way, suitable for further class discussion' (p. 11). It may be that such discussions on slavery and sex trafficking can be sensitively tackled with 10- or 11-year-olds (the upper end of the target audience) particularly if the children or members of their families have experienced such issues. However, the topic seems unsuitable for viewing by or discussion with children of 7 or 8.

Following this production of *Pericles*, NT Primary Classics has presented four more Shakespeare plays, adapted by Heap for children aged 7–11 – *Romeo and Juliet*, *MND*, *Macbeth* and *Twelfth Night* – the four most popular of Shakespeare's plays for study below GCSE level. Each of the plays was cut to around an hour in length, and told on a small, portable set which could be easily toured to a variety of school halls. Heap sees the touring aspect of the productions as an essential part of their spirit. While the professional theatre stage 'can be a pedestal' on which Shakespeare is placed 'like some Wizard of Avon', the school hall is, in Heap's view, 'a more democratic space' in which children are likely to feel more comfortable and, therefore, react more freely (n.d., p. 2). Within the school hall, Heap aimed to create as intimate an environment as possible, based on direct contact between actor and audience. For *Romeo and Juliet* and *Macbeth* the stage was in traverse, creating an even closer proximity between actor and audience than in the thrust stage configuration, and allowing the audience to surround the action. Having worked on a great deal of pre-Shakespearean drama with the Medieval Players, Heap has become convinced of the necessity of directly addressing the audience in Shakespearean drama, making them feel 'that they are important to the event' (2009b, p. 8). This strategy is particularly effective with young audiences who are more likely to be drawn into the action and to remain attentive when being spoken to directly by the actors. As Heap explains, it also permits the performers 'to gauge if their audience is following and understanding' (p. 8). In addition to using direct address to engage the audience, the productions also made use of audience participation, encouraging, in a similar way to the Regent's Park productions, an active involvement in the telling of the story. In *MND*, for example, volunteers were recruited to play 'huntsmen', blowing party horns to wake the sleeping lovers (2009a, p. 41) while in *Twelfth Night* the audience was encouraged to join in with Feste, Sir Toby and Sir Andrew in singing 'Hold thy peace' (2010, p. 33).

With a simple set and costumes, and basic lighting, one of the chief means of telling the story, creating the atmosphere and establishing setting in the 'Discover' productions has been the imaginative use of musical instruments ranging from the violin, oboe and drums used for *Romeo and Juliet* to the unusual garoban (a large wheel-shaped instrument containing beads) to make the sound of the sea in *Pericles*. The use of live sound effects helps to reinforce the sense of a story being conjured up by the actors, while song and dance are elements of live performance enduringly popular with young audience members as many of their comments on the performances attest.[3]

As with the Regent's Park productions, each of the productions has been performed by a severely reduced cast – although, one that has grown steadily in size from *Pericles*, for which Heap was permitted only five actors, to *Macbeth* and *Twelfth Night* for which he used seven. In order to make sense of the doubling and tripling of characters and to help link elements of the edited text, the productions have used the device of storytelling. Each has begun with a pre-show, establishing the actors as storytellers and creating a framing device for the play. In *Pericles*, the cast were fishermen, singing and drinking tea on the beach; for *Romeo and Juliet*, they were the town band rehearsing for the Capulet ball; for *MND* a group of pyjama-clad clowns, informed by the stage manager that they were to perform the play; and for *Macbeth*, a group of ramblers on a Scottish hillside who, due to a sudden storm, were forced to take shelter, making 'a collective decision to tell a story' (Heap, n.d., p. 3).

Similar to the Regent's Park productions, all of the Primary Classics versions have been reduced to just over an hour, a length which Heap describes as 'the optimum tolerance for our audience . . . and long enough to contain a telling of the complete story while preserving some of the best lines' (n.d., p. 4). In order to reduce the length of the plays so dramatically, Heap began, as he explains, 'by looking for at least one substantial cut' (p. 4) – in *Pericles* Act 1, in *MND* all of Puck's lines on the basis that they 'do not advance the plot' (p. 4), in *Macbeth* the murder of Banquo and much of the rather long and often tedious 4.3 and in *Twelfth Night* the play's first scene. Most of these cuts do not detract substantially from the stories of the plays, the information they contain being imparted elsewhere. Possibly Heap's most 'contentious' cut was his removal in *Romeo and Juliet* of the first part of 3.5 (the post-consummation waking scene between Romeo and Juliet). However, Heap is quick to insist that the cut was made not for 'for bowdlerising motives – children see much more graphic material in Eastenders and Hollyoaks' – but because he felt that 'it perhaps heightened the tragedy that Romeo and Juliet's love is only consummated in death' (2009c, p. 9). Although this claim is debateable – the consummation of the pair's love, clearly indicated in Shakespeare's text, seems to contribute significantly to the development of their relationship – Heap's comment exemplifies his anxiety not to patronize his young audience by cutting apparently 'unsuitable' material. Although Heap does remove or alter some words which might seem difficult for a young audience to comprehend – changing 'nuptial hour' to 'wedding day' and 'abridgement' to 'entertainment', for example, in *MND* (2009a, p. 9), his cuts are not motivated by a desire to censor the text for his young audiences.

Heap also explains that in altering the text he had no qualms about occasionally introducing a 'glaring anachronism' in order to bring the piece up to date and to avoid a sense of 'reverence for old language' (n.d., p. 5). In *MND*, for example, Philostrate introduces the available entertainment to Theseus with the inserted iambic 'That Athens has got talent, doubt it not' (2009a, p. 45), while the stage directions suggest that Theseus might insert into the list of 'sports' for performance 'Rhydian' or 'any recent TV talent show contestant' (p. 45). Lines referring to contemporary Renaissance events are a common feature of Shakespeare's plays. Thus, it may be argued that by throwing in some up-to-date references Heap captures some of the spirit of the original performances.

One of the most striking features of the NT Primary Classics has been the extensive education programme that accompanied the productions. Each production toured to around 40 primary schools across London, all of which received a series of 6 workshops exploring areas including character, plot and the play in production. The workshops were designed to 'prepare children for seeing the production', increase their level of engagement with the performance', and 'introduce key elements of theatre practice and the building blocks of performance' (Discover: Primary and Early Years, 2010, p. 8). Within the storytelling sessions the children were introduced to the plot and characters, led through an exploration of the poetry and dramatic form and encouraged to engage in 'in depth debate and exchange about the play' (p. 9).

In addition to educating the young audiences about Shakespeare's work and theatre practice, the workshops aimed, 'through participation in creative activity', to stimulate learning across a range of subject areas, improving literacy, communication and listening, encouraging team work, imagination and inventiveness and boosting self-confidence and self-esteem (Discover: Primary and Early Years, 2010, p. 6). *Children Engaging with Drama* – an evaluation of the NT's drama work in primary schools – also found that the children who took part in the workshops gained a 'statistically higher score in optional SATs mathematics compared to matched children' (Turner et al., 2004, p. 8), suggesting that this method of workshop-based creative learning had a beneficial impact not only on areas connected with literacy and communication but across the curriculum, possibly due to an overall increase in confidence.

As the other major national theatre with a repertoire based almost exclusively on Shakespeare, the RSC may be seen to have been rather slow in mounting their own productions exclusively for young people. Of course, the RSC has, for many years, welcomed school audiences to performances in their main repertoire, and has run a strong education programme of workshops and resources, supporting their viewing experience. In addition, regional tours accompanied by educational workshops have been part of the company's repertoire from its early years, under the artistic directorship of Peter Hall, when the company's small-scale touring project, 'Theatregoround', toured to 'unconventional performance spaces' (Chambers, 2004, p. 42). However, Theatregoround's work mostly took the form of 'anthologies, "docudramas" and short plays' (p. 42), rather than cut-down versions of Shakespeare's work, and subsequent tours to a range of spaces including schools, universities and community centres have comprised of full-scale, full-length plays drawn from the company's repertoire rather than productions aimed at or adapted specifically for young people. The company did produce a one-off young people's production of *Macbeth* at the Other Place in 2004 ('the first time we really explored creating work specifically for a young audience' – Jacqui O'Hanlon, Director of Education, 2011) which subsequently toured to primary schools in Warwickshire. However, as O'Hanlon explains, the production was directed by an assistant director and employed a cast of understudies.

It was not until 2009 that the company launched their Young People's Shakespeare (YPS), using established actors, directors and designers from the main company to create child friendly, shortened versions of Shakespeare's play. The project, a collaboration between the Production and Education wings of the theatre, was launched with *The Comedy of Errors (Err.)*, a condensed 80-minute version of the play aimed at a Key Stage 2 audience. The production was directed by Paul Hunter of 'Told by an Idiot', a company famous for their playful, larger-than-life storytelling, and was performed in the RSC's Courtyard Theatre by members of the Ensemble, as well as touring to local schools. Combining the text with improvisation, lively music, tap-dancing and slapstick physical comedy, the production was praised by reviewers for its 'zest' (Gardner, 2009), 'daft visual gags' (Grimley, 2009) and its ability to make an audience feel that 'Shakespeare is your contemporary' (Gardner, 2009) even if some felt that the pantomimic aspects overshadowed the delivery of the text.

YPS Err. was remounted in 2010, alongside *YPS Hamlet*, directed by Tarell Alvin McCraney, for the RSC's inaugural YPS week, a week of performances and activities for schools, young people and families, including street theatre and art and drama workshops. As O'Hanlon explained, the YPS week brought 'to life' the RSC's 'Stand up for Shakespeare manifesto' (see Chapter 1) placing 'children of all ages and abilities . . . at the heart of the RSC's artistic programme' (RSC, 2010). Both YPS productions subsequently toured schools in the Midlands and Newcastle-upon-Tyne, before transferring to the Roundhouse Theatre in London during the RSC's 2010–11 winter residency and then touring to London schools in January 2011. Like *Err.*, *Hamlet* was praised for its 'lively' (Billington, 2010), 'fun' (Lee, 2010) approach. Reviewing online, Peter Kirwan described the production as 'my ideal *Hamlet*' – skilfully striking 'a fine balance between streamlining and clarifying with tremendous skill' and crediting its young audiences with the ability 'to cope with serious business' such as Ophelia's madness and suicide (2010). The RSC's YPS continues in 2011 with *The Taming of the Shrew*, adapted and directed by Tim Crouch, which will play at the Swan Theatre in September and October, and 'from 2012 will evolve into a new small-scale tour across the country, playing to a mixture of schools and venues' (O'Hanlon, 2011). *The Taming of the Shrew* is an unusual choice for a primary school audience. However, Tracy Irish (RSC Education) explains that the company are keen to 'encourage directors to think of a non-traditional text for an 8–13 age group' and to 'shy away from old favourites like *Macbeth* and *Dream* as we want to open up the canon for young audiences' (2011). Although Irish admits that '*Shrew* is a controversial choice' which required 'confidence in Tim [Crouch] from all involved', she explains that Crouch felt that the play's themes of 'sibling rivalry, pressures to conform, domestic violence etc.' could be of potential relevance to a young audience (2011).

For Irish 'the key' to the productions are the 'accompanying workshops' which help young people to see 'the relevance of the play to their own lives'. For both *Comedy of Errors* and *Hamlet*, the schools to which the production toured were 'offered an INSET day for teachers so that those teachers had ideas and activities with which to support their students' seeing of the performance' (Irish, 2011) as well as a post-show workshop and Q and A session with an RSC Education practitioner and members of the acting company, many of whom had completed a postgraduate award in teaching Shakespeare with the University of Warwick.

Like many of the productions of Shakespeare for children the RSC's YPS productions are also supported by online educational resources which provide a number of suggestions for exploring the action, themes and characters of the plays in a practical way, fulfilling one of the three major elements of the 'Stand up for Shakespeare' manifesto – 'do it on your feet' (RSC, 2008). The exercises suggested for use in the classroom for both *Err.* and *Hamlet* were mainly drawn from those put into practice in the rehearsal room by directors Paul Hunter and Tarell Alvin McCraney, empowering the young audiences to use the same exploratory techniques as those used by the professional casts. As with the NT 'Discover' workshops, in addition to exercises designed to directly engage children with the plays and the productions, the resources suggest ways of using the plays across the primary curriculum. For *Err.*, for example, the resources suggest ways of exploring the play in Citizenship, by tackling themes of treatment of foreigners, servants and employees, and notions of justice; in Maths, by looking at 'selling and trade'; in PE, through mirroring exercises; in Art by making a map of Ephesus and undertaking costume and set designs and in Science, by exploring the genetics of twins. The productions thus become a resource for a creative approach to a range of subjects (RSC, 2009, p. 14).

The RSC YPS, NT Primary Classics and Regent's Park reimagined productions share a number of elements in common with Propeller's 'Pocket Shakespeare' – the actors' engagement with the audience in the performance space prior to the start of the play, use of live music and sound effects, direct audience address, elements of audience participation and improvisation, all of which are clearly strategies chosen for their ability to capture and retain the attention and enthusiasm of a young audience. Like these other productions, Pocket Propeller also uses a small cast of six actors, working with the Shakespearean text, edited to around an hour in length. Where Pocket Propeller differs from the other productions discussed is in their use of an all-male company of actors, whose physical energy and rough-and-tumble style defines their work.

Like the RSC YPS, Pocket Propeller draws its cast members from a professional company of actors who perform full-scale Shakespeare productions with the main company – in this case Propeller, Edward Hall's all-male company established in 1997, with its chief aim being to 'find a more engaging way of expressing Shakespeare and to more completely explore the relationship between text and performance' (Propeller, 2011b). The company has toured its productions worldwide and has received numerous awards for its work. Propeller's highly physical approach and use of an eclectic range of styles and music have already earned them a following among secondary schools in Britain and abroad, but in 2010 Propeller launched 'Pocket Propeller' with the aim of delivering 'a first class theatrical experience' to young audiences unfamiliar with Shakespeare's work (Hall, 2011). The use of actors, and indeed production team members, from the main company is an important part of delivering this 'first class' experience. Most of the actors will have performed in full-length productions of the plays in established theatres across the world, 'allowing them', as Hall asserts, 'the freedom to concentrate on improvising with their young and very lively audience', while ensuring that they are 'given access to an experience of the highest standard delivered by experienced and skilled classical actors' (cited in Propeller, n.d., p. 5). Although each of the Pocket plays is reduced to around 60 minutes in length, the production values remain high and the commitment and energy of the cast equal to that evident in their full-scale productions.

Pocket Propeller's first production – *Pocket Dream* – performed in various venues since 2009, was based on Propeller's full-scale production of *MND*, performed by the company in 2002–3 and 2008–9 in over 200 worldwide venues, and will be followed in 2011 by *Pocket Comedy*, based on the company's 2010–11 world tour of *Err*. The philosophy of Pocket Propeller is based on freedom of expression and reaction. The company actively encourage the young audiences to 'explore their own reactions' in 'the freest possible way', and encourage teachers not to make their students 'behave' (Hall, 2011). The relationship between the actor and audience is at the heart of this approach, and is one of flexibility and openness, with the actors responding to and improvising with the young audience members. Each performance is followed by a talkback session in which the actors encourage the young audience 'to articulate and explore the responses to the show' (Hall, 2011).

All of the productions discussed thus far retain Shakespeare's language and, for the most part the structure of the plays, but cut the texts to a length considered manageable for a young audience of around 8–11 years old. Both YSC and S4K, who specialize exclusively in productions of Shakespeare for primary school children, use rather different, if contrasting, approaches to introducing young people to Shakespeare's plays.

YSC, established in 1988 by Christopher Geelan and Sarah Gordon, provides a programme of workshops and performances for primary schools, working with over 800 schools and 100,000 children each year. The company's work, which has been cited by the Arts Council as an example of excellence in arts education practice, centres around the strategy of 'active storytelling' – 'a practical, collaborative discovery process' through which the young audiences help to tell the story of a Shakespeare play, and to 'explore and define' its world (YSC, n.d.). Their productions involve a group of four or five actors who take some of the play's central roles, performing certain scenes in a mostly uncut version of Shakespeare's text, while members of the young audience take other roles, performing heavily edited extracts of Shakespearean dialogue linked by narration from the actors. Even if not playing roles in the play, all the members of the audience are involved in the process of creating the performance, making suggestions about how characters might react or behave, echoing lines spoken by the actors, and helping to evoke the setting and atmosphere through the creation of sound effects. The productions thus involve some elements of the Shakespearean text, encouraging the young audiences to engage with Shakespeare's language and imagery, while also including elements of narration and explanation. The use of Shakespeare's language stems from the company's recognition of the fact that 'young children have an innate love rhythm and rhyme' and 'enjoy speaking Shakespeare's words and exploring different ways of saying them' (YSC, n.d.). By putting into the children's mouths short, accessible sections of Shakespearean dialogue, the company encourages an embracement rather than a fearful suspicion of the language.

S4K take a quite different approach to introducing young audiences to Shakespeare. Describing themselves as 'THE National Shakespeare Company for Children and Young People in the UK' (Chenery and Gimblett, 1997–2011a), they have been touring full-scale musical versions of Shakespeare's plays, running at around 2 hours in length, accompanied by workshops, throughout Britain since 1997 and in locations abroad since 2007. In addition to touring these professional productions, the company also produces 'Put on a Play' packs for schools, providing teachers with the necessary resources – a synopsis, brief character descriptions, script and score – to mount a S4K production themselves.

Unlike all of the productions discussed thus far, although the S4K productions follow closely the structure of Shakespeare's plays (with some cuts), they 'translate' Shakespeare's texts into the modern vernacular in order to make them easily intelligible to children, adding contemporary songs in the place of some speeches. The focus of the productions is thus on the stories of Shakespeare's plays and not on his language.

As the use of the slang '4 Kidz' in the title of the company suggests, the emphasis is on making Shakespeare seem 'cool'. In defending this choice of name, founder Julian Chenery explains that they 'wanted something that sounded catchy, innovative, was a bit irreverent and anarchic, showed that we were different, was not a name that sounded elitist or "posh"'

(Chenery and Gimblett, 1997–2011b). This irreverent, non-elitist approach to Shakespeare is at the heart of the company's work and has proved extremely popular with young people, the productions playing to 'millions' (1997–2011a). However, one might question whether the company is, in fact, bringing 'Shakespeare' to children any more than might a production of *West Side Story*. Their claim that 'our unique easy-to-understand musical adaptations of Shakespeare's plays form the basis of a complete understanding of his work' (1997–2011a) is extremely hard to justify given that a 'complete understanding' of Shakespeare's work includes an understanding of his language – his imagery, symbolism, rhetoric, use of rhythm, rhyme and the different registers of verse and prose, all of which elements enhance the meaning of the lines.

One finds in the S4K productions many of the same problems associated with the graphic novel translated texts. Although in places the modernized dialogue used in the productions provides a useful simplification of some of the more complex lines, in many cases such a 'translation' seems unnecessary, and results in rather stilted lines, devoid of the elegance, rhythm and sometimes humour of Shakespeare's own words. In S4K *Hamlet*, for example, the first exchange between Hamlet and his mother

> *Queen Gertrude* Good Hamlet, cast thy nightly colour off,
>   And let thine eye look like a friend on Denmark.
>   Do not for ever with thy vailed lids
>   Seek for thy noble father in the dust.
>   Thou know'st 'tis common – all that lives must die,
>   Passing through nature to eternity.
>
> *Hamlet* Ay, madam, it is common.
>
> *Queen Gertrude*   If it be,
>   Why seems it so particular with thee?
>
> *Hamlet* Seems, madam? Nay, it *is*. I know not 'seems'.
>   'Tis not alone my inky cloak, good-mother,
>   Nor customary suits of solemn black,
>   Nor windy suspiration of forced breath,
>   No, nor the fruitful river in the eye,
>   Nor the dejected havior of the visage,
>   Together with all forms, moods, shows of grief
>   That can denote me truly. These indeed 'seem',
>   For they are actions that a man might play;
>   But I have that within which passeth show –
>   These but the trappings and the suits of woe. (1.2.68–86)

is translated to

> *Queen*: Good Hamlet, it's time to stop grieving for your dead father.
>   You know that everything that lives must eventually die.

Hamlet: Ay, madam, that's life.

Queen: If you think so, why do you seem to be so down?

Hamlet: Seems, madam! No, it is; I know not 'seems'.
I don't wear black for nothing. Within me I am deeply sad.

(Chenery and Gimblett, 2007, p. 7)

While the basic sense of the lines remains, so much is lost in translation. The verse form is obliterated, and hence the rhythm and sometimes the rhyme. As Alex Preminger and T. V. F. Brogan note, the 'effect' of rhyme 'on audiences and readers both inside and outside poetry is well known' (1993, pp. 1059–60). Indeed, studies have shown that young children take enjoyment in rhythm and rhyme even before they learn to read and write (Bradley and Bryant, 1991, pp. 37–45). Shakespeare uses rhyme within his plays to mark the ends of scenes and acts (particularly in his early works), to emphasize comic dialogue, to highlight wordplay and to frame aphorisms, 'concentrating the listener's attention' on the lines (Raffel, 1996, pp. 195, 204). In this passage, the rhyming couplet which ends Gertrude's first speech frames a key aphorism about life and death, while Hamlet's last couplet provides a summation of his emotional state. A further couplet, 'Ay madam . . . particular with thee', shared between Hamlet and Gertrude indicates the swiftness of the exchange, Gertrude completing Hamlet's line, and attempting to trounce him with her rhyme. Each of these moments, key to an audience's aural appreciation of the arch and artificially formal tone of the exchange, is lost in the modernized dialogue. Also, in translating 'Why seems it so particular with thee' into 'If you think so, why do you seem to be so down?' the informal tone of which appears, in any case, unsuited to the Queen, the wordplay on 'seems' is lost. Hamlet's 'Seems, madam! No, it is; I know not "seems"' does not make sense when the word is absent in that form from Gertrude's line. Granted Hamlet's anaphoric verses – 'Nor customary . . . visage' – may seem overly rhetorical, and are often cut by theatre directors; however, the remainder of this exchange seems relatively straightforward, not requiring 'translation' in order to be understood. The aural pleasure and indication of tone that is lost in the modernization of the lines is surely greater than what is gained by the simplification.

Far easier to accept than the claim to be providing children with the 'basis of a complete understanding of' Shakespeare's work is Chenery's suggestion that the genre of musical theatre, 'readily accepted and enjoyed by people of all ages' can act as 'a bridge' to the understanding and enjoyment of Shakespeare (Chenery and Gimblett, 1997–2011a). The songs used in the productions, the music for which is specially composed by Matthew Gimblett, resemble those of many popular modern musicals and animations. Written in a variety of styles and tempos and each with a catchy refrain their appeal is obvious to a young audience familiar with the Disney mode of storytelling. While these productions may not provide children with a comprehensive introduction to the work Shakespeare, they may help them to engage with Shakespeare's stories and take away some of the anxiety about studying his work at a later stage in school. However, there is also a danger that these productions may encourage a fear of Shakespeare's language as something too difficult to be encountered in children who, as the work of YSC demonstrates, are perfectly capable of engaging with Shakespeare's language when introduced to it gradually and with some elements of explanation and clarification.

Young Shakespeare Company and Pocket Propeller: *A Midsummer Night's Dream*

The Young Shakespeare Company
A Midsummer Night's Dream

On 17 January 2011, around 40 Year 5 pupils gathered in the school hall at Bush Hill Park Primary. The hall, in which they had just eaten lunch, had been swiftly transformed, with the help of some up-ended tables covered with a painted cloth and benches arranged in traverse, into the playing space for the Young Shakespeare Company's 'active storytelling' production of *A Midsummer Night's Dream* directed by Christopher Geelan. 'Active storytelling' is a process which works best, the company suggests, 'when the children do not know the story first', since they can 'live through the story, discovering it as they go' (YSC, n.d). Over the next 2 hours, the young audiences would 'discover' Shakespeare's play through a mixture of narration, discussion, audience participation and performance.

The play began with the entrance of an energetic 'storyteller' (Anna Haf Morgan) who explained to the assembled audience that some of them would be taking roles in the performance, but that all would be playing an active part in the unfolding of the tale. This initial direct communication and clarification is an essential part of the all-inclusive, non-competitive process of active storytelling. Reassured that all would have an important role to play in the afternoon's proceedings, there were no obvious displays of disappointment or jealousy when volunteers were selected to embody the characters in the first scene – Theseus and Hipplolyta, Lysander, Demetrius, Hermia, Egeus and finally Helena.

The whole of the play's first scene was narrated, with the children being given short, simple tasks to perform, gradually introducing them to the nature of the performance and to Shakespeare's language. Having established the location and the identity of Theseus and Hippolyta, the storyteller asked all the children to greet Theseus by repeating three times the line – 'Happy be Theseus, Duke of Athens', a simplified version of Egeus' first line – 'Happy be Theseus, our renowned Duke' (1.1.20). This triple repetition became the default method of delivery for the lines assigned to the young audience members, ensuring the reinforcement of certain important pieces of information concerning character identity and relationships. In addition to speaking to the characters, the audience was also asked, at points in the play, to assume the persona of one of the characters, supporting the actor playing the role. Having informed the audience, for example, that both Lysander and Demetrius were in love with Hermia, the storyteller asked the audience to echo their lines – 'Dear Hermia' and 'Sweet Hermia' – one side of the traverse joining each lover. This mode of delivery was used again for the lovers in 2.2 when both fall for Helena, highlighting the change of affection. Lysander's sudden infatuation was expressed with the phrase 'O Helena, O Helena, O Helena', while Demetrius declaimed 'Dear Helena, Dear Helena, Dear Helena', both lines again being echoed by the audience.

Just as one feared that the process of narration and repetition in 1.1 was in danger of becoming tedious, with the start of 1.2 the professional actors begin to assume roles and to take on the Shakespearean text. With only four actors the mechanicals were reduced to Quince (Harriet Rose), Bottom (David Timmins), Snug (Louise Beresford) and Flute (Benjamin Wells), the essential participants in the performance of 'Pyramus and Thisbe', and the text cut down accordingly. For most of the acted sections of the performance the actors delivered an edited version of Shakespeare's lines without alteration. However, occasionally, when encountering a difficult word, the comprehension of which was deemed necessary, the actors used the technique of miscomprehension by one of the characters resulting in an explanation by another. For example, Quince's line, 'You may do it extempore' (64), clearly baffled Snug, leading Quince to explain 'Make it up as you go along'. Later, in 3.1, when Quince conceded, 'Well, we will have such a prologue' (3.1.21), the other mechanicals showed a similar lack of apprehension, with Quince once again elucidating 'A speech'. This technique enabled the actors to clarify words for the audience without seeming to patronize them or make assumptions about what they might or might not understand.

Following the playing of 1.2 by the actors, the storyteller returned, quizzing the children to check that they were following the plot and then involving them once more, this time in the creation of the forest – the weather and the creatures living there. In keeping with the company's policy that no suggestion is ever wrong, the actors gamely accepted all ideas from the young audience, even when their enthusiastic affirmation of 'wolves' led to the suggestion of 'werewolves' and their search for 'fairies' as the forest's inhabitants took them via all manner of winged creatures. Having established a stormy location awash with dangerous and fantastical animals, the audience were then tasked with creating the forest soundscape, different groups being appointed to make the sounds of wolves, lions, rain and wind, while the storyteller 'conducted' them, taking the volume up and down. The final stage of this episode of audience involvement was the introduction of a section of text – an apt appropriation of lines from Puck's Act 5 speech 'Now the hungry lion roars' (5.1.1–2) – the lines of which the children were asked to repeat, adding in appropriate sound effects. This exercise bore out Sarah Gordon's assertion that young audience members 'enjoy speaking Shakespeare's words and exploring different ways of saying them', the children producing a lively rendition of the lines and roaring and howling enthusiastically.

The combination of the performance of a simplified text by the children as the lovers, the performance of the Shakespearean text by the actors as the mechanicals and fairies, and the narration of sections of the story with the aid of audience suggestion was now established, and the actors skilfully and seamlessly manoeuvred from one mode to another throughout the remainder of the play, pausing at points to ensure that the audience were keeping up with the story. This varied means of storytelling, which credits the audience with the capacity to engage with the Shakespearean text while providing clarification of plot elements, character relationships and some words, clearly enabled the young audience to follow the play easily, as indicated by their accurate, enthusiastic responses to the questions.

While clearly able to understand and appreciate some of the verbal humour of the play, the audience perhaps inevitably responded most enthusiastically to the play's physical humour, with the most popular section of the play being the mechanicals' play within the play, in which the potential for physical comedy was fully exploited. Flute appeared with two huge balloons down his top, one of which burst when he stabbed himself, Bottom died with his sword sticking up from between his legs in a obviously phallic manner and Pyramus and Thisbe found their lips locked when Snug as Wall ducked after the line 'O kiss me through the hole of this vile wall', removing the barrier between them.

The reactions of the young audiences to the kissing, sexual humour and the storyteller's remarks about the lovers, played by their peers, being 'in love' or 'going to marry' was predictably similar to that of the Playing Shakespeare audiences at the Globe – an audible mixture of amusement and disgust. However, the young audience at Bush Hill Park settled down again quite quickly, obviously keen to hear the remainder of the play and apparently less self-conscious in their responses than their older counterparts. As the enthusiastic applause and cheering at the end of the performance indicated, the children were clearly enraptured and entertained, one small boy needing to be moved from his seat by a teacher concerned that in his hysterical laughter he might fall off.

Following each performance, YSC provides all schools with follow-up materials containing a range of suggested activities with which to continue an exploration of the play. The materials, like those provided by NT Discover, encourage the use of the play for a range of activities across the curriculum – in drama, literacy and art – with suggestions for improvising 'off-stage' episodes, designing wedding invitations and costumes, writing an account of the argument between Titania and Oberon from the point of view of the changeling boy, writing rhymed and unrhymed lullabies for Titania and writing newspaper reports of the final wedding in the style of different broadsheet and tabloid newspapers (Gordon, n.d., pp. 4–6). These activities encourage pupils to think, in particular, about language – rhyme, metre, style and tone – drawing on their experiences of watching the play performed.

The suggested activities are clearly also designed to open up interpersonal and social discussions within the classroom, urging pupils to draw parallels between events in the play and those in their own lives. For example, a section on father/daughter relationships suggests that having improvised the 'unwritten' scene between Hermia and her father that takes place before the play, the children might imagine a modern-day scenario in which a father is telling his daughter what to do (Gordon, n.d., p. 4). Such an exercise might well lead to discussions on the authority of fathers over their daughters across different cultures as well as time periods.

Pocket Propeller: Pocket Dream

Having toured to theatres and schools in 2009 to early 2011, Propeller's *Pocket Dream*, directed by Edward Hall, opened at the E4 Udderbelly in London on Saturday 30 April 2011. An upside-down purple inflatable cow which contains a 400-seat venue used mainly for comedy shows at the Edinburgh Fringe Festival was not perhaps the most obvious choice for the Pocket company's first residency. However, the festive spirit which surrounded the venue in its temporary Jubilee Gardens location – with a specially erected courtyard, containing a bar and various food stalls – had, one couldn't help but feel, something of the atmosphere of the Elizabethan theatre – the inn-yards and outdoor amphitheatres with their street sellers and plentiful supply of alcoholic refreshment. Granted the company were forced to compete with the noise of people eating, drinking and being entertained on London's Southbank, but then arguably so were Shakespeare's fellow players. Indeed, Propeller's use of this lively south-of-the-river venue in the heart of London's popular entertainment area seems one more feature of the company's work – alongside their all-male casting, use of contemporary dress, live music and sound – which captures the '"spirit" of the original staging' (Rokison, 2010, p. 73).

However, while the venue may have recalled some of the original performance conditions and, with its simple lighting wash over the stage and auditorium, enabled the sort of direct communication between actor and audience for which the company is well known, the choice of venue did not chime readily with the target audience for the show – an audience of young people. Although there were noticeably more children of primary school age in attendance during the run than one might expect to find at a professional Shakespeare production, there were also a number of adult-only parties, particularly at evening performances, undoubtedly changing the dynamic of the performance from those staged in school venues or marketed exclusively to schools. The original tour was funded by the Arts Council, designed for and offered free to school children around the country, many of whom had not seen Shakespeare performed before. Their reactions were, as Tam Williams explains (below), more vocal and unforgiving than those of the audiences at Udderbelly where most of the children in the audiences have been accompanied by their parents, engendering a different reaction to one in which young people are surrounded by their peers.

Pocket Dream began, very like the YSC production, with the actors all appearing on stage to greet the audience, Tam Williams, the actor who would serve as a narrator figure, as well as playing Puck and Flute, introducing the company – Babou Ceesay (playing Lysander and Snout), Alastair Craig (playing Demetrius and Quince), Richard Dempsey (playing Helena, Titania and Starveling), Vince Leigh (playing Bottom and Oberon) and Jonathan McGuinness (playing Hermia and Snug). By acknowledging the audience, this introduction set the scene for a production in which the spectators would be regularly addressed and involved, and established the company as actors who would 'tell the story' of *MND*. There was no illusion of reality but a spirit of play and informality, often absent in a darkened proscenium arch auditorium. Williams also explains (below) that the introduction was devised by director Edward Hall as one of a variety of means of slowly drawing the audience in to the production, a device particularly useful when dealing with schools' audiences.

Williams made a point of asserting in the introduction that the company of men would be playing women as well as men, an assertion which was often met in the schools' productions with 'heckles' and 'wolf-whistles' (interview below). However, the all-male casting is an important feature of the company's style both in their full-scale and Pocket productions. In addition to drawing on the original practices of the Renaissance stage, it is another feature of the company's work which helps to emphasize the fictive nature of the production, encouraging, in both actor and audience, an imaginative engagement and willing suspension of disbelief.

As Dempsey also comments, the all-male casting, far from hampering or complicating the storytelling, 'may have actually allowed [the actors] more liberty' (cited in Propeller, n.d., p. 20) since, as Leigh explains (below), the actors are more physical with each other than they might be with female actors. Certainly the lovers' fight in *Pocket Dream* was an energetic and quite brutal affair, with the male lovers hurling Hermia around, and all four slapping one another. This 'physicality', a 'trait' of Propeller's work (Williams, cited in Propeller, n.d., p. 20), has an evident appeal to young audiences who enjoy the excitement of a stage fight, a number of the younger members of the audience gasping as the slaps and punches were delivered.

Following the introduction of the actors, the start of the performance was signalled by the actors beginning an acapella rendition of the Everley Brothers' 1950s hit 'All I Have to Do Is Dream'. This song became the 'theme-tune' of the production, sung and hummed at various intervals in different musical styles. Live music and sound are key features of all Propeller's productions, many of the actors being also musicians and singers. In *Pocket Dream* the use of simple sound effects, performed live by the company, was one of the main storytelling devices, creating atmosphere, humour and clarity. Williams, as the Puck/Narrator figure had a pair of finger cymbals which he used to mark significant moments, such as the putting to sleep and awakening of the lovers, or character asides. In the scene of Puck's transformation of Bottom into an Ass, Williams used the finger cymbals to freeze the other actors while he moved skilfully between the figures of Flute and Puck, making each transition clear to the audience.

Another particularly effective sound effect used in the production was the 'hum' achieved by running a wet finger around the rim of a glass. This mystical-sounding noise was used to accompany dialogue relating to the magic purple flower, 'love-in-idleness' – during Oberon's first speech about the flower to Puck (2.1.155–74), in his speech about Titania – 'I know a bank where the wild thyme blows' (2.1. 249–67), and during the anointing of Titania and the lovers' eyes. This effect not only helped to create a magical atmosphere, but also aurally united all the points in the play relating to the flower, again enhancing the clarity of the storytelling.

Perhaps the most inspired use of music in the production was Jimi Hendrix's 'Purple Haze' as the song which Titania sings to Bottom while he sleeps on 'pressed flowers' (3.1.151). Although the appropriateness of one of the best known psychedelic drug songs of the 1960s to Titania's state of being under the influence of a purple flower might have been lost on most young audience members, Dempsey's perfect falsetto delivery, with an acapella accompaniment by the rest of the cast, added to the playful feeling of the production.

During the initial rendition of 'All I Have to Do Is Dream' the actors, clad in white tops, long johns and corsets, their neutral 'chorus' costume, began to draw items of costume from the tea chest which dominated the stage, Helena and Hermia adding Victorian nightgowns, Lysander and Demetrius striped pyjama tops with their initials embroidered on the pocket (serving as a vital reminder to the audience throughout as to which was which), Oberon a black cloak, Titania a huge black feather collar and sparkly net skirt, Puck a white ballet tutu and the mechanicals a range of brown working-men's coats and a variety of hats. With each of the actors playing two or three quite different roles, this Brechtian-inspired act of assuming a character by donning items of clothing in view of the audience was extremely helpful, enabling them to easily identify which character an actor was playing at a particular time.

As the song ended, Williams introduced the lovers to the audience, explaining who was in love with whom, and inviting the audience to follow them in their flight into the forest. This introductory narrative replaced the whole of 1.1, the most dramatic cut in the production, and one which largely removes the court (Egeus, Theseus and Hippolyta) from the play, a decision made for the sake of timing, number of available actors and the desire to 'get into the forest as quickly as possible' (Williams, below). Although the events which take place in the forest are undoubtedly the most engaging section of the play, some of the darker atmosphere of the play was lost in the absence of the threat of death or a cloistered life hanging over Hermia.

The play began, following a brief introduction of the fairy characters, with Act 2, with the actors assuming the roles of Titania, Oberon, Puck and the Fairies and beginning to speak an abridged and slightly altered Shakespearean text. The reordering of scenes in the production was skilfully done in order to tell the story with the greatest possible economy. The reversal of 1.2 and 2.1 also served to establish clearly the forest setting and the fairy inhabitants as central to this telling of the play. Indeed, in contrast to the cutting of Puck's lines and representation of the character as a puppet in Heap's NT version of the play, here Puck became the central figure, the puppeteer, directing the other characters' actions and guiding the audience through the play. The manipulation of scenes also allowed the merging together of the two early mechanicals' scenes – 1.2 and 3.1 – a seamless edit achieved by Quince ordering the characters not to leave to 'con' their parts (1.2.93), but to begin rehearsing (scripts in hand), reducing the number of character transitions.

With the cutting of 1.1, the actors were required to play only 13 characters between them, a manageable feat given the simple strategies established to indicate a change of character. The paucity of actors was also wittily exploited in the production – first when Leigh was unable to play Bottom and Oberon simultaneously, and secondly when there were insufficient actors to play Duke Theseus and Hippolyta in Act 5. At the end of 3.1, as Leigh changed from Bottom to Oberon, he handed the fairy queen a stuffed-toy donkey which she wound in her arms, later kissing it passionately, much to the amusement of the audience. Bottom having been transformed back into a human, in 4.1, Leigh delivered his speech, ending with the line 'And I will sing it in the latter end of a play, before the Duke' (4.1.213–14) which was followed by a trombone fanfare apparently indicating the Duke's entrance. Leigh exited, only to be thrust back on stage by his fellow actors, no longer in character, informing him that he was supposed to be playing the Duke. This metatheatrical moment exploited the humour inherent in apparent theatrical mistakes, and neatly allied the actors with their 'Mechanical' characters, also about to perform a play replete with error. It also permitted the use of audience participation as the actors finally decided to find a Duke and Duchess among the younger members of the audience, seating them on stage in the umpire-chair 'thrones' to watch the performance of 'Pyramus and Thisbe'. The use of audience participation has been a feature of most of the Shakespeare productions for young people, breaking the barrier between actor and audience. Although in Hall's production the active participation was confined to two actors, as opposed to the full-audience participation encouraged by the YSC and NT productions, the actors' relationship with the audience is established from the beginning of the production and, as Leigh comments, the company spends a lot of the production 'directly talking to' the audience 'and including them' (interview below).

As was evident with YSC's production, the mechanicals' play-within-a-play has an obvious attraction for a young audience, offering up a series of opportunities for slapstick physical comedy – in this case Starveling as Moon bringing in a dog on wheels with which he succeeded in tripping up Snug as the Lion; Moon shining his 'sunny beams' directly into Bottom's eyes, blinding him before falling asleep in the audience and having to be woken to 'take [his] flight'; Bottom's sword (a sink plunger) getting stuck to the floor and forcing Bottom to launch himself from one of the 'thrones' in order to kill himself and Thisbe killing herself while sitting on Pyramus' face before dying with her head in his groin. It is interesting to note that some of the decisions made by Propeller in creating 'business' for *Pocket Dream* were very similar to those of YSC – mild sexual jokes of the sort that appeal to children: Flute stuffing two balloons down his blouse in order to play a woman and Flute and Bottom having an accidental kiss when Wall shirked his duties, both of which were greeted with laughter.

The reactions of the young boy and girl, cast as Theseus and Hippolyta, sitting aloft on the thrones to watch 'Pyramus and Thisbe' evidenced the appeal of the humour of the Mechanicals' play. Once they had lost their inhibitions, they reacted with obvious enjoyment and amusement, a far more positive and generous reaction than that of the Theseus and Hippolyta in Shakespeare's text. As Williams, divesting himself of Puck's tutu, asked the audience to 'give me your hands' (Epilogue, 15) adults and children applauded enthusiastically – perhaps indicating a lack of clear distinction between what children and adults find entertaining and engaging. The question and answer session with which each performance closed, brought questions from both generations, and indicated a surprising level of understanding from some extremely young members of the audience. Amidst the inevitable practical questions – 'Why only boys performing?' 'Is it tiring?' and the rather charming 'Is it hard to remember what part you are supposed to be playing?' – came the remarkably insightful question from a very small girl – 'Is any of the play supposed to be a dream?' Craig's answer that the play was '[a]s much a dream as you perceive it to be' was characteristic of the company's unpatronizing, sincere responses to all the questions asked.

Like YSC, Propeller does not run workshops to accompany their Pocket productions, but produce an education pack supporting the production, incorporating useful general information about the play – a synopsis, outlines of the main characters, a production history, discussion of some of the play's key themes and wider information about Shakespeare and his works (Propeller, n.d.). The pack also contains information specific to Hall's production, in the form of interviews with the director, designer and cast which provide insight into the creation of *Pocket Dream* – the all-male casting, rehearsal process, delivery of the verse and nature of the adaptation. The pack seems perhaps more aimed at teachers than pupils, the interviews being quite sophisticated; however, it serves as an extremely useful resource for provoking discussion on the production following a school visit.

In addition to providing information, the pack includes suggestions for exercises for use in the classroom. Like those proposed by YSC, there are exercises in designing costumes and speaking the text. Some exercises draw explicitly on the work of Hall's company, for example, the suggestion that students might act out a scene between the lovers in three groups – one all-male, one all-female and one male/female. This concern with the effect of cross-gendered casting on the dynamics of the character relationships is of particular interest in considering Propeller's all-male productions, and also raises important considerations about the play's original performances by the Lord Chamberlain's Men which would have used boy actors to play the female roles. Other of the exercises, like those suggested by the RSC, stem from rehearsal techniques used by the actors both in Pocket Propeller and in the company's full-scale productions – mining the script for facts and clues about a particular character, improvising 'off-stage' action which is mentioned but not enacted in the play, and using 'actioning' as a means of working out what a character wants to achieve from any given line. The exercise of actioning, derived from the work of Max Stafford Clark, with its roots in the rehearsal practices of Stanislavsky, encourages young people to think in detail about what the characters are saying and why, as well as encouraging an expansion of vocabulary through the identification of appropriate transitive verbs to accompany each line. All of these exercises are useful both for students writing essays about character, plot and language, and those focusing on dramatic art, and combine to support an in-depth academic and practical approach to the study of the play.

Conclusion

It is surely a testament to the success and popularity of the various projects discussed that most seem set to continue, at least into the foreseeable future, with Regent's Park, Pocket Propeller, the RSC as well as YSC and S4K having projects in the pipeline for 2011 and 2012. One cannot help but feel that part of their success is due to the seriousness with which the actors, directors and production teams take their work and their commitment to putting on theatre of the highest quality for young people.

Although the productions which do use the Shakespeare text are often forced to reduce it to less than half, expunging characters and sometimes plot lines, they surely provide a far more welcome, and valuable introduction to Shakespeare than a narrative storybook, giving children a chance to hear Shakespeare's language, spoken by experienced actors who are able to make it come alive in a way that it rarely does when read out in class. They also, perhaps most importantly, allow them to experience the pleasure of live theatre, and, in particular, a genre of theatre in which the fourth wall is actively broken, allowing actor and audience to interact in a shared space. Gardner may be right in asserting that young people are capable of understanding a full-scale production of a Shakespeare play when it is clearly and brilliantly performed, but often clarity is sacrificed in the professional theatre for the sake of quirky interpretation or an attempt to make the play more interesting for an audience who may have seen in many times. The strength of these productions is that, with an audience of young children specifically in mind, they prioritize clarity, brevity and active involvement, all elements which, as has been seen, have the potential to involve and enthral young audiences.

Interview with Propeller's Tam Williams, Babou Ceesay and Vince Leigh – Conducted at the Udderbelly, London on 14 May 2011

HOW MANY OF YOU WHO ARE DOING THE SHOW NOW WERE INVOLVED IN THE ORIGINAL TOUR?

Williams   Al [Alistair Craig], Dickie [Richard Dempsey] and me.

Ceesay   This is my first time doing it, and Vinnie [Vince Leigh] and Johnny's [Jonathan McGuinness].

Williams   Johnny has done the full-scale *Dream*.

Leigh   Playing the same part. And I did Demetrius in the full-scale production.

ON THE ORIGINAL TOUR, DID YOU MAINLY TOUR SCHOOLS?

Williams   We toured schools, and some theatres and a factory and places where you would never normally take a play, but because it's just two umpires chairs and a mat we can do it anywhere, so I think they tried to get us to do it anywhere. I think it has probably played around 30 to 40 different venues in the past 2 years.

WERE YOUR AUDIENCES EXCLUSIVELY COMPRISED OF YOUNG PEOPLE?

Williams   It was mainly for schools, and we performed in schools, or in places where the Arts Council was providing free transport to the venues for schools. It was basically a free theatre trip for hundreds of kids, everywhere we went. It was an Arts Council funded outreach programme for Propeller. It was very rewarding but it was much harder work than this. Here, at the Udderbelly, we've had a mixed bag of parents and their children and it's an easier combination. The kids see their parents enjoying it, and they enjoy it. It used to take a much longer time to warm the audience up when we were just playing to kids, but, by the end of the play they were listening and laughing, often despite themselves.

WHAT AGE WERE THE CHILDREN YOU PLAYED TO ON TOUR?

Williams   Sometimes 13- and 14-year-olds, which was tricky, particularly with the male on male stuff. Sometimes younger.

WHAT AGE GROUP DO YOU THINK IT WAS DESIGNED FOR?

Williams   Well, for people who have never seen a Shakespeare. But having done it here in the Udderbelly it seems that it works for most ages, for adults as well as children.

Ceesay   Some as young as 6.

Williams   My five-year-old came and saw it and loved it.

Leigh   And I had a 4-year-old god-child who was absolutely transfixed.

Williams   Al's daughter was probably a tiny bit too young – she's 3.

WHAT HAS BEEN THE RATIO OF CHLDREN TO ADULTS IN THE UDDERBELLY AUDIENCE?

Leigh   We've had more adults.

Ceesay   Well, in the first two or three shows we had mainly half and half, but recently, we've had a couple of night-time shows where the audience has been predominantly adults.

HOW HAS THE AUDIENCE MAKE-UP CHANGED THE DYNAMIC OF THE PRODUCTION?

Leigh   I think the children feel safe with their parents, rather than being in an aggressive school environment where they might be bullied for enjoying it.

Williams   One of the joys of doing it in schools is that I often would single out the ring leader – and there is always one – and I would get him up on stage to play the Duchess. Or I would get the teacher who was telling them to be quiet all the time to play the Duchess. I made a thing about that as the narrator, saying, 'Whatever your teacher has just said, ignore it. You can make as much noise as you want'.

Leigh   It's actually more disruptive if you have a teacher saying 'Be quiet, shush, be quiet'.

Williams   I think that on the whole the audiences are better here because there's a sense of an environment for listening and enjoying the play.

IN WHAT WAY ARE THE REACTIONS DIFFERENT FROM OR INDEED SIMILAR TO THOSE YOU RECEIVE WHEN DOING A FULL-SCALE PROPELLER PRODUCTION?

Ceesay   I find that with the full production, because we have all that time to draw the audience into the story, we have more of an opportunity to get enjoyment from moments that are story-related. In the shorter version there's not so much of a pay-off, for example, when they realize what's happening with the Lysander, Demetrius, Helena, Hermia relationships.

Leigh   In this version, the only thing we've really cut is Theseus, so you do get most of the story; you just lose a lot of the detail, which is what enhances moments like that.

DID YOU FEEL THAT YOU NEEDED TO CHANGE YOUR STYLE OF DELIVERY FOR THE YOUNGER AUDIENCES?

Williams   For me, no.

Ceesay   I would say yes, only in so far as – I was going to say clarity – but in fact even for an older audience you may well have someone in there who has not seen Shakespeare before.

Leigh   In the tent we're performing in here at the Udderbelly Festival, we've had to be so big and over-the-top and pantomimic, which has, in fact, added another level. I'm loving it, because I'm getting to do a lot of things that I'd normally be booed off the stage for doing.

IS THAT BECAUSE OF THE SIZE OF THE VENUE OR THE NOISE, OR BOTH?

Leigh   Everything – the size of the venue, the wind, the noise from people outside and the planes.

Williams   It's been a very difficult venue. But, what is great is that Ed wrote a prologue for the top of the play, which is a great 'in'. We come in and introduce ourselves and tell the audience a tiny bit about Propeller, which starts to draw them in, and then we sing, and then Ed has begged me to slow the first bit down so that when we first go into verse it is slightly easier on the ear, and so the audience are gradually submerged into the play, like a diver.

SO IS THE INTRODUCTION YOU DO AT THIS VENUE DIFFERENT FROM THE ONE YOU DID IN SCHOOLS?

Williams   It's the same, but with the schools' audiences we would often be fighting over a lot of whistling and heckling – basically they wanted to kill us. The introduction was a good way of diffusing everything and saying 'we're all right', 'we're not scary', and then we were able to take them into the play. But Propeller always does something before a show. Out in the foyer beforehand there's often music or when we did *Taming of the Shrew* there was a wedding reception with someone playing the piano and us all greeting the audience. It's a nice way of drawing the audience in.

Leigh   I think that we do tend to talk to the audience a lot more than in a lot of productions – directly talking to them and including them – as opposed to acting with the other people on stage.

IN THE INTRODUCTION YOU TELL THE AUDIENCE THAT YOU, AS MEN, WILL BE PLAYING WOMEN. WHAT WAS THE USUAL RESPONSE FROM SCHOOLS' AUDIENCES?

Williams Heckles, wolf-whistles. The kissing was much more dangerous in the schools' productions. With Hermia and Lysander, when the first moment came there would literally be a mini riot. And Ed was all for that.

BUT DID THOSE WHO INITIALLY FOUND IT DIFFICULT TO COPE WITH EVENTUALLY CALM DOWN AND ACCEPT IT? YOU GET SCHOOLS' AUDIENCES AT THE FULL-SCALE PROPELLER PRODUCTIONS AND PRESUMABLY THEY ACCEPT THE CONVENTION.

Ceesay   Even in the full-scale productions there is the potential for a riot when at some performances you have a few schools in and they are trying to out-cool each other. You have people over-laughing or over-screaming just to be an attention-seeker.

Leigh   My strangest reaction was when we did a festival in Barbados where I think homosexuality is illegal, and we had four polo-pitches full of school children and when we started kissing we were almost mobbed, but they calmed down and eventually went with it, and they loved it.

WHAT ARE THE BENEFITS OR DISADVANTAGES OF HAVING AN ALL-MALE COMPANY?

Leigh   I played Demetrius in the original production and the freedom that you get when you're working with all men is incredible, because, if I'm playing opposite a woman, I'm six foot two and if I went to hit a woman I would always have a worry that I might actually be hurting her, or going beyond a professional line that I shouldn't cross; but with men who you actually play-fight with anyway off-stage, you can actually enjoy it and really go for it, so it becomes hugely physical. You don't worry and it becomes fun and a bit like rugby.

WHAT DO YOU FEEL LIVE MUSIC AND SOUND CONTRIBUTES TO THE PRODUCTIONS?

Leigh   It really focuses the story when the ensemble are all there, making the sound effects and concentrating, and all adding a certain level to whoever is speaking. We're all telling that story together and that really helps the audience to focus, because we're all watching the action and we're all involved, rather than the traditional process of saying your lines and going to the Green room and watching the football.

Ceesay   I think that it adds atmosphere. I remember when I first watched the full-scale production, the magic in *A Midsummer Night's Dream* came alive because of the music. We're the film generation so we love sound effects happening in the background. When they happen live, all the better.

Williams In the Q and A sessions afterwards the children always want to come up onto the stage and try out the sounds for themselves. It's so much more interesting than having recorded sound.

THE ORIGINAL PRODUCTION WAS SET IN A VICTORIAN ATTIC. THIS ONE HAS A TEA CHEST AND SACKS OF TEA ON THE STAGE. WHO CAME UP WITH THE DESIGN AND WHY TEA?

Williams Michael Pavelka came up with the idea. I think that he thought that because we were touring it the tea bag idea would be useful, and initially we had more tea bags that the children could sit on. I think he decided on tea because of the Indian connection – the Indian boy. I think that that was his inspiration for it. So, much as I loved the attic, and that works for the full-length version, I think that with touring the tea works rather well. There's something transient about tea and the tea-clippers.

I DID WONDER WHETHER IT HAD ANYTHING TO DO WITH THEORIES THAT SOME OF THE EARLIEST PRODUCTIONS OF SHAKESPEARE'S PLAYS TO TOUR ABROAD WERE THOUGHT TO HAVE BEEN PERFORMED ON THE SHIPS OF THE EAST INDIA COMPANY.

Williams That may well have had something to do with it as well.

CAN YOU TELL ME SOMETHING ABOUT HOW THE PRODUCTION WAS CREATED?

Williams Yes, I was in the original group who devised it, and we were basically paid by Ed to sit in a room for three weeks and work out how to do an hour's versions of *A Midsummer Night's Dream*. We had a lot of pizza and did about an hour's work a day and we worked out that if Puck became the narrator and he had a device by which he could freeze the action we could insert plot when we needed to, and jump in and out of character. A lot of it developed, of course, when we got in front of an audience. We have a confidence within the group and we trust each other and are able to play.

WHY WAS ACT 1 SCENE 1 CUT?

Williams   In getting in down to the bones of the play we decided to just deal with the lovers, the forest and the mechanicals, and with six actors that is just about manageable. Those are the strongest three strands of the play, although Theseus is a wonderful part and has some wonderful language.

Leigh   I think it's because we want to hook the kids immediately.

I JUST WONDER WHETHER IT LOSES SOME OF THE DARKNESS WITHOUT THE THREAT AGAINST HERMIA.

Williams   Yes, it does. I just think that Ed wanted us to get into the forest as quickly as possible.

WHEN YOU BRING THE TWO AUDIENCE MEMBERS UP ON STAGE HAVE YOU HAD ANY RESISTANCE?

Williams   I think that because of the way we begin, with the introduction, the audience are aware that we are aware that they are there all the time. I think that because of this they are not particularly surprised when we ask them to come up on stage.

Ceesay   Hands shoot up quite quickly when we ask for volunteers, and it just adds another dimension.

WHAT ABOUT DISRUPTIVE BEHAVIOUR ONCE YOU HAVE GOT THEM ON STAGE?

Leigh   Not really. One little boy refused to get up on the umpire's chair the other day. He was absolutely terrified, but it was actually rather lovely, because we had to play to him, where he sat on the floor. Whenever we talked directly to him he seemed a bit shy, but when we turned away we could see him, out of the corner of our eyes, giggling and clearly enjoying it.

WHAT REACTIONS HAVE YOU HAD FROM THE VARIOUS YOUNG AUDIENCES YOU HAVE PLAYED TO?

Ceesay   I teach, and I've taught in some very rough places where the most difficult thing to do is just to get someone's attention. What's amazing about this production is how concentrated and attentive the young audiences are, and at the end how they are still sitting on the edges of their seats.

Leigh	And still curious. I remember once we opened up the question and answer session and one little girl – she was only about 6 – asked 'what happened to the Indian child'.
Ceesay	And another time, one young kid asked why we had tea bags on the stage, and another kid answered before us: 'It's because of the Indian boy'. It's amazing that they pick up on something that happens early in the play and is not really mentioned again.
Leigh	They are really paying attention.

Notes

1 Last accessed on the Regent's Park Theatre website in 2009 – http://openairtheatre.org/. This quote is no longer available.

2 The theatre's website claims that 'over 140,000 people attend our four annual productions between May and September with many people telling us they saw their first theatre production here' (Regent's Park Theatre, 2003–10a).

3 One young audience member commented of *MND* that 'when they did the silvery moon song I kept on singing it all the way home' and another of the witches' singing in *Macbeth*, 'I will never forget the moment the three witches sung around the pot . . . when they started I was blown away' (Heap, n.d. p. 6).

Web resources

Pocket Propeller:
    www.propeller.org.uk/education
RSC (2009), Education Pack for YPS *The Comedy of Errors*:
    www.rsc.org.uk/downloads/rsc_Edu_coe_2009_full_pack.pdf
— (2010), 'YPS Week 2010': www.rsc.org.uk/education/yps/2010/yps-week.aspx
Shakespeare 4 Kidz:
    www.shakespeare4kidz.com/
Young Shakespeare Company:
    www.youngshakespeare.org.uk

CHAPTER SIX

Shakespeare: The Animated Tales

The final 'short Shakespeare' to come under discussion in this section is *Shakespeare: The Animated Tales* (*Tales*). Produced jointly by Channel Four Wales (S4C), BBC Wales and Russian animation studio Soyuzmultfilm between 1992 and 1994, and scripted by Leon Garfield, the project comprised versions of 12 of Shakespeare's plays, each reduced to a half-hour animation. On the advent of their release, Terence Hawkes dismissed the *Tales*, arguing that since 'they are packages of stories based on the Shakespearean plots, which themselves were not original . . . they aren't going to provide much insight into Shakespeare' (quoted in Lewis, 1992, p. 12). This is, of course, one of the main criticisms levelled at the storybook Shakespeares discussed in Chapter 3, on the basis that, since Shakespeare took most of his stories from preexisting sources, a retelling, devoid of his language and dramatic style, is essentially un-Shakespearean. Hawkes' criticism in this respect is valid; as Garfield himself asserts, in adapting the plays for the *Tales*, 'the demands of the story' always came first (2001, p. 36) and the viewer is certainly more likely to gain a sense of the basic story of the plays than of Shakespeare's characterization or style, and even then one that lacks the nuances and complexities of Shakespeare's plots. However, three points may be raised against Hawkes' assertion. The first is that, unlike most storybook Shakespeares, the *Tales* are not simply 'stories' – they are largely dramatized versions of the plays in which the dialogue emanates from the mouths of reacting and interacting characters. The second is that the dialogue used, again unlike that of most of the storybook retellings (excluding Garfield's), is Shakespeare's own dialogue, albeit, as will be discussed, heavily cut and rearranged. Thirdly, in describing the animations as 'packages of stories', Hawkes fails to mention their visual dimension, which plays a vital role in the retelling of the plays.

As Gregory M. Colon Semenza points out, most critical writing on the *Tales*, of which there has been relatively little, has tended to focus on the 'textual cutting', reading the films 'as adapted literature – not as film' (2008, p. 37). Semenza's is an important point. While the texts and their treatment are undoubtedly one significant factor in considering the mediation of the plays, the visual aspects of the animations are of equal significance in terms of their effect on the viewer's perception of the story and, in particular, its characters. If emphasis is placed on the *Tales* purely as a means of relaying Shakespeare's texts, or even his stories, then they will, almost certainly, fall short; but, if they are discussed as animations, their artistry analysed and the relationship of their visual imagery to the verbal imagery of the plays unpicked, then they may encourage discussion of the intricate ways in which animation is able to convey mood and tone, reflect differences in genre, and depict theme and character. They may also contribute to debates about the afterlife of Shakespeare's plays more generally, and to an understanding of the process of adaptation.

This chapter will begin by considering the intended audiences for the *Tales* and the nature of their potential engagement with the material. It will then proceed to a discussion of the filmic elements of the animations and the way in which these relate to the themes and content of the various tales depicted and viewers' impressions of the plays and their characters. The discussion then moves to the, albeit according to Semenza, overemphasized area of textual cutting, looking at the ways in which the cuts affect perceptions of the plays' plots, characters, themes, and, in particular, metre, rhythm and rhyme.

Stanley Wells proposes two different audiences for the *Tales*, suggesting that they are suitable 'for people who either don't know them [the plays] or who, knowing them, are interested in seeing what can be done with and through them in a different medium' (1992). These are, of course, two quite distinct constituencies, whose experiences of the animations are likely to be quite different. As Janet Bottoms asserts, 'it would certainly be very difficult for a child, or anyone who does not know the plays well, to grasp all the ideas and images in many of the *Animated Tales*' (2001, p. 11), and yet, the marketing of the animations was clearly aimed at young people unfamiliar with the plays, rather than at seasoned playgoers. The question must, therefore, be raised as to what the *Tales* can offer as introductions to Shakespeare, and what appeal they might have to the viewer already familiar with the plays.

The publicity material for the *Tales* presents them predominantly as preparatory materials, introducing 'Shakespeare's valuable cultural heritage . . . in an accessible, exciting form'. It also asserts their capacity to 'educate', and, in stating their 'targeted audience' as that of '10–15 year olds' (quoted by Semenza, 2008, p. 40), suggests that they are aimed at those young people for whom Shakespeare is, or will soon be, a part of their educational and examinable curriculum. There is, of course, nothing wrong with introducing Shakespeare to children predominantly through his stories, particularly when presented in new and innovative forms. Like the graphic novels discussed in Chapter 4, the *Tales* skilfully combine the verbal and visual, emphasizing the status of the plays as drama rather than narrative. In addition, they include an aural dimension – one that has rarely been discussed in critical appraisals of the animations – Shakespeare's words spoken by some of Britain's most experienced Classical actors. As such, they have some of the appeal of the Young Shakespeare Company's active storytelling productions discussed in Chapter 5 – introducing young people gradually to the language of Shakespeare, spoken not by their peers in stilted classroom readings of the plays, but by actors skilled in performing his work.

However, while, as Bottoms discusses, there are numerous potential educational benefits in the use of the *Tales* in the classroom, there are 'dangers in their uncritical use in schools' (2001, p. 3) in particular in their employment as replacements for the study of the complete plays at Key Stage 3 and above. A particularly worrying example of this potential use of the *Tales* is evidenced in Peter Thomas's article, 'A Present for Mr Patten' (1992). Thomas, a teacher and senior moderator for GCSE Literature, welcomes the *Tales* not as a resource to accompany young people's study of Shakespeare, but as a substitute for reading the whole of a play, asserting, 'teachers of real kids will find the *Animated Tales* a blessing: short enough to hold interest and long enough to prepare Key Stage 3 questions which meet Lord Griffiths' taxing criterion that they test knowledge of the story' (1992, p. 37). If knowledge of the story, and a simplified one at that, is deemed to be the prime goal of secondary teaching of Shakespeare then the *Tales* might indeed serve such a purpose. However, Shakespeare's work is, as previous chapters have discussed, defined by more than just his stories – his characterization, language, combination of verse and prose and metrical variety. As Garfield himself admits of his texts, 'in terms of the totality of the plays, the losses are enormous' (1992, p. 36). A study of the plays at GCSE level, and even to an extent at Key Stage 3, can surely not sustain such 'losses', and must take into account the structural and stylistic features of the plays. Although Thomas refers to the *Tales* not only as presented on screen but also in Leon Garfield's published texts, which are 'more than twice as long as those in the videos' (Bottoms, 2001, p. 5), even these are a fraction of the length of the complete plays and with their layout of the verse as prose, are surely unsuitable as replacements for study of the complete texts.

This is, of course, not to say that the published texts have no value. As Bottoms argues, they are 'valuable resources' which 'offer a base for comparison of isolated scenes or incidents, opening up possibilities for discussion about the reasons for, or effect of, the differences between text and video, or between either of these and the original play' (2001, p. 13). As Bottoms' remark suggests the greatest potential in the *Tales* – both in their printed and animated forms – is in their capacity as educational devices to be used *alongside* the study of the plays, in discussions of varying ways of adapting and interpreting Shakespeare's work. For a viewer already familiar with the plays, there are to be discerned, as Laurie Osborne suggests, a wealth of skilful techniques of animation which enhance the themes and characterization of the plays – the 'literalization' of metaphors and sophisticated blending of different 'artistic modes' – 'sculpture, painting, engraving, film and puppetry' (2003, pp. 140, 144). Garfield similarly speaks of the ability of the animators to devise 'images of their own that were wonderfully potent and revealed dimensions of the plays out of all proportion to the all-too-short time allowed' (1992, p. 36). However, many of these images and metaphors are likely to be discernible only to viewers who have already read or seen the plays in a fuller form, and are thus able to identify visual manifestations of textual imagery absent from the edited dialogue.

This tension in the *Tales* between apparent simplification and accessibility and complexity and sophistication is undoubtedly partly the result of the conflict identified by Bottoms between the chief aims of the British producers and those of the Russian animators. While Executive Producer Christopher Grace saw the *Tales* predominantly as appealing to 'children', the Russian animators were approaching their task from a tradition accustomed to reinterpreting stories not for children, but for 'mature audiences', placing emphasis on 'personal artistic freedom' (Bottoms, 2001, p. 6).

The choice of plays for the first series coheres with the producers' aims of targeting them at children, being those most frequently considered suitable or appealing to young people – *A Midsummer Night's Dream* (dir. Robert Sahakyants), *Hamlet* (dir. Natalya Orlova), *The Tempest* (dir. Stanislav Sokolov), *Macbeth* (dir. Nikolai Serebryakov), *Romeo and Juliet* (dir. Effim Gamburg) and *Twelfth Night* (dir. Mariya Muat). The plays chosen for the second series were slightly less typical and less obviously child-friendly, including *Richard III* (dir. Natalya Orlova), *Julius Caesar* (dir. Yuri Kulakov), *As You Like It* (dir. Alexei Karayev), *The Winter's Tale* (dir. Stanislav Sokolov) and *The Taming of the Shrew* (dir. Aida Ziablikova) and *Othello* (dir. Nikolai Serebryakov), both often deemed controversial for their respective sexist and racist elements. This may indicate a greater level of risk-taking on the part of the producers in light of the success of the first series; however, the plays remain those commonly found on GCSE or A-Level syllabi and, in the case of *Richard III* and *Julius Caesar* have a cross-curricular appeal. Garfield, discussing the choice of plays, states that they needed to have 'an international appeal . . . which rather ruled out the Histories', to give 'some hint of the enormous variety of Shakespeare's work', and to lend themselves 'most readily to drastic abbreviation' (1992, p. 36). The first two criteria seem somewhat at odds with each other, since a representative sample of Shakespeare's 'enormous variety' would seem, necessarily, to include the Histories, one of the three genres into which his plays are commonly divided. Indeed, on release of the box set of the animations, the films were divided, as in the First Folio, into the three genres of Comedy, Tragedy and History. However, presumably since only one History play (*Richard III*) had been produced, both *The Tempest* and *Julius Caesar* are included on the DVD labelled 'History'. While a case can be made for *Julius Caesar*, more often categorized as a tragedy, as a historical drama, I can see no justification for including *The Tempest* under this heading, the play having no clear historical basis and containing significant elements of fantasy. Indeed, such a categorization may prove extremely misleading to young people studying Shakespeare and his works. Garfield's third criteria – based on the extent to which the plays selected lend themselves to 'drastic abbreviation' – will be discussed later in the chapter.

Although seeking to appeal to a young audience, as Executive Producer Christopher Grace explains, the *Tales* sought to position themselves against the Disney mode of animation with its 'sentimentality' and degree of 'kitsch' (quoted by Osborne, 1997, p. 105). Instead, the project employed Russian animators, using a range of animation techniques – oil painting on glass, puppets, and Russian cel animation, which although akin to the Disney style of animation is, according to Osborne, 'wholly distinctive' in style, characterized by a different style of illustration from Western cartoons (p. 108).

In addition to this attempt to distance the *Tales* from the style of Disney, critics have noted other strategies by which the animators have sought to escape the films' association with children's cartoons. Osborne finds references in the animations to famous film versions of Shakespeare, including Orson Welles' *Macbeth* and Laurence Olivier's *Hamlet*, which, in her view, 'serve to associate the cartoons more closely with Shakespearean films than with narrative children's versions or with Saturday morning cartoon programming aimed solely at children' (1997, p. 107). Semenza similarly notes the metafilmic associations with the films of Welles, Kurosawa and Eisenstein (2008, p. 56), which serve to link the animations to sophisticated renderings of Shakespeare's plays rather than popular commercial entertainment and, as such, encourage their perception as serious artistic enterprises. In Semenza's eyes, the allusions not only to film but also to 'iconic paintings' 'call attention to . . . the process of adaptation' emphasizing, particularly in the case of *Hamlet*, the animation's status 'as a stylized work of art' (p. 53).

Hamlet, produced through the process of oil painting on glass, is mainly black and white or sepia-toned, with small splashes of colour, which gain a symbolic significance – the prominent yellow, a sickly hue that marks the dis-ease and 'rotten[ness]' of Denmark, and red, used particularly strikingly in the final scene, in which the means of death (the bloody wounds of Hamlet and Laertes, and the poisoned wine that kills Gertrude) are highlighted in similar tones. This process of painting on glass, as well as having an obviously painterly quality which often appears two-dimensional, produces an effect of jerkiness in the movement of the characters, creating an awareness in the viewer of the process of the film's creation. That *Hamlet* is the most 'stylized' of the films, rich in metafilmic and artistic references and drawing attention to its own artifice, seems appropriate for a play that is consistently metatheatrical, employing not only a play-within-a-play, but numerous soliloquies and explicit references to the art of theatre.

This is one example of the appropriate matching of the mode of animation to the mood and tone of the individual play, a relationship which Osborne suggests was particularly 'dynamic' in the second series of animations (2003, p. 141). Oil painting on glass is similarly used for *Richard III*, also directed by Natalya Orlova, and similar in style to *Hamlet*. Its largely black-and-white images, appropriate for the shadowy gothic-style buildings that dominate its landscape, serve to enhance the play's themes of obfuscation and deception, and the obvious artifice seems appropriate to another highly metatheatrical and rhetorical play. By contrast, the style of painting used for *As You Like It (AYL)*, that of oil on film cel, is highly colourful, recalling at points the paintings of Raoul Dufy and Henri Rousseau, the latter particularly apparent in the image of the lioness, lurking to attack Oliver (4.3.115–17) which is strongly reminiscent of *Tiger in a Tropical Storm* (1891). This vibrant style is, perhaps, more appropriate to the genre of comedy, although it obscures some of the play's darker elements, in particular in the depiction of the forest throughout as a sunny pastoral idyll, despite the characters' description of Arden as a 'desert' (2.4.71; 2.6.16) and 'uncouth forest' (2.6.6), and references to the 'bleak air' (2.6.14) and dangerous creatures that inhabit its environs (4.3.110–19).

Different styles of cel animation are used for *A Midsummer Night's Dream (MND)*, *Macbeth*, *Romeo and Juliet*, *Othello* and *Julius Caesar*, according to the genre and mood of the play. The animation style of *Macbeth*, for example, is angular, employing a palette of muted, stone-like greys and browns, which lend a harsh, flinty tone to this tale of ambition and war, while that of *MND*, in particular its forest, is rounded and richly coloured, with Puck and the fairies clad in a range of bright hues, more akin to the saturated tones of Disney cartoons. However, unlike Disney's protagonists, the lovers in *MND* are, as Martha Tuck Rozett notes, 'adult' looking, 'ugly and unromantic with angular features and visible body hair', helping to emphasize the 'grotesqueness and disorientation' inherent in the play (1997, p. 13). The only one of the cel animations to have a Disney-like tenor is *Romeo and Juliet*, the big-eyed characters in colourful pseudo-Renaissance costumes resembling those of Disney's fairytales. This choice of style emphasizes the play's status, akin to many Disney films, as a story of romantic young love. However, in doing so it softens the play's more violent elements. The fights, for example, are strikingly unbloody, depicted most frequently in wide shots in order to demonstrate the skilful sword play, and with no close-ups of the injuries or pain caused.

The remainder of the *Tales* – *The Tempest*, *Twelfth Night (TN)*, *The Taming of the Shrew* and *The Winter's Tale (WT)* – were made using puppet animation, a style which gives a more three-dimensional quality, and, as a consequence, a greater humanity to the characters, particularly appropriate to these stories of family relationships, separation and reunion. Although the range of expressions capable of being conveyed are limited – the lack of movement in Hermione's face making her appear serene and martyr-like throughout her trial, even when Leontes refutes the words of the Oracle, and similarly unmoved in the final scene, when she discovers that 'Perdita is found' (5.3.122) – the puppets are capable of highly effective movements of the eyes and mouth, which help to convey mood. The former is used particularly strikingly in *WT* in the trial scene (3.2), in which Leontes' sideways looks at Hermione clearly portray his suspicion at her declarations of innocence.

Osborne suggests that the choice of puppetry for *The Tempest* is particularly appropriate, having 'explicit, even thematic connections' to the play (1997, p. 114). Certainly Prospero is spoken about in academic criticism on the play as a 'puppet-master', pulling the strings of the other characters (Ray, 2007, p. 134; Lipmann, 1976, p. 242). Although in the film he too is a puppet, he is the most obvious manipulator of the other characters – in particular of Ariel, Miranda and Ferdinand. *The Tempest* then, like *Hamlet* and *Richard III*, provides another example of an animation drawing attention to its own method of production. The choice of puppetry foregrounds the metaphor of the play as Prospero's puppet show, just as Michael Grandage's 2002 and Trevor Nunn's 2011 stage productions, with their crumbling proscenium arches, foregrounded the metaphor of Prospero as theatre director.[1]

The Tempest's magical elements are also heightened by the use of animation – in Ariel's varying degrees of translucency, the subtle appearances of faces in the rocks of the island that give it an air of enchantment and the magical appearance and disappearance of the banquet. Such transformations, which in live action films are evidently result of special effects, are part of what Rozett calls 'cartoon magic' (1997, p. 213), and seem natural to the genre of animation. Indeed, Bottoms asserts that in the case of the *Tales* the emphasis 'on fantasy and imagination' is greater than that on 'human drama', with the plays selected being 'predominantly those that involve the fantastic or supernatural to some degree' (2001, p. 9). This is certainly true of *MND*, *Hamlet*, *The Tempest* and *Macbeth*, with one of the most chillingly brilliant elements of *Macbeth* being the transformative power of the witches, who are one moment ghostly and masked and the next skeletal, their bones transmuting into the medal of the Thane of Cawdor and the crown during their prophesy of Macbeth's accession to power.

Even in the plays that lack an obvious fantastical or supernatural element, such features have, as Bottoms remarks, 'been added'. Bottoms cites the magical elements of the Forest of Arden in *AYL*, and those of *WT* (2001, p. 9). In the case of *AYL*, although the fantastical features are rather twee – white unicorns whose horns form a heart in the wooing between Orlando and Ganymede, and plump cupids who dart arrows from their bows – they are not out of keeping with the play as a whole, with its appearance of the god Hymen in the final scene. The Forest of Arden is, after all, an indefinable location containing common features of a rural setting – 'sheep' (2.4.83), 'goats' (3.3.2), 'brooks' (2.1.16) and an 'oak' tree (4.3.105) – alongside a 'palm-tree' (3.2.171–2), 'olive trees' (4.3.78), a 'snake', and a 'lioness' (4.3.109; 115). However, in the case of *WT*, with the exception of the allegorical figure of Time, the play does not contain elements of the supernatural, and hence, such features have the potential to be somewhat misleading. When Leontes speaks of his jealousy (2.3), for example, the demons that cluster around his head are in danger of making his irrational behaviour seem motivated by supernatural forces, rather like Macbeth. More misleading is the final statue scene, which Bottoms describes as 'simply, and literally "magical"' (2001, p. 9). Hermione's statue is surrounded by a glowing light that brightens suddenly when Paulina calls for music, surrounding Hermione with a white haze. Both this light and the breeze that flutters Hermione's veil as she 'comes to life' have no obvious source, and thus appear to be caused by some enchantment. The inference is thus that Paulina is effecting a genuine resurrection of the dead queen, rather than staging the return of the still-living Hermione. This moment is not helped by the fact that, although Leontes delivers the giveaway line about Hermione being 'not so much wrinkled, nothing / So aged' as the 'statue' that he beholds (5.3.28–9), the puppet Hermione, like that of Polixines, Camillo, Leontes and Paulina, does not age at all over the 16-year period, not only making no sense of Leontes' exclamation, but also making Hermione indeed appear magically preserved.

A similar, apparently magical transformation occurs in *TN*, when Orsino's expressed desire to see Viola in her 'woman's weeds' is met, not with the usual response that 'The captain that did bring me first on shore / Hath my maid's garments' (5.1.272–3) but with Viola's '"Cinderella" twirl' (Rozett, 1997, p. 213) into her dress. While Rozett is undoubtedly right in asserting that children 'would enjoy' such a moment (p. 213), it distorts the ending of the play. The visual image with which the play ends – that of two men paired together (Orsino and Cesario) – has been viewed as an important part of the play's final message. R. W. Maslen, for example, suggests that when Viola leaves the stage in male clothing, 'her clothes seem to promise that their marriage will be an egalitarian one' (2006, p. 137), while Stephen Orgel suggests that the failure of Viola to regain her clothing is her failure to regain her identity, and thus testifies to the 'impossibility of concluding the plot' (1996, p. 104). The retransformation of Viola back into her female guise restores the conventional patriarchy, and removes some of the ending's potent ambiguity.

In my view, the most successful matching of animation style to the tone, mood and themes of the play is in the tragedies and histories – the sometimes monochrome oil paintings of *Hamlet* and *Richard III* and the angular style and muted colours of *Macbeth* and *Othello*. While the medium of animation does bring out the magical and charming qualities of the Comedies, even with the resistance to a Disney mode of animation, there is a tendency to create fairytale-like environments which belie the plays' darker qualities. Like the magical pastoral idyll of Arden with its abundance of flora and fauna, bright blue waters and fantastical inhabitants, Illyria in *TN* is a 'green and pleasant land' (narration) with Orsino's fairytale palace, Olivia's garden with its statue of Cupid, heart-shaped swan fountain, and box trees made partly of lace and the streets whose houses are decked with flowers. This serves to place the themes of romance and love at the play's centre; however, it obscures the melancholy, bitter notes in the play, an obfuscation enhanced by the removal of the imprisonment of Malvolio and his subsequent threat of revenge.

The mood, tone and themes of the plays are enhanced not only by the mode and style of animation but also by the dense visual imagery which augments and sometimes replaces the imagery of the texts. Semenza speaks of Orlova's *Hamlet*, for example, as 'a stunning achievement whose visual language serves quite adequately to compensate for words, words, words' (2008, p. 52). *Hamlet*, like many of Shakespeare's plays, is awash with bird imagery invoking, among other birds, hawks (2.2.381), doves (4.5.168) and ravens (3.2.241). Many of the references are cut from the dialogue; however, Orlova employs a series of visual bird images which replace, and even move, beyond these brief allusions to take on a more profound thematic significance. Ophelia, for example, is linked in death with the heron, a bird often used in art as an allegory for 'Christians rising above the storms of life' (Werness, 2004, p. 214). Having followed Ophelia's point of view from the castle to the river, the camera focuses on a heron at the water's edge which, as the splash of Ophelia hitting the water is heard, takes off into the sky. As this white bird soars further skywards, it begins increasingly to resemble a white dove – another bird with religious connotations, associated, in particular, with 'purity' (p. 143). This image not only associates Ophelia, the innocent victim of others' actions, with endurance and purity (the latter a feature of her traditional stage presentation in white (Teker, 2006, p. 114)), but, as Rozett notes, 'offers the audience a reassuring vision of the soul's escape from bodily limitations' (1997, p. 210) providing Ophelia, as in the novels discussed in Chapter 7, with a form of happy, or at least transcendent, ending.

The antitheses of the dove are, according to Werness, 'the sparrow, the raven and the crow' (2004, p. 145), the latter two in particular having a 'negative symbolic significance' particularly in nineteenth-century art, in which they are associated with 'dreams of ill omen' (p. 106). Shakespeare himself provides a number of negative references to the raven, which is by turns, 'hateful' (*2HVI*, 3.1.76), 'fatal' (*Mac.* 1.5.37–8; *Tit.* 2.3.97) and, in *Hamlet* itself, 'the croaking raven' that 'doth bellow for revenge' (3.2.241). This last reference seems particularly pertinent to the use of the raven in the animation in which, following Hamlet and Laertes' fight over Ophelia's grave, and immediately preceding the final scene of widespread vengeance, a cawing raven takes off from one of the gravestones, and flies away.

The use of the raven as an image with which to evoke a sense of doom and fatalism is present in Orlova's other animation – *Richard III*. The image is used initially after Richard's declaration that he will send Clarence's soul 'to heaven' (1.1.120), and then becomes mainly associated with the young princes and their fate. Following Richard's insistence that Prince Edward should reside in the Tower (3.1.65), the camera pans up to show ravens circling in the sky around the tower. Images of ravens flying across the screen also occur after the princes enter the Tower (3.2.149), after Queen Elizabeth asks the Tower to 'use my babies well' (4.1.102),[2] and, finally, during the murder of the princes, when a number of ravens fly up from the Tower. The raven has a double significance in relation to a play set around the Tower of London, since legend famously dictates that the kingdom will fall when the ravens leave the Tower. Thus both the presence and absence of these birds have ominous connotations in relation to the succession and the death of kings and princes.

Visual imagery is also used in the animations to enhance the significance of relationships, particularly those in the Romantic Comedies, which seem otherwise underdeveloped in the short duration of the films. In the animated *AYL*, for example, there is little to suggest Rosalind and Orlando's initial affection for one another. They exchange only three lines following the wrestling, Orlando's asides (1.2.247–50 an 277–9) in which he confesses his passion are cut, and Rosalind's early admission of her feelings (1.3) are similarly absent. However, when Rosalind gives her chain to Orlando – 'Gentleman / Wear this for me' (1.2.234–5) – it is adorned with a red heart, providing a clear visual allegory for her literal giving of her heart to Orlando. Throughout the rest of the animation, Orlando only has to look at the heart, to indicate that he is thinking of Rosalind, and, in referring to it when he describes her as 'just as high as my heart' (3.2.64), explicitly links his heart with that of Rosalind, despite having said nothing about her, or to her, up until this point.

In addition to being used to replace images or sentiments which are cut from the text, visual imagery is also used to enhance the words – providing emphasis, aiding an audience's comprehension of complex passages or creating a visual realization of narrated events in the form of flashbacks. As Jaques' 'All the World's a Stage' speech in *As You Like It* (2.7.139–66) begins, Karayev moves to an image which closely resembles the Elizabethan woodcuts of London's Bankside with the Globe theatre at its centre, linking Jaques' speech with the Globe theatre's own motto – 'Totus mundus agit histrionem' (the whole world is a playhouse). The animation moves from this establishing shot into the theatre, where a series of images illustrates the various 'ages' of man, ending with the appearance of a skeleton at the end of the 'sixth age', clearly representing the figure of death. Thus, Jaques' otherwise potentially static speech is given a visual realization, and one that ties it firmly to the metatheatrical evocation of the theatre in which it was originally performed.

A similar strategy, and style of animation, is used for Rosalind's description of the behaviour of men and women in marriage:

men are April when they woo, December when they wed: maids are May when they are maids, but the skychanges when they are wives. (*AYLI*, 4.1.139–41)

The drawings which appear in the corner of the screen show a man wooing his love at a window, followed by an image of the same man holding his now wife's yarn while she spins, and finally an image of the wife beating her husband with a household implement. The images serve to clarify what is otherwise a rather obscure series of metaphors in a concise, imaginative and humorous way.

Surprisingly, given the imaginative approach of the directors in their creation of such resonant visual images, the depiction of the characters in many of the animations often conforms to unimaginative stereotypes – Shakespeare's complex and often ambiguous figures 'reduced, quite literally, to cartoon types' (Semenza, 2008, p. 42). Semenza discusses the depiction of Prospero and Caliban in *The Tempest* as examples of characters whose 'psychological and moral complexities . . . largely disappear', mainly due to the reduction of the text, and thus 'the absence of the cumulative textual evidence of Prospero's multiple character flaws, which undermine simple readings of Prospero as virtuous and Caliban as monstrous' (p. 42). It is undoubtedly true that the textual cutting has a profound effect on the presentation of these characters; however, one might argue that the animations themselves are equally culpable in encouraging such a dichotomous perception. As in many of the storybook illustrations discussed in Chapter 3, we find Caliban depicted as a monstrous figure – in this case, a web-footed, toad-like creature with black tufts of hair and pointed, devilish ears, played by Alun Armstrong in an inhuman, oddly Yoda-like voice, while Prospero is a white-haired, bearded figure with a commanding stance, a blue cloak, which as Lisa Hopkins points out is 'the colour associated with holiness in the iconography of religious paintings' (Hopkins, 2008, p. 49) and a calmly authoritative voice provided by Timothy West. Although Semenza argues that the balance between the characters is somewhat redressed in the contrast between 'Prospero's violent and unnatural artistry', and the spirits of the landscape who are 'understood by and actually seem protective of Caliban, the island's true native' (p. 60), an awareness of such a distinction requires a sophisticated reading of the animation. While it is possible that a 'perceptive teen viewer' would be capable of recognizing 'the clash between the dark and unnatural magic of Prospero and the beautiful and graceful magic of these island spirits' (p. 60), the average viewer is more likely to come away with an impression of Caliban as an inhuman monster and Prospero a wise, powerful magician.

Lady Macbeth is another character discussed by Semenza as lacking in complexity. Described by the narrator as 'fiend-like', she is explicitly linked to 'traditional cartoon villainesses' (2008, p. 55), illustrated in the vein of Disney's wicked stepmothers, and linked to the witches by her apparent ability to transform herself through magic. In the sequence in which she calls to the spirits to 'come to my woman's breasts', for example, as she rips open her top, a horse and a dragon charge from her bosom towards the camera. The depiction of Lady Macbeth as a villainous figure is, however, tempered by, and at points even appears at odds with, her voice, which is provided by Zoe Wanamaker, and which does not resemble the stereotypical 'evil' voice of many Disney villains, or indeed of the witches in this animation. Wanamaker's voice gives the impression of a strong and determined, but not inherently wicked character, and helps to return to Lady Macbeth some of the ambiguity inherent in Shakespeare's characterization.

Another example of a jarring between the depiction of a character and their voice, which again serves to prevent the character from fulfilling a visual stereotype, can be discerned in the depiction of Viola in *TN*. The puppet Viola has the appearance of a rather fragile young girl, with a wide-eyed, innocent face which often seems at odds with Fiona Shaw's mature and often powerful voice. While at points the pairing sits uncomfortably, it prevents Viola from coming across as a naive little girl. A very similar, slight, puppet figure is used for Perdita in *WT*, the character, with her long red hair resembling the Pre-Raphaelite painting by Frederick Sandys (1866). However, this visual depiction coupled with the light, young voice provided by Lynn Pearce means that the character becomes the epitome of the idealized Renaissance young woman – beautiful, chaste, obedient and silent (Aughterson, 1995, p. 67), an impression enhanced by the cutting of many of her lines, including those in which she is shown to be thoughtful, practical and capable of speaking out – asserting in realistic terms to Florizel the impossibility of their marriage (4.4.38–40); taking control of the 'hostess-ship' of the sheep-shearing festival (4.4.70–2) and asserting her bravery and belief in equality:

> Even here undone.
> I was not much afeard, for once or twice
> I was about to speak, and tell him plainly
> The selfsame sun that shines upon his court
> Hides not its visage from our cottage, but
> Looks on alike. (*WT*, 4.4.441–6)

The reduction in character complexity is, then, partly the result of the characters' physical depiction, and partly the result of the brevity of the animations. Bottoms argues that the latter is most noticeably responsible, since 'depth and human complexity' require 'time to build' – 'What human drama requires is time, and time is precisely what the *Animated Tales* lack'

(2001, p. 9). Although Garfield states that 'the Tragedies presented fewer problems' in terms of cutting of material than the Comedies since 'their stories tend to be monolithic', his comment, once again, operates on the assumption that the transmission of the stories is of prime importance. For Bottoms, while the 'multiple and interwoven stories' are the greatest casualty of the Comedies, the loss in the Tragedies is greater, coming 'in terms of human reaction and interaction' and 'ethical complexity', and rendering a morally complex play such as *Othello*, in which the protagonist suffers a gradual descent into jealousy and lack of control, 'frankly a disaster' (p. 10).

While there is not sufficient space to discuss all the significant changes to character or relationships brought about by the cuts, one might mention the cutting in *Romeo and Juliet* of most of the role of Mercutio and his interaction with Romeo such that Romeo's grief at his death and his subsequent revenge on Tybalt seems largely unmotivated; the cutting of Malvolio's imprisonment in *TN* such that he seems mildly humiliated rather than cruelly destroyed; and the excision of much of Iago and Othello's exchanges in 3.2. *Othello*, diminishing Iago's role in provoking Othello's jealousy, and making it appear not gradual, but more akin to Leontes' sudden, irrational suspicions in *WT*.

Semenza's argument in relation to the obliteration of much of the psychological and political complexities of the stories and the ambiguities of characterization is that 'these films are not intended for literature professors who will meticulously evaluate them in relation to the Shakespearean source texts. They are made for an audience of young teens and pre-teens whose analyses will be confined mainly to what they see before them. And what they see before them, in this case, is a challenging series of visual images accompanied by sound' (2008, pp. 44–5). It is certainly true that the intended audience was a teenage one, and there can be no doubt that the visual images provided are in some cases vividly evocative; however, the question of whether the reduction of the plays' complexities is problematic depends on the perceived function of the animations. If they are to be enjoyed for their 'challenging' and visually stimulating images, or indeed viewed alongside a study of the whole play, as an example of one form of interpretation or appropriation, then the absence of elements of the political, moral and psychological complexity is not a problem, and might indeed provoke discussion and comparison with other versions. If, however, they are to be used in the classroom, in place of the study of the whole text, prior to students studying one or two scenes in depth, then this lack of complexity and ambiguity does seem problematic and potentially misleading.

Thomas, commenting on the intended market for the *Tales*, asserts that 'those who despise abridgement will carp at cuts . . . and purists will be annoyed that the blank verse is laid out as continuous prose. Carpers and purists can stick to the uncut texts, but teachers of real kids will find *The*

Animated Tales a blessing' (1992, p. 37). The implication in Thomas's tone is that those who mourn the loss of certain characters, or levels of complexity, or who comment on the problems inherent in the textual layout, are being pernickety and are out of touch with the realities of teaching, whereas, both these areas can prove extremely misleading to students studying the texts.

In cutting the plays to 30 minutes, Garfield was, of course, forced to make quite substantial excisions, which he concedes were 'to the plays' detriment' (1992, p. 36). As discussed above, these cuts often lead to rather two-dimensional characters and to the removal of elements of the plots which contribute to their complexity and, at points, deliberate ambiguity. Another problematic effect of cutting, whether for students studying the plays with the aid of the printed texts, or indeed for those familiar with the plays watching the animations, is in the obliteration of the iambic pentameter – both in terms of the rhythm and rhyme of the lines, and in the removal of any clear distinction between verse and prose in the dialogue. Bottoms cites the first encounter between Romeo and Juliet in 1.5 as an example of a cut which destroys 'the rhyming structure of the whole dialogue' (2001, p. 5). The lines between the pair famously form a sonnet, a form which, as Thomas Honegger elucidates, is pivotal to the scene and to the subsequent development of their relationship:

> The final couplet, with its verbal parallelisms (move, prayer) and the fact that the two adjacent lines spoken by the protagonists share the same rhyme, immediately precedes and foreshadows the harmonious physical union by means of a kiss . . . Lastly, Juliet's participation in the composition of the sonnet foreshadows her active role in the developing relationship with Romeo. (2009, p. 170)

The cutting thus eradicates a verse structure central to this moment in the play, and one which is surely key to students' study of *Romeo and Juliet*.

Rhyming couplets are a casualty of the cutting throughout the plays. The cutting of these metrical devices, which commonly occur either at the ends of scenes or are used to mark significant lines in the plays, seems detrimental both to those studying the plays from the texts of the *Tales*, leaving them unaware of Shakespeare's dramatic use of this structure, and to those familiar with the plays, particularly in the removal of famous saws:

Phebe   [Dead shepherd, now I find thy saw of might]
       Whoever loved that loved not at first sight? (*AYLI*, 3.5.82–3)

Viola   I'll do my best
To woo your lady – yet [a barful strife –]
Whoe'er I woo, myself would be his wife. (*TN*, 1.5.41–2)

This may seem like the 'carping' described by Thomas; however, Shakespeare's use of metre is often as potent for a transmission of meaning as the words themselves, and, in the case of rhyming couplets is, as Bottoms asserts, 'important for its effect on the education of the ear' (2001, p. 5).

As the cutting of both Carl Heap's National Theatre productions and those of Pocket Propeller (discussed in Chapter 5) indicate, it is possible to cut a Shakespeare play with some regard for the metrical structure of the verse. Garfield makes no attempt to retain the metre, cutting out odd words, and sections of lines such that the whole spoken text sounds like prose. There is some irony in the highly experienced actor, Antony Sher, who plays Richard III, observing the accented 'ed' ending in his line 'I am determinéd to prove a villain' (1.1.30) for the sake of the preservation of the pentameter, when the metre of most of his lines is shot to pieces. It is to the credit of many of the actors, clearly experienced in delivering Shakespeare's lines, that they manage to make some distinction apparent between the verse and prose.

The layout of all the lines as prose in the published texts is even more misleading. Even when the essential metre of passages such as the witches' rhyming iambic tetrameter in *Macbeth* is preserved, the lines are printed in a way that makes the distinctive structure of their magical incantation difficult to discern:

1st Witch	When shall we three meet again? In
	thunder, lightning, or in rain?
2nd Witch	When the hurly-burly's done, when the
	battle's lost and won (Garfield, 2002, p. 394)

Thus, irrespective of Thomas's claims about their convenient length, the published texts seem entirely inappropriate for the study of Shakespeare in the classroom.

As this chapter has discussed, the *Tales* are by no means solely aimed at young audiences. However, elements of their interpretation, in particular the eschewing of the darker elements of the comedies, and tendency to stress the possibility of hope or transcendence at the end of the tragedies, seem geared towards children as opposed to adults. In addition, the setting of all the plays in either the Renaissance, or, in the historical period in which they are set (Ancient Rome for *Julius Caesar*) warrants comparison with the BBC Shakespeare television productions of the 1970s and 1980s which, in being intended to serve a predominantly educational function, shied away from modern dress or from interpretative takes on the plays, their originator, Cedric Messina, instructing the directors 'to "let the plays speak for themselves"' (Bulman, 1984, p. 572). Also, while the animations do not pander to perceptions of what is suitable for young audiences to nearly so great a degree as the storybook Shakespeares discussed in Chapter 3, some elements of the depiction of sex and violence in the plays seem motivated by perceptions of suitability for young viewers. As in the storybook *Hamlet*, for example, the references to 'incestuous sheets' and 'the rank sweat of an enseamèd bed' in the 'closet scene' (3.4) are cut, and although the audience is briefly permitted a glimpse of Gertrude and Claudius in a lascivious embrace when the ghost refers to 'the will of my most seeming-virtuous queen' (1.5.46), a curtain soon closes over the pair, before their behaviour becomes 'unsuitable' for universal viewing. Semenza suggests that in this moment Orlova may be explicitly commenting on the censorship of material, drawing 'attention to what young viewers are not allowed to see' and hence highlighting it (2008, p. 53). What 'young viewers are not allowed to see' appears to include violent deaths – those of both Lady Macduff and her children in *Macbeth* and of Elizabeth's brothers in *Richard III* being depicted through the use of stained glass images that allude to slaughter – and certain degrees of nudity. As Bottoms explains, there were 'reported difficulties over the depiction of Romeo and Juliet's marriage night. While nudity was permissible – even requisite – nipples were not, and a compromise was apparently achieved only with difficulty' (2001, p. 6). Nipples seem equally problematic in *Macbeth*, in which although the animators seem to have no objection to sexualizing the character of Lady Macbeth, dressing her in a 'tightly fitting, nearly transparent dress' (Semenza, 2008, p. 42) and having her expose her breasts as she calls to the spirits, her naked bosoms have no nipples.

The *Tales* are skilled artistic works, which have an intricate and often sophisticated relationship to the imagery, themes and production history of the plays. They merit analysis, of the use of visual imagery to invoke textual metaphors, and interrogation of the choices made about styles of animation and depiction of the plays' characters, positioning them in the fertile area of discussion of the interpretation of Shakespeare in performance. They also provide audiences, new or seasoned, with the opportunity to hear highly experienced actors like Antony Sher (Richard III), Pete Postlethwaite (Quince), Timothy West (Prospero), Brian Cox (Macbeth) and Roger Allam (Orsino) giving skilled and sensitive readings of the lines. However, despite the fact that the animations may, as Semenza argues, provide 'numerous additions . . . to the Shakespearean text' (2008, p. 64), one cannot help but feel that if each had been allowed a little more time (even an extension to an hour in length, which is surely not too long to hold the attention even of the 'cartoon' generation), and the cutting of the texts had been a little more sensitive to the verse form, then they would have an even greater appeal, both for use in the classroom and as productions of Shakespeare in their own right.

Notes

1 Michael Grandage's production played at the Crucible Theatre, Sheffield from 24 September to 19 October 2002 and subsequently at the Old Vic theatre, London from 16 January to 15 March 2003. Trevor Nunn's production played at the Theatre Royal Haymarket from the 27 August until the 29 October 2011.

2 Reference unique to the Folio, taken from Hammond (1981).

PART THREE

Rewriting Shakespeare

CHAPTER SEVEN

Novel Adaptations of Shakespeare: *Hamlet*

Hamlet is one of Shakespeare's most frequently performed, adapted and appropriated plays. Numerous authors have taken the themes and characters of *Hamlet* to create novels, plays, films and even television skits for adult audiences with the aim of reinterrogating the play's themes and characters. Less well known but equally abundant are adaptions, particularly in novel form, for teenagers.

As Megan Lynn Isaac comments, 'Hamlet seems like an especially ripe text for revision by young adult authors; the themes embedded in this single play serve as a virtual catechism for the field of adolescence' (2000, p. 66). Hamlet is a student, grappling with his mother's remarriage, his relationship with his young girlfriend, his sense of identity and feelings of responsibility, themes which feature regularly in adolescent literature. As Mike Cadden writes, 'the YA novel's primary subtext is usually about identity construction' (2010 p. 308), and Hamlet is surely the character in Shakespeare who struggles most with a construction of a sense of self – a character 'who tries relentlessly to talk himself – and a self into being' (Bartels, 1994, p. 173).

Writing in 2000, however, Isaac asserts that despite the seeming relevance of the play to modern adolescents, 'oddly . . . the thematic richness of *Hamlet* has inspired surprisingly few revisions of the play in young adult literature', finding only three novels which in her view 'significantly develop a vision of *Hamlet* as part of their own stories' (2000, p. 67). Those she does explore have, for the most part, what she admits are 'tangential connections to Hamlet' (p. 67). Laura A. Sonnenmark's *Something's Rotten in the State of Maryland* (1990) and Lois Duncan's *Killing Mr Griffin* (1978) are less adaptations of *Hamlet*, than novels which include the study of the play in High School as part of their narrative, and while Katherine Paterson's *Bridge to Terribithia* (1977) may have some thematic relationship to *Hamlet*, to describe it as an adaptation or even a 'development' of Shakespeare's play is stretching the comparison.

In the years following the publication of Isaac's book, however, a number of Young Adult novels firmly based on Shakespeare's play have emerged, the most notable being Lisa Fiedler's *Dating Hamlet* (2003), Rebecca Reisert's *Ophelia's Revenge* (2003), Matt Haig's *The Dead Fathers Club* (2006), Lisa M Klein's *Ophelia* (2006), Alan M. Gratz's *Something Rotten* (2007) and John Marsden's *Hamlet* (2009), all of which take the themes, characters and elements of the plot of *Hamlet* and rework them, frequently with the apparent aim of demonstrating the proximity of the issues of Shakespeare's play to those of contemporary young adults. *Hamlet* is not the only one of Shakespeare's plays to have undergone such revision, a number of his works, most notably *Romeo and Juliet* and *Macbeth*, having also spawned a series of adaptations in novel form. This relatively recent profusion may be explained perhaps by two phenomena – an increase in the market for 'serious young adult fiction' (Giblin, 2005, p. 57) and an ever-increasing desire to find ways of making Shakespeare's plays more accessible and appealing to young people.

As Janet Alsup argues, when they 'are allowed to read books that . . . focus on characters, settings, or situations familiar to them . . . teens often respond more positively to reading' (2010, p. 7). As a consequence, much Young Adult literature demonstrates a desire on the part of authors to write books in which 'teen readers can identify with the main characters and their struggles' (p. 9). A common method by which authors adapting Shakespeare seek to make the characters, situations and settings more familiar is by updating the events of the plays to the present day, a feature of Haig, Gratz and Marsden's adaptations of *Hamlet*.

Another notable feature of a number of these adaptations and one which seems designed to appeal particularly to young, modern, particularly female readers is their focus on the character of Ophelia. Fiedler, Klein and Reisert all make Ophelia the narrator and protagonist of their novels, giving her far more agency and opportunity for self-expression than her Shakespearean counterpart. As Marsha M. Sprague and Kara K. Keeling observe, adolescent girls respond particularly well to reading books about other girls – in particular about 'female characters who are suffering' (2007, p.viii). For them, historical fiction 'presents real opportunities for present-day girls to situate themselves as observers rather than participants in looking at girls' issues' (p. 89) – to explore the restrictions and social expectations which affected young women in the past, and relate these to their own lives and experiences rather than essentially reading about themselves. Putting Ophelia at the centre of the story may help to draw girls into what is essentially a male-dominated play, and to encourage them to consider Ophelia's treatment and behaviour in relation to their own experiences.

These strategies in adapting Shakespeare for young adults are not particular to *Hamlet*. Updatings of *Romeo and Juliet* include Sharon M. Draper's *Romiette and Julio* (2001) which updates the play to reflect racial tensions between Hispanics and African Americans in contemporary America and *Son of the Mob* (2002) by Gordon Korman, in which the son of a crime boss falls for the daughter of an FBI agent; while *This Must Be Love* (2004) by Tui Sutherland relocates the story of *A Midsummer Night's Dream* to Athenwood High and Gratz's second Horatio Wilkes novel, *Something Wicked* (2008) updates the story of *Macbeth* to the twenty-first century, with Horatio investigating the suspicious murder of Duncan MacRae at a Scottish Highland Fair.

Other adaptations also demonstrate a tendency to give voice to marginal or silent female characters in the plays. Both Klein (*Lady Macbeth's Daughter*, 2009) and Reisert (*The Third 'Witch'*, 2001) retell *Macbeth* from the point of view of Lady Macbeth's absent child about whom, in the play, we only hear in her line 'I given suck' (*Mac.* 1.7.54), while Caroline Cooney (*Enter Three Witches*, 2007) reimagines it as the story of Mary, daughter of the deceased traitor, the Thane of Cawdor. Similarly, Fiedler (*Romeo's Ex: Rosaline's Story*, 2006) writes the story of Rosaline, in *Romeo and Juliet*, a young woman mentioned only in passing in the play. As such, these novels may be aligned with the third-wave feminist movement which demonstrates a concern with 'issues facing adolescent girls' and in particular with giving 'voice to girls who had been silenced in society' (Starr, 2003, p. 474) or in this case, in literature.

One of the main ways in which these novels allow their female characters a 'voice' is in writing the narrative in the first person, a strategy employed by Reisert, Klein and Fiedler. It is also the technique employed by Gratz and Haig, who respectively write from the point of view of Horatio Wilkes (Gratz's equivalent of Shakespeare's Horatio) and Philip (Haig 'Hamlet' figure). The capacity to tell a story in the first person is one of the key differences between prose and drama, an important consideration in thinking about the transfer of the story of *Hamlet* from the medium of drama to that of prose. While Shakespeare's play offers a multiplicity of unmediated character-voices, these adaptations in novel form transmit the story either through the eyes of a single character, or, in the case of Marsden's *Hamlet*, through a skilful combination of omniscient narration and free indirect speech, presenting elements of the story from the point of view of Hamlet and Ophelia, and to a lesser extent, Horatio. Indeed, in Canada, Marsden's book was published as *Hamlet and Ophelia* (2008), a title which acknowledges the significant role played by Ophelia, at least in the early part of the novel, where entire chapters focus around her memories and feelings.

Although the original story of Hamlet (or 'Amleth', as told by the Danish Historian Saxo Grammaticus) is set in the twelfth century, Shakespeare's play seems firmly located in 'a sophisticated and Christian Renaissance court' (Thompson and Taylor, 2006, p. 24), and, as critics have sought to demonstrate, is intimately related to the political and social circumstances of Renaissance Europe.[1] While Klein, Fiedler and Reisert retain the play's pseudo-Renaissance Danish setting, Haig and Gratz update their novels to identifiable twenty-first-century locations: Nottingham, England and Tennessee, USA respectively. This updating of the story's locations is clearly motivated by the notion, discussed by Alsup, that young readers react well to recognizable settings in novels. Certainly the locations of these novels are more familiar to contemporary teenagers than that of the sixteenth-century Danish court, if only through the medium of television and film. While one might, as does Alsup, question the value in authors consistently attempting to bring their narratives too close to young people's real-life experiences – the experience of reading texts 'which are different in some ways from the teen students' real worlds' being equally as important (Alsup, 2010, p. 11) – in the case of both these novels the contemporization is highly effective, and in Gratz novel, despite the more familiar setting, the experiences of his characters are at a substantial remove from those of most teenagers.

Marsden's apparent updating of his novel to a modern setting seems less effective. Indeed, the period in which the novel is set is not immediately apparent. Words like 'bum' and 'semester' and references to 'smoking' and 'drugs' seem to suggest a contemporary setting, one which seems later confirmed by the description of Hamlet as wearing 'jeans' (Marsden, 2009, pp. 2, 38, 47–8, 50); however, anachronisms abound. The castle of Elsinore appears firmly medieval, with stone floors, gargoyles and a portcullis; the ghost of Hamlet's father is clad in 'a full-length cloak'; and young Hamlet and Horatio carry swords in scabbards, weapons which we are told 'befitted boys of their age' (pp. 1, 9, 19, 112). Also, the troupe of actors who arrive at Elsinore are all male, as was characteristic of the Renaissance period and we are informed that 'any other arrangements, involving the use of unchaperoned girls or women would have been unseemly' (p. 73), which does not reflect twenty-first-century attitudes to women on the stage. These anachronisms permit Marsden to adhere closely to Shakespeare's play, in many cases including close approximations of whole scenes transferred into a modern prose vernacular, while at the same time enabling him to make elements more immediately accessible to his young readership through the inclusion of modern customs, clothing and phrases. This is a technique which has proved effective in theatre productions of Shakespeare's plays, as seen in the Globe's 'Playing Shakespeare' *Romeo and Juliet*, discussed in Chapter 1; however, I would argue that within the context of a novel, written essentially in a realistic mode, the anachronisms seem jarring, and the contemporary references, mostly inconsequential, and in some cases at odds with Marsden's tight adherence to the Shakespearean plot.

In Haig and Gratz's novels it is not only the setting but also the characters which are adapted to make them contemporary. While Marsden, Klein, Fiedler and Reisert retell the story of Shakespeare's characters, Haig's and

Gratz's are modern figures whose lives partly mirror those of Shakespeare's play. Horatio Wilkes, Gratz's narrator, is the best friend of Hamilton Prince (Gratz's 'Hamlet' figure) whose father, manager of the Elsinore paper plant, has recently died under slightly suspicious circumstances, while his uncle Claude (Claudius) has taken over the business. Horatio narrates the story in a Raymond Chandleresque noir fiction style which sometimes appears crude:

> One thing was for sure. Something was rotten in Denmark, Tennessee, and it wasn't just the stink from the paper plant. (Gratz, 2007, p. 17)

However, like the futuristic *Manga Shakespeare: Macbeth* discussed in Chapter 4, the change of style offers a new perspective on the play, and one that has proved appealing to the teenage market, earning the book a number of awards for writing for Young Adults.[2]

There are several aspects of Gratz's text which have evident appeal to teenagers – the crime fiction genre, the modern setting and the central characters. As Diane L. Chapman elucidates, mysteries and detective stories 'rank among the most popular of juvenile genres' with 'successful series' having 'a protagonist with whom readers can identify' (2005, pp. 572–3). Horatio Wilkes is just such a figure – 'a wry, sarcastic seventeen year-old detective' (Gratz, 2006) – bright, witty and prepared to take risks to solve the crime. One might argue that Gratz is taking a similar strategy to the novels discussed above, narrated by Ophelia, in making Horatio, a character who in Shakespeare's play is something of an 'impotent bystander' (Thompson and Taylor, 2006, p. 137), the book's protagonist. While in Shakespeare's play Horatio stands by, wanting to help but 'unable to do so' (p. 137) in Gratz's novel he is given the agency to intervene and alter the course of events and thus becomes the tale's true hero.

Like Horatio, Gratz's other young protagonists Hamilton and Olivia (Ophelia) are also teenagers, students at the Wittenberg Academy in Knoxville. They are thus not much older than the intended readership for the book, and, as such, demonstrate concerns with which young readers are likely to be able to identify: relationships, parental conflict and an anti-establishment, anti-capitalist fervour. This is a world of videos, DVDs, PlayStations and Xboxes, and, like Michael Almereyda, in his film version of *Hamlet*, Gratz updates various aspects of the story to fit with his modern-day setting, with Claude (Claudius) and Paul (Polonius) using the 'intercom' (Gratz, 2007, p. 107) to eavesdrop on Hamilton and Olivia, and the Norwegian threat being transmuted into a takeover bid from Branff Communications owned by Ford Branff (Fortinbras). In this environment, rather than having a ghost – a character at odds with the literary genre in which Gratz is writing – the details of Claude's crime are brought from beyond the grave by a CCTV video recorded by Hamilton's father prior to his demise. Viewed first by the security guards Bernard (Bernado) and

Frank (Francisco) and then by Hamilton and Horatio, the recording is a clever device which permits the revelation of certain details of the poisoning without straying into the realm of the supernatural – at odds with the noir detective genre.

The use of a contemporary setting for a story which shares with *Hamlet* many elements of plot and characterization helps to emphasize, much like the modern-dress productions and films discussed in earlier chapters, the contemporaneity of many of the play's themes. However, as the online reading guide, created to accompany study of the book, suggests, there are also a number of deliberate departures from Shakespeare's text in Gratz's book. Students are usefully encouraged to think about the differences as well as the similarities between the two texts (Gratz, n.d. p. 3), an important consideration in thinking not only about the way in which the experiences of contemporary youth might mirror that of their Renaissance counterparts, but also how lives of young people in modern-day America differ from those of Early Modern Europe.

The question of departure from the source text also raises the important issue of dramatic irony in relation to the novel, an issue of significance with all adaptations of Shakespeare's plays. Dramatic irony functions on various levels in Gratz's text, but is, of course, dependent on knowledge, of the Shakespearean original. The novel quite clearly subverts dramatic irony by undermining the reader's expectations of the fates of the various characters, leaving most of the protagonists alive, a subversion shared, to some degree, with many of the novels discussed. This alteration of the ending seems, in Gratz's novel, less motivated by a desire to produce a happy ending than a necessary consequence of the genre of detective fiction, in which the detective must solve the crime and save the day. If, as the reading guide suggests is intended the novel is studied alongside Shakespeare's *Hamlet*, it may usefully encourage classroom discussion, not only of the differences prompted by the transfer of the story from one period to another, but also of those provoked by the conventions of different literary styles and genres.

For a reader familiar with Shakespeare's play, there is also humour to be gleaned from the self-reflexive references to *Hamlet* within Gratz's text. Horatio's mother, for example, an 'English lit. professor', leaves Horatio a voice-mail message which includes a quote from *Hamlet* – '"What a piece of work is man! . . . How noble in reason. How infinite in faculty. In form and moving, how express and admirable. In action, how like an angel, in apprehension, how like a god." And yet you can't be bothered to call your mother when you get to Hamilton's house?' (Gratz, 2007, p. 91).[3] This message, amusing for its ironic undermining of Hamlet's elevated language by its association with Horatio's failure to call home, is one of a number of witty references to Shakespeare's text embedded in the novel. Perhaps the most complex self-reflexive reference in the novel is its acknowledgement of its own status as 'pastiche of *Hamlet*' (Gratz, n.d., p. 3) through reference to another pastiche of the play – Tom Stoppard's

Rosencrantz and Guildenstern Are Dead, which is used in place of 'The Murder of Gonzago', a performance arranged not by Hamilton, but by Rex and Trudy Prince – '"It's – um . . .". She blushed. "To tell you the truth, I can't remember. I think it's based on some Shakespeare play"' (Gratz, 2007, p. 47); 'A sign on the wall advertised their upcoming performance. *"Rosencrantz and Guildenstern Are Dead,"* I read aloud' (p. 83). The reading guide invites students to look beyond *Something Rotten*, considering it in relation to the genre of 'pastiche' (Gratz, n.d., p. 3), and to Stoppard's play, which, similar to Gratz's novel, puts two of *Hamlet*'s more minor and less proactive characters at its centre, giving a similarly oblique look at the events of Shakespeare's play and its protagonists.

The reading guide also points out that both these adaptations are part of a larger 'tradition of retelling classic stories' of which Shakespeare himself was a part (Gratz, n.d., p. 3), another significant point in discussing adaptations of the plays, and one which raises the question of the extent to which they might be viewed as adaptations of adaptations. Just as Shakespeare took Saxo Grammaticus' legend and adapted it to comment on Renaissance society – theological uncertainty, the ethics of revenge and the culture of spying – so Gratz adapts Shakespeare's *Hamlet* to comment on the concerns of contemporary America – corporate greed, industrial pollution and a similarly pervasive culture of surveillance.

Haig's novel is quite different from Gratz's – narrated by Philip Noble, a disturbed 11-year-old boy. Although Philip is much younger than Shakespeare's title character and indeed the 'Hamlets' of the other novels, the key themes of the play – parental death, remarriage, self-doubt, madness, sexuality and religion – are all explored by Haig, and seem as strikingly relevant to this contemporary tale of a working-class Nottinghamshire childhood as they do to that of a university student from Renaissance Denmark. Like Shakespeare's Hamlet, Philip's recently murdered father returns as a ghost to tell Philip that his uncle Alan was responsible for his death and has designs on Philip's mother, and urges his young son to take vengeance.

Haig's novel is presented as an uncorrected piece of Philip's writing, devoid of punctuation and apostrophes, and often deliberately awkward in expression in a way that is sometimes comic – 'Mum used to live in Sunderland but she hates it and says it is a Ghost Town and she doesnt talk Sunderlanguage only a bit when she talks to Nan but most of the time she talks normal' (Haig, 2006, p. 2) – and sometimes touching – 'And I saw Mum and she saw me but didnt see me properly and she went to the corner of the hall by the radiator and sat down in a ball and cried and shook her head in her hands and said No no no no no and everywhere round us looked the same but bigger and I wanted to go and tell her it was OK but that would have been a lie and so I just sat there and did nothing' (p. 9). This style of writing allows the reader apparently uncensored access to Philip's thoughts and emotions. It also serves to endorse the value of a child's honest expression of feelings, however crudely or inexpertly communicated.

Philip is not a conventional literary hero like many of the Hamlets featured in these novels – a handsome, tortured, romantic soul – but a pensive, isolated little boy, bullied by his peers at school. Alice Trupe suggests that in contemporary young adult literature 'a postmodern hero with weaknesses, an antihero, or an unlikely hero may well be more satisfying than the classic hero' (2006, p. 107) and it is perhaps in his status as this type of protagonist that Philip has such appeal for young readers.

In addition to exploring the issue of bullying, a 'common theme in children's literature' (Barone, 2010, p. 114), and one often recommended for use in provoking classroom discussion (Scaglione and Scaglione, 2006, p. 69), Haig uses Shakespeare's play to explore the less frequently examined, but equally relevant, themes of sexuality, mental illness and bereavement. Death and dying are taboo subjects, 'historically . . . not considered appropriate material for children's books' (Gilbertson, 2005, p. 221) and although some books have been written on the subject, they remain rare, 'especially those that deal with the death of a parent or sibling' (p. 223). The death of a parent is, however, something that many young people experience, and many may 'find comfort in knowing that [they] are not alone, that others suffer – and survive' (Pyles, 1998, p. 8). Haig explores the subject with sensitivity and insight, depicting the various manifestations of grief suffered by his protagonist – the initial 'pain' in his stomach (Haig, 2006, p. 9), nightmares, anger, resentment and panic.

In 1.5 *Hamlet*, Hamlet tells Horatio of his plan to assume an 'antic disposition' (1.5.173); however, much discussion has revolved around the question of whether Hamlet eventually becomes genuinely mad. In performance, a number of Hamlets have 'straddled the boundaries between sanity and insanity' (Hapgood, 1999, p. 86). These boundaries are, of course, fragile ones, and what the Elizabethans might have viewed as 'madness' is now more frequently recognized as a manifestation of a range of mental illnesses. Similarly, Ophelia's madness, regularly portrayed from the late nineteenth to mid-twentieth century as 'picturesque' (Showalter, 1994, p. 228) has been presented in more recent productions of *Hamlet* as manifesting itself in the form of recognizable psychological disorders such as schizophrenia and bulimia.[4]

Mental illness is another subject long excluded from fiction for young people. However, as Hugh Crago discusses, 'the growing popularity of psychotherapy has in turn influenced narrative which has becomes increasingly confessional . . . and increasingly concerned with abnormal mental and emotional states' (1999, p. 166). Haig's protagonist, Philip, does not, like Hamlet, attempt to feign any form of insanity. However, he is depicted as suffering from a number of psychological disturbances including sleep-talking and nightmares which result in his peers calling him 'skitso' (2006, p. 32) and lead to him being referred first to a school counsellor and then, following a panic attack, to the doctor who diagnoses 'Panic Disorder' and prescribes 'diazepam' (p. 225). Elements of Philip's erratic behaviour are seen to stem from his bereavement, while others are shown to be the direct result of his visions of his father's ghost. His behaviour in Leah's bedroom, which mirrors that of Hamlet in Ophelia's closet – 'I took her wrist and held her hard' – and leads Leah to ask 'Why you acting mental' (Haig, 2006, p. 145) is shown to be caused by the presence of Dad's ghost, urging Philip to break up with Leah.

The reading guide provided by Viking asks readers to consider 'the most useful way to understand the spirit we come to know as Philip's father' – 'Should he be thought of as a character, as an embodiment of Philip's anxieties, as a demonic presence, or as something else? Why does Philip trust him for so long?' However, the question of whether the ghost of Philip's father is real, or a further manifestation of his psychological distress, is never resolved in the novel, which ends with Philip certain of 'only six things':

> Dad died on the bridge near Kelham
> Three men came and smashed the Pub
> My fish melted
> Mr Fairview died in the fire at the Garage
> Uncle Alan saved my life (Haig, 2006, p. 302)

Leah's emotional turmoil is viewed only briefly through the eyes of Philip, scaled down from that of Shakespeare's play to appear more psychologically convincing. Rather than running around hurling flowers at people, Leah is shown sitting on her bed, not crying but 'digging her right thumbnail into her left hand' (p. 273). Although she sings songs approximating those of Ophelia – 'Dead and gone dead and gone' (p. 273) and 'Tomorrow is Saint Valentines Day' (p. 275), these are established as pop songs which she sings quietly to herself.

The Viking reading guide also poses the question: 'How might Philip's mental disturbances be influenced by matters relating to sexuality, for example, his recent circumcision, his attraction toward his mother, and his ambivalent feelings about Leah?' The question of sexuality – in particular Hamlet's feelings about his mother – is one that has dominated discussions of the play, since Ernest Jones' attribution of Freud's Oedipus complex to the relationship between Hamlet and Gertrude (1949). However, in Haig's novel, Philip seems more attracted to his young teacher, Mrs Fell, whom he describes as 'the prettiest Teacher because she has green eyes that look into you and black curly hair and a big smile' (Haig, 2006, p. 54) than he does towards his mother.

In *Hamlet* itself, the question of Hamlet's incestuous desire for his mother is open to debate. His obsession with his mother's relationship with Claudius seems to stem more from a horror at her betrayal of his father, and a sense of personal rejection than a desire to sleep with her, which he never voices. Similarly, Philip's feelings for his mother seem motivated by a need for support and resentment at Uncle Alan's intervention into their family unit. Indeed, writing about his mother's relationship with his uncle, Philip asserts – 'Uncle Alan hasnt pinched Leah he has pinched my Mum. I dont fancy my Mum even though she is pretty because if you fancy your Mum it is DISGUSTING!' (Haig, 2006, p. 96), clearly a wry reference to the much discussed Freudian interpretation of the play.

Haig's novel is peppered with such witty references – Uncle Alan refers to the Real Ales in the pub as 'Stale flat unprofitable' (Haig, 2006, p. 72), an echo of Hamlet's line in 1.2;[5] Mr Fairview, the Polonius character brings a fish as a gift for Philip's mother, leading Philip to utter 'Fishmonger' (p. 74), recalling Hamlet's line to Polonius in 2.2[6] and Dad's Ghost utters a variation on Hamlet's most famous line – 'To be or not to be that's the question Philip' (p. 95)[7] as means of urging his son to vengeance. In addition to echoing lines from *Hamlet*, Haig makes reference to some of the themes in a similar vein. Although in Haig's novel, Philip's father has been killed in a car crash, Haig alludes briefly to the method of murder in *Hamlet* – poison. When Philip is imagining ways to kill his Uncle Alan, he writes – 'POISON. You can pour poison into someone's ear when they sleep and it kills them. But there are no poison shops any more. Weedkiller is poison but I don't know if you can pour it into ears' (p. 122). These intertextual references to *Hamlet* are quite sophisticated, and only likely to be recognized and enjoyed by those familiar with the Shakespearean text. In this respect Haig's novel seems designed to have an appeal beyond that of children and young people, to an adult market, a crossover not uncommon in literature originally marketed for children.[8]

By using the outline of Shakespeare's play but with new and contemporary settings and characters, and with distinctive narrative styles, both Haig and Gratz succeed in creating original novels which stand alone as pieces of young adult fiction in their own right. Although the two books are clearly recognizable as related to *Hamlet*, *Something Rotten* is equally concerned with establishing itself as a piece of noir detective fiction – indeed the online 'Discussion Guide' invites the reader to investigate this element of the book prior to exploring its relationship to Shakespeare (Gratz, n.d., p. 2). Similarly, Haig's primary motivation for writing his novel was not a desire to reexplore Shakespeare's play, but to tackle the issue of parental death:

> I didn't begin with a conscious desire to rewrite *Hamlet*. I began with the desire to tell a story about grief from a child's perspective and found myself gravitating increasingly toward these grand Shakespearean themes . . . my intention was to write a story that connects with people emotionally and hopefully that connection works the same with or without an in-depth knowledge of *Hamlet*. (Haig, n.d.)

The reviews suggest that Haig achieved this end, James Stuart in the *Guardian* describing it foremost as a 'darkly comic and a painful, touching account of bereavement' (2007).

Although these novels, aimed perhaps particularly at boys, have male protagonists, and in the case of Marsden and Haig's novels, male narrators, their respective Ophelia figures are, perhaps inevitably given their modern setting, more assertive and vocal young women than the character depicted in Shakespeare's play. In Gratz's *Something Rotten*, the Ophelia figure – Olivia – plays a central role as an environmental activist who opposes pollution of the Copenhagen river by the 'Elsinore' paper plant – owned by the Prince family (a name which permits Larry to tell Olivia, in a punning equivalent of Polonius' line in 2.2 *Hamlet*, that she is 'not marriage material for a Prince') (Gratz, 2007, p. 25).[9] Olivia is depicted as an intelligent and passionate modern woman, studying alongside Horatio and Hamilton (the 'Hamlet' character) at Wittenberg Academy in Knoxville. When we first meet her she is standing defiantly in the driving rain at the front gate of the paper plant wielding a protest sign. Unlike Shakespeare's character who, up until her madness, says little, Olivia is voluble and assertive; as Horatio says, 'she seemed to like the sound of her own voice, so I let her talk' (p. 80) Although she is clearly still in love with Hamilton, with whom she has split up at the start of the novel, in the equivalent episode to Shakespeare's 'nunnery scene' (3.1), in which she returns his love letters, she is far from submissive, tossing them at him and calling him a 'son of a bitch' and 'a bastard' (p. 105). Similarly, at the point at which she discovers that Hamlet has shot her father (albeit not fatally) she does not become mentally unbalanced but 'mad' with rage:

> 'Stand up you bastard!' she screamed.
> . . .
> 'Take off your sunglasses and look me in the eyes.'
> . . .
> I figured it would be a slap, but Olivia reared back and socked him a good one in the eye. (p. 143)

Indeed, Olivia is so strong and passionate in her beliefs that Horatio even considers her potential culpability in the murder of Hamilton's father – 'At first I had thought that Elsinore's pollution was just a convenient knife to stick in her ex-boyfriend for spite, but it was clear her passion for the cause went well beyond the fury of a woman scorned. But just how far did it go?' (p. 61). Certainly her 'passion for the cause' extends to risking her life in a clever play on Ophelia's method of demise in Shakespeare's play, drinking the polluted water from the river as a publicity stunt and collapsing on camera (p. 167).

Marsden's Ophelia is also a more independent and confident character than Shakespeare's, credited by Marsden with an innate intelligence spurred by 'instinct and emotion' (2009, p. 91) in contrast to Hamlet. Marsden expands her role from her frequently silent and passive presence in Shakespeare's play, providing her with a voice, narrating elements of the story through her eyes, and thereby allowing the reader access to her feelings about the other characters – in particular her father, brother and Hamlet. Like all of the modern-day Ophelias, she is less inclined than Shakespeare's character to accept the sexist comments made about women, by Hamlet in particular, thinking angrily of his comment on the performance of 'The Murder of Gonzago' that 'A woman's love lasts no longer than her words':[10] 'Is that all he thought of women then? Would he treat her as mere trash?' (2008, p. 93). However, from the moment of Ophelia's madness, related in very brief and abrupt terms by Marsden – 'And Ophelia went mad' (p. 152), she loses her voice within the novel, and, like Shakespeare's Ophelia becomes the object of others' uncomprehending gaze.

While Haig's Ophelia figure, Leah, plays a smaller role in *The Dead Fathers Club* than her counterparts, largely because the novel is so firmly focused around its male protagonist, she too is depicted as a feistier figure than Shakespeare's Ophelia – a year older than Philip, and the initiator of their relationship. When Philip breaks up with her, rather than breaking down as does Ophelia, she is at first amazed: 'You? Youre finishing with me?' and then kicks Philip hard in the back (Haig, 2006, pp. 184–5). The greater assertiveness and freedom afforded these 'Ophelia' figures is undoubtedly partly the result of the setting of the novels in the twenty-first century where perceptions of what is appropriate in terms of behaviour for girls has altered significantly since the Renaissance. As such they provide an instructive contrast to Shakespeare's figure and encourage debate about the way in which the role of women has changed over the past 400 years.

In Shakespeare's play, Ophelia has only 4 per cent of the lines and appears in only 5 of the play's 19 scenes (Bate and Rasmussen, 2007, p. 1922). As Elaine Showalter notes, 'for most critics of Shakespeare Ophelia has been an insignificant minor character in the play, touching in her weakness and madness but chiefly interesting, of course, in what she tells us about Hamlet' (1994, p. 220). Indeed, Ophelia has no real story independent of that of the protagonist – 'We can imagine Hamlet's story without Ophelia, but Ophelia literally has no story without Hamlet' (Edwards, 1979, p. 36). While Hamlet speaks a series of soliloquies which expand on his thoughts and feelings, Ophelia has only one brief soliloquy, in which she tells us more about Hamlet than about herself: 'Oh what a noble mind is here o'erthrown! . . .' (3.1.149). Fiedler, Klein and Reisert's reverse this tendency, electing to make Ophelia the protagonist and narrator through whose eyes the reader sees the events unfold and to whose motivations and feelings the reader is privy. Towards the end of Klein's novel, Ophelia, considering her actions, seems to challenge explicitly her Shakespearean counterpart's lack of an independent story – 'I had wanted to be the author of my tale, not merely a player in Hamlet's drama or a pawn in Claudius's deadly game' (Klein, 2006, p. 241).

Although Klein, Reisert and Fiedler's novels are set, like Shakespeare's play, in Renaissance Denmark, their protagonists have the sensibilities of modern young women. They are proactive, strong, bright and sexually aware and engineer much of the action of the story. In an overt rejection of the line spoken by Shakespeare's Hamlet – 'Frailty, thy name is Woman' (1.2.146), Klein's Ophelia asserts her strength – 'We women are not all frail. I for one am strong and true' (p. 99). Fiedler's character, perhaps the most overtly feminist of the three Ophelias, similarly rejects this notion. When Hamlet utters his views on Gertrude's 'feminine frailty' she immediately responds – 'I prefer we talk not on your notion of frailty and women, sir. In fact, I warn thee – go not there' (2002, p. 63). The deliberate twisting of this famous reference constitutes an overt rejection of common critical perceptions of Ophelia 'as a weak character, in both form and function' (Resetarits, 2001, p. 215).

This emphasis on the strength of women and their rights to equality with men may appear ahistorical for a Renaissance protagonist. Indeed, this is one of the issues raised by Sprague and Keeling in discussing the challenges of writing historical fiction for Young Adults: while 'many girls in the past accepted their roles with equanimity', 'the happy conformist does not work well as a heroine', and thus, most heroines of Young Adult historical fiction are, like the Ophelias depicted in these novels, those who fight against the system, and triumph over the odds or resist 'the pressures of conformity' (2007, pp. 89–90). Sprague and Keeling also suggest that 'when writing historical fiction, authors must decide how to negotiate the disparity between past and present modes of expected female behaviours so their readers will find the heroines' problems and solutions relevant to their own experiences' (p. 90). In refusing to passively accept the notion that women are necessarily weaker and less capable than men, the protagonists of these novels challenge historical perceptions of women. They also encourage girls to think about the differences in expectations about the behaviour of young women in the Renaissance, and the extent to which Shakespeare's Ophelia is a victim of a patriarchal society.

Juliet Dusinberre argues that in Shakespeare's play, 'Ophelia has no chance to develop an independent conscience of her own, so stifled is she by the authority of the male world' (1975, p. 94) – in particular that of Claudius, her brother and most notably her father. As Marvin Rosenberg writes, 'no father in the tragedies has so much control over a daughter as Polonius' (1992, p. 251). Polonius tells Ophelia how she should behave and what she should do; he manipulates her actions and forces her to choose between her loyalty to him and her feelings towards Hamlet. In the first scene in which Ophelia appears (or at least, speaks) in Shakespeare's play she is told first by her brother and then by her father how to conduct her relationship with Hamlet, advice which she appears to passively accept – 'I shall the effect of this good lesson keep, / As watchman to my heart' (1.3.45–6); 'I shall obey, my lord' (1.3.136). Although these lines could be played sarcastically or without sincerity, such an interpretation is rare in the theatre, where Ophelia has generally been portrayed as quietly obedient. As Robert Hapgood comments, even in modern productions where Ophelias have 'been more assertive than their predecessors . . . they all in the end obey male authority' (1999, p. 91).

In these three novels, the action of this episode is subverted, in *Ophelia* with an overt defiance, and in *Dating Hamlet* and *Ophelia's Revenge* with Ophelia, as narrator, making plain her real feelings and intentions in a way that is, of course, not possible on stage in the absence of a soliloquy. Klein's Ophelia responds angrily to Laertes' lecture – 'You cannot control me' (Klein, 2006, p. 106), and when her father repeats the warnings in similar words to Shakespeare's Polonius – 'Do not believe his vows! They are traps to catch a woodcock!' – she loses her temper, shouting, 'I trust Hamlet! . . . Why do you not trust *me*. I am not a child, a green girl as you seem to think' (p. 108). It is at this point in the novel that she makes her decision to defy her father – 'I decided that from this moment on, I would no more be my father's daughter. Yet I would let him think that he still ruled me' (p. 109). Although Fielder does not depict the episode itself, it is later related by Ophelia to her confidante, Anne, with Ophelia expressing 'rage' (2003, p. 31) that Polonius sees fit to advise Laertes, 'To thine own self be true' (1.3.78), while forbidding her to speak with Hamlet: 'You see? My father is a fool, and a cruel-hearted one at that' (p. 32). Meanwhile she mocks Laertes' advice: 'He urged me to think on Hamlet's attention as a condition not permanent. Sweet, but not lasting. I tell you Anne, it was all I had to keep from breaking into laughter when talked he of a growing body as – believe you this? – a "*temple*"' (p. 32). Like Klein's Ophelia, she chooses not to take their advice – 'whatever I do *not* do with Hamlet, I do not not do because I am ordered against doing it but because I do choose not to do it!' (p. 34). Reisert's Ophelia goes through the motions of seeming to acquiesce to the advice of her brother and father, in a passage which closely echoes Shakespeare's *Hamlet*; however, she tells the reader of Laertes' advice that, 'I wanted to laugh' and of her father's that 'I wanted to slap him' (2003, pp. 278–9). Twisting his words 'you're not to waste your time with Lord Hamlet', she utters almost exactly the same final line as Shakespeare's Ophelia – 'I will obey you, my lord', while confiding in the reader that 'time spent with Hamlet was never wasted' (p. 279).

The depiction of Ophelia as struggling with her relationship with her father and his intervention in her relationship are aspects of these novels which coheres with much young adult fiction. Trupe suggests that 'parent-child relationships play a significant role in literature for all ages, but the conflicting needs for connection and separation vie most vigorously during the teen years, when children begin making choices – of friends, dating partners' and so on (2006, p. 169). If one accepts Lynn Ponton's argument that 'adolescents define themselves through rebellion and anger at parents or other adults' (1999, p. 55), then Ophelia's challenge to the authority of her father (or the man she believes to be her father) and other authority figures at the court seems an aspect of the novels likely to appeal to teenage readers. Equally, in having Ophelia rebel against her father, defying his orders, these writers are able to prolong her love affair with Hamlet, making their relationship central to the novels' stories, a move undoubtedly partly motivated by the popularity of material about romance and sexual relationships in teen literature – subjects which, like parental conflict, have an evident relevance to adolescent readers.

In order to permit the development of Ophelia's relationship with Hamlet, each of the novels cleverly subverts the events of Shakespeare's play. In all three, Ophelia is privy to Hamlet's feigned madness and an active participant in his deceit of the Danish court, a conceit which turns the character, at least initially, from the victim of Hamlet to his collaborator. Ophelia's outburst to her father about Hamlet's behaviour in her closet is deliberately 'staged' in each of the novels, with Ophelia and Hamlet devising the plan of deception together, Klein's Ophelia actually coming up with the plan to 'feign love to hide love' (2006, p. 129).

The uncertain nature of Hamlet and Ophelia's relationship prior to the start of Shakespeare's play has been much commented upon. The question of whether they have engaged in sexual intercourse is one which has notoriously become the subject of theatrical jokes and the punch lines range from 'In *my* company *always*' (Olivier, 1986, p. 55) to 'only in Baltimore'. For centuries, Ophelia was portrayed on stage as 'a young, beautiful, obedient and pious girl in stereotypical white dress' (Teker, 2006, p. 114) in contrast to Hamlet's 'nighted colour' (1.2.68) and her madness was presented on stage as 'the predictable outcome of erotomania' (Showalter, 1994, p. 225) – the result of a suppression of her sexual desire. However, in recent productions, a number of Ophelias have been portrayed as sexually involved with Hamlet, including Kate Winslet's in Kenneth Branagh's film version, who is shown making 'tender love' with Hamlet, in flashback scenes intercut with 1.3 (Branagh, 1996, p. 28).

In both Klein and Reisert's novels Ophelia and Hamlet engage in sexual intercourse, while Fiedler's Ophelia is portrayed as physically intimate with Hamlet, resisting sleeping with him until after their marriage, but enjoying with him a 'delicate exploration' of each other's bodies (Fiedler, 2002, p. 40). The acknowledgement of Ophelia's sexual desires in these novels helps to liberate the character from stereotypes of repressed virginity and encourages a shift from a focus on frustrated sexuality as the principal cause of her madness, a diagnosis which distracts from an interrogation of the sociopolitical and familial culpability in Ophelia's demise. As Susan Lamb argues,

> [i]t is not woman's sexual desire but the place of women in the social and political web that is problematic. Ophelia's position as the daughter of a powerful courtier, the lover of the Prince who kills her father, the

sister of a man with considerable political power, and as a woman whose speech in madness has political implications for her hearers is lost in what has become a long-term focus on her sexuality. (2002, p. 117)

In a series of further parallels between the three novels, Ophelia, in each, feigns her madness in a similar manner to Hamlet, fakes her death (in the case of Fiedler and Klein's novels through self-administration of a sleeping draught in an allusion to *Romeo and Juliet*) and escapes in disguise (in Fiedler and Klein's novels in male disguise – another 'Shakespearean' conceit) to take on the role assigned to Horatio in Shakespeare's play – telling the truth about the events at Elsinore. One might argue that the story is thus turned from that of *The Tragedy of Hamlet, Prince of Denmark* to 'The Comedy', or in the case of Klein and Reisert, the 'Tragi-Comedy of Ophelia', with all three novels offering a voice to the silenced character of Shakespeare's play, a voice which permits Ophelia the emotional outlet denied her in *Hamlet* and ultimately allows her to escape the fate of madness and death.

None of the novelists follows Shakespeare in sending Ophelia to her watery grave; however, they are quite different in the fate which they devise for Ophelia. Fiedler's novel is the simplest, with Hamlet and Ophelia united throughout in their defiance of Polonius and Claudius. In a convenient twist of fate, the Gravedigger turns out to be Ophelia's real father, resolving any conflict which might have occurred in Hamlet stabbing Polonius, and both he and Laertes, Horatio and Ophelia's maid Anne, assist Hamlet and Ophelia in their plans. The story ends happily with Ophelia and Hamlet planning to remove themselves from Denmark, and, in a series of rather clumsy self-conscious references to other of Shakespeare's plays, to go 'to some sweet-scented isle of flowers, where we may spend our midsummer nights among fairies' (Fiedler, 2003, p. 190) or to 'the city of Verona' to visit Hamlet's 'impetuous' friend Romeo (p. 191).

Although Ophelia is alive at the end of Klein and Reisert's novels, both are tinged with sadness and sacrifice. Although Klein's Ophelia becomes Hamlet's wife, and is determined to assist him, she becomes the casualty of the patriarchal society in which she resides – forced, as an 'unwilling player' by her father and Claudius into the equivalent of the 'nunnery scene' and disowned by Hamlet, she does not fall into genuine madness, but, dresses as a boy to escape to France. It is interesting to note that Klein gives to Ophelia not only some of the attributes of Juliet but also of Shakespeare's more feisty comic heroines who defy the strictures of Renaissance gendered behaviour, assuming traditionally masculine traits along with their male attire. On donning her new garb Ophelia exclaims 'How delightful it is to be a man and free!' (Klein, 2006, p. 229). Although ultimately she remains the victim of her gender, forced to take 'refuge' (p. 234) in a convent where, as she discovers, 'man's power still holds sway' (p. 260), she succeeds in convincing the bishop of her story, and the novel ends with a degree of hope as, having given birth to young Hamlet, she is reunited with Horatio with whom she shares a kiss.

Reisert's Ophelia plays a greater role than the other Ophelias in determining the action of the events at Elsinore. She is not only Hamlet's collaborator, but also acts as collaborator with Claudius, telling him of her suspicions that King Hamlet means to murder the queen, and persuading him to poison his brother – 'I was the one . . . who gave Claudius the vial of poison and explained to him exactly what to do when he caught the king asleep' (Reisert, 2003, p. 237). It is Ophelia who, having discovered that Claudius intends to dispose of Hamlet on his arrival in England, sends her friend Ragnor and his associates to intercept his crossing; Ophelia who comes up with the notion of stirring the populous into support of Laertes for his protection and Ophelia who devises the elaborate plan to fake her own suicide and the deaths of Hamlet and Laertes. However, Ophelia's role as engineer of the main events is somewhat tempered by the revelation, in the final moments of the novel, that she has been manipulated by the ghost of Yorick into being the agent by which he has gained revenge against Hamlet – 'All the while I thought I was controlling everything, and I myself had been the weapon of a ghost' (Reisert, 2003, p. 503). Thus, Ophelia is made responsible for the death of her husband and her brother, becoming not the victim of Hamlet and the society of the court, as in Shakespeare's play, but the 'weapon' of Yorick and his victim. Although the bravery and intelligence of the character is not compromised by this final revelation, Ophelia's status as a feminist heroine, triumphing over patriarchal control is, to some extent, diminished. However, at the end of the novel, despite recognizing that after her ordeal, 'the easiest thing would be to lie back, to let Erik Strong Arm (Fortinbras) assume control of my life, to drift into the queenship that lay at the end of the present stream' (p. 509), she makes the decision to leave the court in order to save her unborn child. Her final action – boarding a ship to England – is one of uncertainty, but also one of hope: 'Come what may, I could have a fine life' (p. 519).

The happy or at least hopeful endings of these novels are in keeping with 'the optimism generally considered a hallmark of YA literature' (Sprague and Keeling, 2007, p. 90). They are also a necessary means of achieving what Sprague and Keeling describe as the '"triumph" that is usually necessary to most mainstream YA fiction' (p. 90), a sense which would be lost either through Ophelia's death or her quiet acceptance of an easy life.

The treatment of the character of Ophelia in all of these novels as a more assertive and intelligent figure is a strategy undoubtedly motivated by a desire to provide the character with a voice that is muted in Shakespeare's play. There is an obvious appeal, as is apparent in adult literature – in Stoppard's *Rosencrantz and Guildenstern Are Dead*, Margaret Atwood's, 'Gertrude Talks Back' (1992), Christine Bruckner's *Desdemona, If Only You Had Spoken* (1992) and Jean Betts's *Ophelia Thinks Harder* (1994), among others – in expanding on the thoughts and feelings of characters who are not permitted full expression of their feelings in a play, in particular, in the case of the latter three, in giving an ill-treated female character a voice – an opportunity, as the title of Atwood's monologue suggests, to 'talk back'.

Gulsen Savin Teker remarks that 'until the impact of feminist criticism on the reading of most canonical texts, mainstream critics of Shakespeare drew attention almost exclusively to the submissiveness and madness of Ophelia' (2006, p. 114), and even though stage and screen interpretations may have moved on from the seventeenth-century portrayals of 'her melancholy, erotomania, or hysteria' and the eighteenth- and nineteenth-century inclination to depictions of 'picturesque madness', in productions of the twentieth-century Ophelia has been 'denied personhood . . . not a speaking subject but an object "to-be-looked at" (Mulvey 272)' (Teker, 2006, p. 115). Klein, Fiedler and Reisert's novels invert the situation outlined by Teker, turning Ophelia from a submissive figure to an assertive one, from object to subject and her madness from a genuine affliction to play-acting. Permitting Ophelia to tell the story of the play from her own point of view allows her to become a far more rounded figure than that of Shakespeare's play, defined by more than merely her submissive nature and insanity. By making the reader privy to Ophelia's thoughts and motivations for her actions, these novels also invite young readers to interrogate the extent to which Ophelia's apparent weakness in Shakespeare's play is inherent, or the result of her treatment by a society which does not allow women to voice their true opinions and feelings.

The novels are, of course, also part of the ongoing association of the figure of Ophelia with adolescent girls, in the tradition of Mary Pipher's highly successful *Reviving Ophelia* (1994) and the 'obligatory parade of reactionary works that employed the term Ophelia to refer to the teenage self' (Hulbert, 2010, p. 200). As Jennifer Hulbert elucidates, through these works 'Ophelia inadvertently became the Shakespearean spokeswoman for a generation'; 'an apt representative of the silent sufferings of adolescent girls', given 'a voice independent of her family and male peers' (pp. 200, 202, 204). However, while such criticism seems to suggest that 'Ophelia is just like the modern day teenage girl' (p. 213), eschewing the obvious differences in contemporary and Renaissance culture, these novels open up both the similarities and the differences, allowing identification but also objectification, and thus raise the important point that while teenagers may identify with elements of Ophelia's struggle, it is not, as Hulbert brilliantly outlines, commensurate with their own.

Notes

1 See Gallagher and Greenblatt (2001) and Codden (1989).

2 The American Library Association, 2008, 'Quick Picks for Reluctant Young Adult Readers' and the Young Adult Library Services Association, 2010, 'Popular Paperbacks for Young Adults: Twists on the Tale'.

3 See *Hamlet* (2.2.305–8).

4 See Hapgood (1999), p. 91.

5 'O God, God / How weary, stale, flat and unprofitable/ Seem to me all the uses of this world!' (*Ham.* 1.2.132).

6 'Excellent, excellent well. You're a fishmonger' (*Ham.* 2.2.176).

7 'To be, or not to be; that is the question' (*Ham.* 3.1.58).

8 A similar crossover has been apparent with J. K. Rowling's *Harry Potter* series, Philip Pullman's *His Dark Materials* trilogy, Mark Haddon's *The Curious Incident of the Dog in the Night-Time* and Markus Zuzsak's *The Book Thief*, all of which have been reissued with adult covers.

9 'Lord Hamlet is a prince out of thy star' (*Ham.* 2.2.142).

10 The line mirrors Hamlet's exchange with Ophelia in Shakespeare's 3.2:

> Ophelia: 'Tis brief, my lord.
> Hamlet: As woman's love. (*Ham.* 3.2.146–7)

Web resources

Gratz, Alan, *Something Rotten*:
  http://alangratz.blogspot.com/2010/01/something-rotten.html
— *Something Rotten: Discussion Guide*:
  www.files.alangratz.com/rotten_readers_guide.pdf
Haig, Matt, *Dead Father's Club* Reading Guide:
  http://us.penguingroup.com/static/rguides/us/dead_fathers_club.html

CHAPTER EIGHT

Original Plays Based on Shakespeare

Original plays that take their themes, characters and plot elements from Shakespeare's work abound in the dramatic cannon, taking the form of sequels, prequels, plays which explore off-stage action, plays in which modern-day characters encounter Shakespeare's and those which update the action to a contemporary setting. In 2006, motivated by a desire to get writers to 'think big' (Edwardes, 2008), the Royal Shakespeare Company (RSC) Artistic Director Michael Boyd, along with Literary Manager Jeanie O'Hare and Associate Director Dominic Cooke, launched a project designed to help writers create new work inspired by Shakespeare's texts, a project which has resulted in an abundance of new writing that draws on the Shakespearean originals in a variety of ways – Leo Butler's *I'll Be the Devil* (2008) loosely based on *The Tempest*, Roy Williams' *Days of Significance* (2007) inspired by *Much Ado About Nothing*, Marina Carr's *The Cordelia Dream* (2008) and Dennis Kelly's *The Gods Weep* (2010), both of which draw on *King Lear*, and David Greig's *Dunsinane* (2010), a sequel to *Macbeth*. Original plays for young people based on Shakespeare are, however, far less numerous. Although the American company Playscript, Inc., which publishes a wealth of plays for schools and youth groups, has produced a number of Shakespearean-inspired plays for young people, almost all are unsophisticated texts which either revolve around the High School performance of a Shakespeare play, or update the plays to a contemporary High School setting featuring baseball teams, cheerleaders and games of spin the bottle.[1]

Of the few British plays for young audiences and casts which have emerged in the past 10 years, three of the most significant have been generated by the National Theatre (NT) in London – Sharman MacDonald's *After Juliet* (1999), commissioned for the BT National Connections Scheme, and Lucinda Coxon's *The Eternal Not* (2009) and Michael Lesslie's *Prince of Denmark* (2010),[2] both commissioned by the NT Discover programme to run alongside productions of Shakespeare's plays in the theatre's main programme. MacDonald's and Coxon's plays are both sequels to Shakespearean texts, MacDonald's a timeless sequel to *Romeo and Juliet* and Coxon's a modern-day sequel to *All's Well That Ends Well* (*AWW*), while Lesslie's *Prince of Denmark* is a prequel to *Hamlet*, set, like Shakespeare's play, in 'Medieval Denmark focalized through Elizabethan England' (2010, p. 1). The three plays bear comparison, focused, as they are, on the younger generations of Shakespeare's plays, freed from the control of the older generations who dominate their Shakespearean counterparts, and as such have an obvious appeal to young audiences.

In addition to being written for young audiences, both *After Juliet* and *Prince of Denmark* were commissioned to be performed by teenage casts, a factor to which the exclusion of Shakespeare's older characters clearly lends itself. *After Juliet* was commissioned as one of ten plays by leading British playwrights, written to be performed by actors aged 13–19 in theatres around the country. *Prince of Denmark*, written as an accompaniment to Nicholas Hytner's production of *Hamlet* which was playing in the Olivier theatre, was planned for performance by members of the National Youth Theatre and the exclusive focus on the younger characters of *Hamlet* was stipulated in Lesslie's commission. However, the focus on the younger generation in both these plays is not merely one of exigency. Both MacDonald and Lesslie use it to reexamine themes of Shakespeare's plays which remain relevant today – MacDonald calling into question the rather 'optimistic' ending of Shakespeare's play and exploring the impulse behind the ever relevant issue of youth violence, and Lesslie examining the teenage formation of identity and the notions of 'free-will and fatalism' (Lesslie, 2011).

Although Coxon's play was not written to be performed by young people, it was advertised in the NT's brochure under events for 'Secondary and Further Education' and offered free to schools and colleges booking for *AWW* in the Olivier theatre. The play's focus is on the young characters of Helena and Bertram – motivated by a desire to give them a fuller voice away from the domineering presence of the older characters of Shakespeare's play. Coxon elucidates – 'It was so interesting re-reading *All's Well*, a play I'd always loved. One thinks of it as being about this young pair, but they're actually given remarkably little stage-time, and when they are on stage, they struggle to get a word in. The older generation is hugely controlling and dominant. At least I've gone some way toward redressing that balance' (Stanford, 2009). This is, in fact, only partially true; while in *AWW* Bertram has only 9 per cent of the play's lines, Helena has the most of any character at 16 per cent (Bate and Rasmussen, 2007, p. 587). However, both characters commune far more frequently with the Countess and the King – the 'older generation' – than with each other, their only lengthy conversation occurring in 2.5, and even then in the presence of

Paroles. Their relationship, which is far too quickly resolved in the play's final scene, is not borne of shared intimacy or mutual attraction, but forced upon Bertram by the King, and manipulated by the Countess both of whom treat him and speak of him like a child, the King accusing him of being a 'Proud, scornful boy' (2.3.152) and the Countess a 'rash and unbridled boy' (3.2.28).

Throughout *AWW*, *Hamlet* and *Romeo and Juliet*, the older generation constantly try to control the younger characters and inhibit their freedom. Indeed the Countess's speech to Bertram on his departure for the French court is remarkably similar to that given by Polonius to Laertes when the latter leaves for France:

> *Countess . . .*
> Love all, trust a few,
> Do wrong to none: be able for thine enemy
> Rather in power than use, and keep thy friend
> Under thy own life's key: be cheque'd for silence,
> But never tax'd for speech. (*AWW*, 1.1.52–6)

> *Polonius . . .*
> Give thy thoughts no tongue,
> Nor any unproportioned thought his act.
> Be thou familiar, but by no means vulgar.
> Those friends thou hast, and their adoption tried,
> Grapple them to thy soul with hoops of steel;
> But do not dull thy palm with entertainment
> Of each new-hatch'd, unfledged comrade. (*Ham.*, 1.3.59–65)

In *Romeo and Juliet*, Juliet is subject to her parents' decision about her betrothal to Paris and is seen only in the Capulet home, Friar Laurence's cell and the Capulet tomb – all contained spaces, under patriarchal control. Ophelia is similarly oppressed by her father who forbids her from continuing her relationship with Hamlet and manipulates her into betraying him, while other members of the younger generation – Hamlet, Laertes, Rosencrantz and Guildenstern – are also subject to the control of their elders, in particular Claudius. Similar to Coxon, MacDonald and Lesslie set out to redress this balance by giving a voice to the younger generation and to characters who have little or nothing to say in Shakespeare's play.

There is an obvious parallel in the work of these dramatists, and that of the novelists discussed in the previous chapter in seeking to provide a voice for marginalized characters, in particular adolescents, and in exploring the issue of parental conflict which, as Alice Trupe suggested, plays a key role in literature for teenagers (2006). These themes are also common to many of the plays written for the NT Connections programme since 1993; one of the few sources from which original plays for young people (as opposed to adaptations of novels) have emerged (Arizpe, Styles and Rokison, 2010, pp. 134–5).

MacDonald's protagonist is Rosaline, who never appears in *Romeo and Juliet*, but whom we hear about, first as the woman with whom Romeo is deeply in love, and then as a figure instantly rejected by Romeo on his encounter with Juliet. According to MacDonald, her inspiration came from her daughter Keira Knightley, who, in turn inspired by Baz Luhrmann's *Romeo + Juliet* (1996), reportedly asked her mother, 'Write a play about Rosaline', 'I mean what happened to her . . . Who was she?' (1999). In MacDonald's play, Rosaline is Juliet's cousin, embittered by the loss of Romeo and seeking to become elected 'Princess of Cats' in Tybalt's place. As the truce reached at the end of *Romeo and Juliet* disintegrates, Rosaline falls for Benvolio, a Montague, the only surviving young character from Shakespeare's play, establishing a similar central conflict to that of *Romeo and Juliet*. However, unlike the Shakespearean original the relationship is not a romantic one but a struggle of wills, ending the play unresolved.

Despite his play's title – *Prince of Denmark* – which seems to allude to Hamlet, Lesslie gives his play's central role to Laertes, who, in Shakespeare's play speaks only 5 per cent of the lines and appears in only 6 of the play's 19 scenes. As Lesslie explains, 'When people think about *Hamlet*, so often they think about the brooding young man in practically every scene – it's a protagonist's play – so it's interesting to consider the reality of all the other characters that surround Hamlet. My main thing was looking back on the play and thinking "Wait a minute, who is Laertes?"' (2011). In Lesslie's play Laertes is an ambitious young man, newly arrived at court, who rails against the social strata and attempts to manipulate his sister Ophelia to further his ends of advancement and power, key themes which dominate both Lesslie's sequel and Shakespeare's original. Lesslie's play also seeks to give a more fully formed voice to other characters who play only minor roles in Shakespeare's play, most notably Osric, who serves as the play's 'fool' (2011), manipulated by Laertes into the central deception plot. As in most of the novels discussed in the previous chapter, the often silent and acquiescent Ophelia of Shakespeare's play is also given a more assertive and proactive role, encouraging the interrogation of the treatment and position of women in relation to both *Prince of Denmark* and *Hamlet*.

After Juliet

As MacDonald specifies, the location of *After Juliet* 'could be Verona. Or it could be Edinburgh, Dublin, New York or Liverpool' (2001, p. 9). Indeed, it can be set 'in any town in the world – except Glasgow' since 'one of the characters (Rhona) is from Glasgow and she's very obviously not at home' (MacDonald, quoted by Maxwell, 2007). Chris Barton, who directed the NT workshops, working with MacDonald on the play prior to its various productions, suggests that the primary reason behind this openness of setting is that MacDonald 'wanted to stress the universality of the theme, and encourage directors to work with the natural social references and dialects of their casts' (2009). This is one of the great strengths of MacDonald's play – it is not exclusive; it encourages young people to think about the proximity of the action of the play to their lives and to own the play for themselves. As Barton comments, 'a Connections play will receive numerous productions in its first year of existence. I think Sharman wanted to feel that each would be unique' (2009). It is undoubtedly for similar reasons of openness and relevance that the play is given no specific time setting (MacDonald tells us that the time 'could be 1500; 1900; 2000; or 3000') (2001, p. 25). Indeed, the play's timelessness is invoked through the mixture of anachronistic references to swords and lanterns, alongside 'rollies', an 'electric hand fan', an 'umbrella' and various 'pieces of domestic modernity' (pp. 16, 29, 25). This freedom of setting is akin to the tendency of modern theatre directors to set Shakespeare's own plays in a multitude of different settings and periods and encourages an acknowledgement of the 'universality' of many of the themes of not only *After Juliet*, but also *Romeo and Juliet*.

One of the central themes of both plays is that of love. However, rather than requited love, which forms the basis of Shakespeare's story, MacDonald explores the tensions of love – love destroyed by death, love unrequited and love resisted – as the war between the genders becomes the most prominent of the play:

Men and women Benvolio.
Men and women. There's a war. (2001, p. 34)

At the outset of the play MacDonald brings home to the audience the plight of Rosaline, her protagonist, mourning for the death of Romeo. Rosaline is, in Shakespeare's play, a mere cipher – a dramatic tool used to lure Romeo to the ball where he will fall in love with Juliet. Never seen at the ball, and subsequently dismissed with a single couplet: 'With Rosaline, my ghostly father? No, / I have forgot that name, and that name's woe' (2.3.45–6), the audience is not encouraged to dwell on her rejection by Romeo. She is one of a number of functional characters in Shakespeare whose fate is left unexplored as the plays focus on their protagonists, and as such is ripe for exploration. Also, given her youth and her plight of rejection in love, she is a protagonist likely to appeal to young audiences. Just as teenage readers respond well to books with whose characters they can identify (Alsup, 2010) (see Chapter 7), so Orlin Corey suggests that 'personality and identification are essential to awaken the empathy of the spectator' in children's drama (Schonmann, 2006, p. 84) and rejection in relationships is particularly common in adolescence (Barber, 2006, p. 29).

In *Romeo and Juliet* we hear the name of 'Rosaline' for the first time when, having been listed as one of the guests at the Capulet Ball Benvolio remarks, 'At this same ancient feast of Capulet's / Sups the fair Rosaline, whom thou so loves' (1.2.84–5), giving a name to the 'woman' (1.1.201) whom Romeo has professed to love. In Romeo's impassioned speeches, we learn of Rosaline's beauty – 'the all-seeing sun / Ne'er saw her match since first the world begun' (1.2.94–5) but also of her apparent vow of celibacy – 'She has forsworn to love, and in that vow / Do I live dead that live to tell it now' (1.1.220–1). As such Rosaline appears resistant to Romeo's affections, potentially legitimizing the lack of concern for her feelings about his transfer of affections to Juliet. However, MacDonald sets up Rosaline's seeming resistance as a front – a means of testing Romeo's love:

> I wanted him to see
> I wasn't so easily won.
> He was a Montague after all. (2001, pp. 5–6)

This explanation seems utterly plausible, particularly in a contemporary setting where young women are constantly faced with media exhortations to 'play hard to get', and turns Rosaline from a seemingly priggish figure into a character trying to negotiate the complexities of relationships, complexities with which young viewers are likely to empathize. This potential for empathy is further exploited in Rosaline's long speech in the middle of the play when she goes to lay flowers for Juliet. Here the audience are privy to her feelings of jealousy towards Juliet (a younger, prettier rival) another particularly common emotion experienced in adolescence, particularly with regard to relationships (Malakh-Pines, 1998, p. 39):

> You were too small, too pretty, too rich,
> Too thin and too much loved for me to cope with.
> (MacDonald, 2001, p. 30)

We learn that Juliet stole Rosaline's 'favourite doll' and later her 'best friend', finally stealing Romeo:

> Later still, you took my love
> And didn't know you'd done it;
> Then having taken him
> You let him die. (p. 31)

While Rosaline mourns the loss of Romeo she is, in turn, pursued by Benvolio – a Montague who watches her, as Valentine says, 'day and night' (p. 8). Although this love between a Montague and a Capulet echoes that of Shakespeare's play, unlike in *Romeo and Juliet*, MacDonald is unromantic in her portrayal of their relationship. Indeed, Rosaline explicitly rejects the concept of love at first sight, asking Benvolio:

How can you love me?
You don't know me. (p. 18)

Later in the play she similarly questions the notion of romantic love:

What is love?
. . .
Love is not carried on an evening's zephyr breeze
Love is not in the pulsed scent of a woman's cologne.
Love is not in the turn of a man's head;
. . .
Love is only the rut
A quick pant and it's gone. (pp. 51–2)

This conception of love as primarily motivated by sex undermines that of the young protagonists in *Romeo and Juliet*, but presents a more realistic portrait of many relationships, in which, for boys, 'the heterosexual norm' dictates that they are more likely to 'focus their efforts on sexual, rather than relational, forms of intimacy' (Lerner and Steinberg, 2009, p. 123).

Rosaline's exchanges with Benvolio are similarly not characterized by romantic language but by sarcastic barbs:

Rosaline I bet you always wash your hands.
Benvolio After?
Rosaline Touching a Capulet.
Benvolio Velvet your claws Rosaline. (MacDonald, 2001, p. 18)

Even when she does eventually appear to acquiesce a little towards the end of the play, Rosaline does not fully consent, leaving the status of her relationship with Benvolio ambiguous. In an echo of Shakespeare's *Twelfth Night* in which Orsino asks the disguised Viola: 'Give me thy hand / And let me see thee in thy woman's weeds' (5.1.270–1), Benvolio asks Rosaline, who is wearing men's clothes:

Do you still have the dress?
. . .
Will you put it on for me? (MacDonald, 2001, p. 81)

In *Twelfth Night*, Orsino's sudden shift of affections from Olivia to Viola may sit uneasily with a modern audience; however, a swift conversion to marriage in the final act is a feature of many of Shakespeare's comedies, and frequently appears to transcend past misunderstandings, infidelities and even former rejection.

MacDonald, however, explicitly rejects the conventional happy ending, providing stage directions which indicate Rosaline's failure to fully assent to Benvolio:

> *Benvolio*   Will you put it on for me?
> *The moon is bright. Shadows flutter across it. Chase and chase again.*
>   One day?
>
> *He takes her hand. Twines his fingers in hers.*
>
> *Rosaline*   In the spring.
> *But she doesn't smile at him.*
>
> *Benvolio*   Is that a promise?
>
> *Rosaline*   Maybe.
>   *She isn't close to him. Though she doesn't take her hand away.*
>
> (MacDonald, 2001, p. 81)

Rosaline's resistance to Benvolio's impassioned declarations, and her failure to consent to his desire to dress her in feminine clothes, establish her as an assertive, independent young woman who is not easily won or controlled.

Unlike in *Romeo and Juliet*, where Juliet is isolated as the only young woman in the play, MacDonald creates a series of strong, forthright female characters, who are shown, similar to Rosaline, to have a practical, unromantic view of love. In the first scene Rosaline's half-sister Livia expresses her willingness to conform to the conventional custom of marriage only if she is able to manipulate it to her advantage:

> Marry, Marry money, Rosaline.
> Hire a cook for the kitchen
> A nanny for the children
> And unless he's very talented in that direction
> Hire a mistress for the bedroom. (MacDonald, 2001, p. 6)

Alice, Rosaline's cousin, is similarly proactive in matters of relationships, planning to ensnare a good husband by manipulating the system that values physical attractiveness in women:

> I'll dance with our new Prince of Cats.
> Later I will marry him.
> Not that he knows that.
> Nor will he till it's done.
> Make the dress fine, Rhona.
> I have plans. (p. 42)

Alice's relationship with Petruchio is, like that of Rosaline and Benvolio, based on conflict as much as flirtation and characterized by an unromantic attitude that comes predominantly from Alice:

Petruchio   I never betrayed you
Alice   What was there to betray?
               We made no promises,
               You and me,
               Save a look here
               A touch there.

Petruchio   As long as we have things clear between us.

Alice   Things are clear. Very, very clear
               To me at least.
               You like a woman who fights.

She hits him on the arm. Hits and hits again. A windmill of hitting.
(2001, p. 82)

It is striking that in *After Juliet* much of the violence comes from the young women. They are equally as responsible for the ongoing conflict as the young men who are the principal perpetrators in Shakespeare's play. This inclusion of the female characters in the fighting between the Montagues and Capulets is another feature of *After Juliet* that resonates with contemporary society, where teenage girls are increasingly involved in violent behaviour.[3] As Valentine notes, Rosaline is as viciously committed to the idea of maintaining the feud as any of the men:

I see a spitting cat
In your eyes, Rosaline.
I don't see a truce. (2001, pp. 7–8)

Despite the apparent reconciliation between the Montagues and Capulets at the end of *Romeo and Juliet*, the violence between the two factions persists in *After Juliet*. MacDonald rejects Shakespeare's romantic conception of the death of the young protagonists ending the conflict between the families, explaining '*After Juliet* comes to the opposite conclusion from *Romeo and Juliet* and *West Side Story*. I don't think the death of the young stops conflict. I don't know what will' (1999). As Valentine says,

Can the Prince change the habits of a lifetime with a word?
Did his 'word' bring my brother back to life?
Do the dead live because an amnesty is called?
And if they don't live how can there be peace? (p. 28)

This issue is, of course, hugely relevant in view of the high number of teenage gang-related murders which continue to occur around Britain, despite campaigns, such as that by the family of murdered teenager Ben Kinsella, to raise awareness of the devastating effects of youth violence.[4]

    MacDonald explores some of the motivations behind the characters' persistent desire for conflict – deeply ingrained hatred, revenge and boredom, a motive pertinent to the lives of many contemporary teenagers (Goldson, 2011, pp. 105, 120).

The atmosphere of some of the play's scenes is akin to that of a number of modern-day town centres at night, with young people hanging out in the streets, fighting partly because they have nothing better to do:

> *Rosaline*:   There will be killings anyway
> To fill up the space in our minds
> Wrought by this Prince-ordained peace. (MacDonald, 2001, p. 70)

The play ends not with a truce but with members of the Montagues and Capulets drawing their swords as the lights go down:

> *Two Capulets, one Montague are left on stage. Valentine leaning. Looking up at Gianni looking down. Catches his eye. Gianni tugs on Lorenzo's sleeve. They both fix on Valentine. Valentine pats his sword hilt. Raises an eyebrow in question. Lifts the sword out of the scabbard. Gianni nods. Accepts the challenge. He and Lorenzo jump down. Valentine unsheathes his sword. Wipes it on his jacket.*
>
> *Waits.*
>
> *The drummer points.*
>
> *Lorenzo and Giani draw their swords.*
>
> *The flute trills and falls silent.*
>
> *Blackout.* (MacDonald, 2001, pp. 83–4)

Although MacDonald's sequel to *Romeo and Juliet* does not follow in the tragic mould of Shakespeare's play with the death of the young protagonists, one could argue that its ending is more bleak than that of Shakespeare's tragedy, the final moments of which are characterized by a sense of reconciliation and optimism as Montague and Capulet join hands and promise to honour each other's children (5.3.297–303). In ending on an apparent note of reconciliation and regret, Shakespeare's play glosses over the issue of the culpability of various other characters in the deaths of Romeo and Juliet – most notably the Nurse and Friar Laurence. In the play's final scene, the Friar's speech of contrition which he ends with the words 'if aught in this / Miscarried by my fault, let me old life/ Be sacrificed, some hour before his time, / Unto the rigour of severest law', is met only with the Prince's ambiguous comment – 'We still have known thee for a holy man' (*Rom.* 5.3.265–9), while the guilt of the Nurse, absent from the final scene, is not discussed. As with the apparent uniting of the two families, MacDonald does not accept this neat resolution. Instead, she returns to Shakespeare's source material – Arthur Brooke's *The Tragical History of Romeus and Juliet* (1562) – in which the Nurse, Friar, Peter

and the apothecary are put on trial for their role in the deaths of the young
protagonists, and various punishments meted out:

> The nurse of Juliet is banished in her age,
> Because that from the parents she did hide the marriage,
> Which might have wrought much good had it in time been known,
> Where now by her concealing it a mischief great is grown;
> And Peter, for he did obey his master's hest,
> In wonted freedom had good leave to lead his life in rest,
> Th'apothecary high is hangéd by the throat,
> And for the pains he took with him the hangman had his coat.
> But now what shall betide of this grey-bearded sire?
> Of Friar Laurence thus arraigned, that good barefooted friar
> Because that many times he worthily did serve
> The commonwealth, and in his life was never found to swerve,
> He was dischargéd quite, and no mark of defame
> Did seem to blot or touch at all the honour of his name.
> But of himself he went into an hermitage,
> Two miles from Verone town, where he in prayers passed forth his age;
> Till that from earth to heaven his heavenly sprite did fly,
> Five years he lived an hermit and an hermit did he die. (Brooke, 1562,
> Liiiv–Livr)

As *After Juliet* begins, the trial is starting, reported to the town on a PA:

> The wiser sort Prince Escalus calls to councell streyt
> That a trial may be held in front of the populace
> And justice meted out to those elders of this place
> Judged to blame for the deaths of Romeo and Juliet.
> Angelica the nurse stands accused
> The servant Peter.
> Fryr Lawrence.
> The apothecary of Mantua. (MacDonald, 2001, p. 7)

News of these figures' fates punctuates the action of the play, as the
characters hear of the sentences decreed by the Prince and raises an
important discussion point in relation to Shakespeare's play – the extent
to which any or all of these characters can be held responsible for the fate
of the young lovers, or indeed whether they were victims of their own
generosity and faithfulness towards Romeo and Juliet. Rosaline explicitly
blames Juliet for not considering these 'four lives', forced into court by her
'selfish suicide' (MacDonald, 2001, p. 32).

In the reports of the trial MacDonald quotes almost directly from
Shakespeare's source, putting the words of Brooke into the mouths of
her characters and mixing them with colloquial dialogue. This mixture

of registers is characteristic of the whole of the play, which is essentially composed in free verse, incorporating moments of heightened poetry that occasionally reference Shakespeare's text, into a largely contemporary and informal register of language. This mixture of contrasting registers of dialogue mirrors Shakespeare's own use of verse and prose, and is far from simple, demanding of MacDonald's young actors that they handle complex syntax and rhythms and swift changes of tone.

MacDonald credits the young people for whom she writes with skill, intelligence and maturity, not only in her challenging style of writing, but also in the content of the lines. She does not shy away from using quite violent and sophisticated images:

Why should they live?
Who raped my dream. (2001, p. 49)

Nor does she refrain from using offensive swear-words:

Lorenzo	I know who I made love to.
Gianni	You're a big fuck off liar, Lorenzo.
Lorenzo	You calling me a liar?
Gianni	Fuck-off, fucking liar. (p. 12)

Although she specifies that 'Should "fuck" be a pain and a trouble please change it to "feck" or a rhythmic equivalent' (p. 4), partly as Barton remarks, 'because [she didn't] want people to decide not to do the play simply because of the swearing', once again she leaves this decision up to the individual production, not imposing any censorship of language herself. There is, I think, considerable appeal to young people in a text which does not patronize them by sanitizing the language of the characters in a way that makes it less authentic.

That MacDonald's play, written nearly 10 years ago, remains a popular choice for youth theatres today evidences not only the universality of its themes and approach, but also the fact that young people are able and willing to engage with complex language and serious themes. It is also undoubtedly true that its success has been in part due to the fact that while it interrogates the key themes of *Romeo and Juliet*, and calls into question the expediency of its ending, it also stands alone as an independent play, with well-developed characters, a clear plot line and a satisfyingly open ending.

The Eternal Not

The idea of commissioning companion pieces to NT main-house productions emerged initially from a conversation between Anthony Banks, associate director of the theatre's Discover Programme – the theatre's education wing – and Nicholas Hytner, artistic director of the NT. Hytner was directing George Bernard Shaw's *Major Barbara* in the Olivier theatre, and was concerned by the play's potential inaccessibility, remarking to Banks that some of the weighty classics in the repertoire might benefit from 'side dishes' which could help young audiences to find a 'way in' (Banks, 2011). When Marianne Elliott, having been commissioned to direct a Shakespeare play for the Olivier stage, chose the complex and infrequently performed *AWW*, Banks felt that this might be an ideal opportunity to serve up such a side dish, commissioning writer Lucinda Coxon to write a piece that, as well as providing a 'way in', would also be 'a bonus' for audiences of Shakespeare's problem play. The result was *The Eternal Not*, a contemporary sequel to *AWW* that focuses on the dysfunctional marriage of Bertram and Helena.

Although, as Banks explains, he did not stipulate that the play should be aimed specifically at young people, subsequent to its writing it was marketed by the theatre predominantly at secondary school and college audiences who were attending the main-house production. The play also formed part of the NT's emerging 4-year partnership with the Shakespeare Schools' Festival (SSF), with the script being 'offered by the NT to teachers who had done SSF before' (SSF, n.d.). As a result, Coxon's play has been staged by secondary school groups around the country from Liverpool to Bristol.[5] As part of the play's development Banks also workshopped the play with 200 Year 10 students who, according to Banks, 'all recognized their parents' marriages in the play' (2011).

Coxon's play is a 30-minute piece for four characters – Bertram and Helena, the young protagonists from Shakespeare's play dragged into the twenty-first century; Kelly, a woman who is helping Bertram to 'disappear', and Mike, Helena's health visitor. Its title comes from Bertram's letter to his mother, the Countess, in *AWW* in which he informs her of Helena: 'I have wedded her, not bedded her, and sworn to make the "not" eternal' (3.2.22–3). Although Bertram is eventually tricked by Helena into breaking this oath, the extent to which he rescinds its sentiments is never fully apparent, the suddenness of his seeming conversion and the final scene's conditional statements leaving the ending unresolved. It is not clear from a reading of the text alone whether Bertram's claim that he realized too late that he loved Helena – 'whom myself, / Since I have lost, have loved' (5.3.54–5) – is genuine, or another untruth, following on from the catalogue of lies he has invented in the process of the play. The King's response to this expression of regret – 'Well excused' (5.3.56) – may be played as genuine, or ironic, seeing through Bertram's facade of contrition. When he subsequently discovers that Helena is still alive and with child, Bertram merely utters the line, 'Both, both, O pardon!' (5.3.310), words which seem entirely insufficient to indicate a considered repentance. Certainly it is difficult to believe that a man who has so vehemently denied his love; has sworn that, 'I cannot love her, not will strive to do't' (2.3.146), and who has spoken of his 'hate' for Helena (2.3.284), calling her 'the detested wife' (2.3.289) has suddenly had a change of heart, and will now be a devoted husband, loving his wife 'ever, ever dearly' (5.3.318).

In any case, Bertram does not accept Helena unreservedly as his wife, the 'if' which begins his apparent acquiescence speaking volumes:

> *Bertram*   If she, my liege, can make me know this clearly
> I'll love her dearly, ever ever dearly. (5.3.317–18)

The King's final summary of events contains a similarly tentative 'if', which, along with the word 'seems' calls into question whether the play does actually fulfil the apparent promise of its title:

> All yet seems well, and if it end so meet
> The bitter past, more welcome is the sweet. (5.3.334–5)

Even Helena's happiness at the end of the play seems uncertain. Although she appears to gain what she desires, her lines raise some questions about her feelings for Bertram. On claiming him as her husband, her description of him as 'doubly won' (5.3.316) suggests that she conceives him as a prize rather than a mutual partner in love. Her final speech, picking up on Bertram's 'if', leaves an image not of future joy, but of the possibility of 'deadly divorce' (5.3.320), and finishes with her reunion with the Countess, which presumably breaks the stage image of herself and Bertram as a united pair. Harriet Walter, who played the role of Helena in Trevor Nunn's 1981 RSC production, explains that she could not see in these final moments a happy ending for Helena – feeling that Helena 'would have liked something different, but she can see that everything has got messy, and since that's the case all she can say is, "It's you and me, boy; there's nowhere else to go, so let's try to make a success of it"' (Rutter, 1988, p. 88). As Susan Snyder suggests, the whole conclusion is characterized not only by conditionals, but also by deferrals, with Shakespeare deferring 'beyond the boundaries of the stage action what would seem to be the very foundations of any happy ending – full understanding and rapprochement between principals and full validations by authorities' (p. 51). It is this deferral of a true resolution of events beyond the end of the play that lends itself so well to the creation of a sequel, encouraging audiences to question the apparently 'happy ending' and the relationship between Bertram and Helena. Coxon takes this unstable basis for a successful marriage as the starting point for her play, imagining the lives of Bertram and Helena on the third anniversary of their marriage, in a pseudo-contemporary society.

In *The Eternal Not* Bertram is once again trying to escape from Helena – to 'disappear' (Coxon, 2009, p. 1), this time by completely erasing his identity:

> *Kelly*   I'll be cancelling your credit cards, shutting down your bank accounts, erasing your phone, dental, medical records . . . (p. 3)

Coxon plays humorously on Helena's obsessive perseverance in chasing and ensnaring Bertram in *AWW*: when Kelly suggests that Bertram may, at some stage, wish to resurface – 'perhaps as soon as whoever it is you are evading shows signs of ceasing to pursue you' – Bertram responds, 'They'll *never* cease!' (p. 5). Later in the play, when Helena asks, 'When will you ever stop running away?', he retorts, 'When will you ever stop chasing?' (p. 20). The seemingly relentless patience which Shakespeare's Helena demonstrates in achieving her goal is taken by Coxon to an absurdist extreme, not only through Helena's unremitting efforts to win Bertram round, but also in her waiting unwearyingly for the birth of her child, who, after 2 years, has not yet been delivered:

> *Mike*   You're almost two years pregnant.
> *Beat*
> *Helena*   It's a good thing I have a gift for patience.
> *Mike*   Yes it is.
> *Helena*   I've always been the same . . . (pp. 11–12)

The absence of the baby in Coxon's play is, however, more significant than being simply an extreme and comic indicator of Helena's forbearance. It exposes the key unfulfilled condition of Bertram's acceptance of Helena – their child. In the final scene of *AWW* Helena claims to have fulfilled Bertram's criteria for becoming accepted as his wife:

> When from my finger you can get this ring,
> And are by me with child, et cetera. This is done. (5.3.314–15)

However, in this speech, she misquotes the terms of his original letter, in which Bertram had stipulated that Helena could only 'call me husband' when she could '*show me* a child begotten of thy body that I am father to' (3.2.58–9, my italics).

In Coxon's play not only does this child remain unborn after years, but, the question is raised as to whether Helena is actually pregnant at all, or is desperately clinging on to the idea despite the apparent absurdity of such a possibility. Helena's health visitor, Mike, is clearly suspicious given the apparent length of her pregnancy, insisting that she take a test. However, as the play ends, with Bertram on tenterhooks, Helena reveals that she deliberately prevented this test from working, leaving the matter unresolved once again, and the pair's future as a married couple uncertain:

Bertram   What was the result?
She hesitates . . .
Bertram   Helena . . . ?
Helena   The test didn't work.
Bertram   Why didn't it work?!
She shrugs.
Helena   I put apple juice in the glass instead.
Bertram sinks.
Bertram   I want to disappear. (Coxon, 2009, p. 27)

Bertram's predicament – an unwilling man trapped in a relationship for apparently having got a girl pregnant – is thus brought up to date, a situation no doubt familiar to many members of the young audiences, if not as one of their own fears, in discussions of adolescent relationships in the media.[6]

Coxon similarly brings Helena and Bertram's unhappy marriage up to date through the use of the recognizable contemporary signifier of the unromantic anniversary present – a common bone of contention among many couples. As Helena says when presented, on the morning of their wedding anniversary, with a pathetic bunch of flowers bought in a petrol station – 'nothing says "I have utter contempt for you" like a random bunch in mirrored plastic from a filling station forecourt' (2009, p. 19). Bertram's gesture gains much of its humour from its recognizability (an article in the *Daily Mail* in 2011 suggested that one in four men buy anniversary flowers at a petrol station (2011), undoubtedly one of the aspects which many of the young people who participated in the workshops recognized from their parents' marriages or, indeed, their own experiences.

Although Bertram and Helena's marriage, as depicted in Coxon's play, clearly contains elements recognizable in many contemporary relationships – the bickering, lack of affection and failure to acknowledge an anniversary with a suitably romantic gesture – the play is, perhaps, too intimately related to *AWW* to stand alone as a fully formed drama. Indeed, Banks explains that the play was primarily intended as a 'curtain raiser' (2011), and although the piece was performed at the Latitude festival in July 2009, he saw its main function there as being to encourage young audiences to come to see the National Theatre's production of *AWW* or to read the play (Banks, 2011). However, as a sequel, the play seems far more likely to appeal to those already familiar with *AWW* than to provide an entry point for those unfamiliar with Shakespeare's work.

One might argue that without prior knowledge of *AWW* too many of the play's elements seem underdeveloped or extremely odd – Helena's lengthy pregnancy, Betram's desire to disappear and his explanation of how he impregnated Helena.

In a rather brilliant sequence, Bertram attempts to explain to Kelly about his marriage and the subsequent 'bed-trick'. His claims, which seem utterly ridiculous, only fulfil their comic potential if one is aware of the events of *AWW* that Bertram is attempting to elucidate:

Bertram   . . . Look, I'm not 'married' married.
She looks at him.
Kelly   Be clearer. I mean in legal terms?
Bertram   There was an ambush.
She raises her eyebrows.
Bertram   By which I mean a . . . ceremony.
Kelly   Did you sign anything?
Bertram   My name. It seemed a formality.
              . . .
              Besides, I thought I could have it annulled.
Kelly   Annulled?
Bertram   Non-consummation. I took off straight after the buffet. We
              never had the sex. My plan was: we never would. Then she
              got herself pregnant.
Kelly puzzles a moment.
Kelly   'Got herself pregnant'?
Bertram   Yup!
Kelly   You mean, you're not the father?
Bertram   Oh, I'm the father alright.
. . .
Bertram   She tricked me into believing she was someone completely
              different . . .
Kelly   Well, people can change.
Bertram   No – I mean *literally*. (Coxon, 2009, pp. 14–16)

This exploitation of dramatic irony to create humour is surely more akin to what Banks describes as the 'bonus' rather than the 'way in'.

Coxon also provides some humorous explanations of some of the 'dislocations and gaps' (Snyder, 1998, p. 26) in *AWW* – elements of her play which, again, are most appealing and entertaining to those with a good knowledge of the play and its inconsistencies. In 3.2 Helena writes to the Countess that she has undertaken a pilgrimage to 'Saint Jaques' (3.4.4) in Spain and her 'convenient arrival in Florence' has, therefore, 'troubled many critics who have observed with Dr Johnson that Florence is "somewhat out of the road from Rousillon to Compostella"'(Kastan, 1985, p. 588). In any case, that Helena arrives in the very part of Florence where Bertram is in residence is a rather extreme coincidence which is never explained in the play. Coxon exploits her twenty-first-century setting to play on this unexplained converging of the ways, with Helena explaining to Mike – 'He couldn't believe I'd found him. He thinks I might be psychic.' When Mike responds – 'Do *you* think that you might be psychic?' – Helena replies with a perfectly plausible contemporary explanation – 'No. He had his mobile with him. I traced him with the GPS' (Coxon, 2009, p. 22).

The bed-trick is clearly a vital plot device in *All's Well*; however, it is not dramatized in the text, and one cannot help but wonder how it is achieved without arousing Bertram's suspicion. A number of productions of the play have staged the encounter in a silent mime, making use either of darkness or a blindfold to effect the changeover between the two women.[7] However, in the absence of dialogue, Bertram's submission to being blindfolded can appear unconvincing. Coxon's Bertram provides justification for his acceptance, comically suggesting that he viewed the device as part of a kinky sex game:

> *Bertram* I found it quite exciting. She said she was shy. It was her first
> time. (2009, p. 16)

A further 'gap' in the function of the bed-trick is Helena's apparent decision to detain Bertram for 'an hour' after he has 'conquered my yet maiden bed' (4.1.58–59). As Harold Bloom asks, 'What takes place during that hour? . . . Does the dilation of the trick express a desire on Helena's art for a more sustained intimacy?' (2010, p. 194). Coxon has Bertram outline to Kelly the details of the sexual encounter, stating 'Look, I don't want you thinking this was a tawdry shoot-and-scoot. I made a proper job of it' and proudly describing his engagement in foreplay in the language of a military campaign:

> The blindfold's on . . . I set about it . . . The usual tactics. As the more
> experienced partner I have the strategic advantage. I dominate in the early
> skirmishes, then with an eye to economy of force, I tease her to the point
> of attrition before mounting a full frontal assault. (Coxon, 2009, p. 17)

Elements of the comedy of Coxon's play are thus dependent on a quite sophisticated understanding of *AWW* and its critical reception.

The military language used by Bertram in his description of his sexual encounter is another area in which *The Eternal Not* engages subtly with a key element of Shakespeare's play – the contrast between Bertram's love of war and hatred of love:

> Great Mars, I put myself into thy file.
> Make me but like my thoughts, and I shall prove
> A lover of thy drum, hater of love. (*AWW*, 3.3.9–11)

Although Coxon's play is located in a contemporary domestic setting, she manages to draw on this theme, not only in Bertram's couching of his sexual exploits in terms of a martial conquest, but also in his obsession with his toy soldiers. In the first scene between Bertram and Helena in *The Eternal Not*, Bertram is devoting substantial energy to the reenactment of the battles of Napoleon, criticizing Helena for describing it as a 'hobby' rather than a 'passion' (Coxon, 2009, p. 8), to which she responds archly – 'What does a passion sound like?' – emphasizing the contrast between the amount of time and enthusiasm Bertram puts into his war games and that which he devotes to their relationship.

Bertram's obsession with his toy soldiers, with which he plays sitting on the floor, engages with another feature of his character as depicted in *AWW* – his youth and immaturity. That Bertram is on the brink of adolescence is indicated by the King's initial orders that he should remain at court because he is 'too young' to go to Italy to fight (2.1.28). Later, Bertram is described by Lafew as one of the 'unbaked and doughy' youths of his nation (4.5.3), indicating his unformed character. Thus, although Banks stresses the extent to which the young audiences for Coxon's play recognized their parents' generation in the marriage, it is clear that Coxon's Bertram is, like Shakespeare's, little more than what William Babula describes as 'a foolish adolescent' (1977, p. 94).

Coxon's play seems to redress somewhat the balance of sympathy in *AWW*, which, as Leah Scragg comments, explicitly 'encourages audience alignment with the female point of view' (2005, p. 38). Coxon's play does not present either Helena or Bertram as the wronged party, eliciting some sympathy for Bertram's entrapment and some for Helena's perseverance in a loveless marriage.

Although elements of the humour and skill of *The Eternal Not* may have been lost on some audience members who saw the 5 p.m. foyer productions preceding the evening performances of *AWW*, for those already familiar with Shakespeare's play the piece not only serves as a witty comment on *AWW* but also serves to provoke debate about the play's themes, genre, dislocations and lack of resolution. As such *The Eternal Not* also has potential as a text to study or perform in the classroom alongside *AWW*, generating discussion and emphasizing the ongoing relevance of many of Shakespeare's themes.

Prince of Denmark

Following the success of *The Eternal Not*, Banks commissioned Michael Lesslie to write *Prince of Denmark*, with a slightly more specific brief – to pen a prequel to *Hamlet* with as many characters as the Shakespearean original, set around 10 years before Shakespeare's play. Although the events which immediately precede Shakespeare's play – the murder of Old Hamlet, marriage of Claudius and Gertrude, and the question of their adulterous or otherwise relationship – might seem to have a more obvious appeal for a prequel, as evidenced by John Updike's successful novel *Gertrude and Claudius* (2000), Banks felt that since 'everyone knows what happens just before *Hamlet*', if the play was to have its own life and momentum, it needed to stand at some distance from Shakespeare's play (2011). Banks' decision to commission a play set 10 years before the events of *Hamlet* was also motivated by his desire to create a piece of theatre for young audiences specifically about teenagers, of which, he felt, there were too few, outside of those commissioned for the NT Connections Programme. Such a piece would be led by action rather than talk, characterized by the 'chaos of adolescence' rather than by Hamlet and his friends having discussions in their rooms at Wittenberg (Banks, 2011).

Although the piece was not conceived as a direct response to Nicholas Hytner's *Hamlet*, as Banks notes, the casting of Rory Kinnear in the title role in Hytner's production did influence the brief for the 'side-dish' (2011). Kinnear was clearly a Hamlet in his thirties, as is suggested by the Folio and Second Quarto texts,[8] and, with this in mind, any response that would explore the character, as presented on the Olivier stage, in adolescence, needed to be set some 10 years before the play. Had the NT production been in the vein of Trevor Nunn's 2001 Old Vic *Hamlet*, with Ben Wishaw's 18-year-old protagonist, the brief might, Banks acknowledges, have been different (2011).

As Lesslie elucidates, a sequel to *Hamlet* allows an exploration of the forming of 'the personas' and formulating of 'the decisions' that lead eventually to the action of Shakespeare's play (2011). While in *Prince of Denmark* Laertes takes the central role, the play is concerned with a number of the characters, key events and relationships of Shakespeare's play: the origins of the political conflict between Denmark and Norway, the rule of Hamlet's father, Hamlet's relationship with his father, the seeds of the love affair between Hamlet and Ophelia, the background to Ophelia and Laertes' arrival at court, the absence of their mother and Hamlet's departure for Wittenberg.

One of the key features of Lesslie's play is the way in which it turns the relationship between Hamlet and his father on its head. While Shakespeare's Hamlet speaks of his father as 'Hyperion to a satyr' (1.2.140), 'A combination and a form indeed / Where every god did seem to set his seal' (3.4.59–60), Lesslie's title character describes his father as 'a fool!', cataloguing 'his failings' (2010, Scene 2, p. 7). His Hamlet is thus an adolescent at odds with his father, a theme which, as discussed in Chapter 7, plays a key role in literature for young people, given the adolescent tendency towards 'rebellion and anger at parents' (Ponton, 1998, p. 55). Having played the role of Hamlet at school, Lesslie was interested in exploring whether the 'pro-paternal angst' which Hamlet displays in Shakespeare's play might be his way of 'compensating for something' in his relationship with his father (2011).

While Shakespeare may appear to present a straightforward contrast between the brave, honourable Old Hamlet and the manipulative Claudius,

Lesslie's portrayal of these two characters invites a closer consideration of the details that Shakespeare gives us about each; an interrogation of the text, which reveals a more complex, ambiguous depiction of the two men. Although we hear from Hamlet that his father was 'so loving to my mother' (1.2.140) and from Horatio that he was 'a goodly king', 'valiant' and 'esteem'd' by 'this side of our known world' (1.2.185; 1.1.83–4), Lesslie picks up on two details from the play which call into question his behaviour both as a good leader and a good husband. In 1.1 *Hamlet*, Horatio, describing Old Hamlet's single-combat with Old Fortinbras, states that the King gaged 'a moiety competent' of his land, which, had Fortinbras won the combat, would have been forfeited to Norway (1.2.83–92). As Lesslie comments, 'I thought, this points to a real neglect of your own people; gambling on your own people's lives' (2011). The other detail on which Lesslie picks up is the Gravedigger's comment in 5.1 that he came to his occupation 'that day that our last king Hamlet overcame Fortinbras', the very same day 'that young Hamlet was born' (5.1.140–1; 144–5). All too easily brushed over, the implication of this remark is that while Gertrude was giving birth to Hamlet, Old Hamlet was away, fighting. Lesslie's Hamlet angrily comments on both these points in his first substantial speech of Scene 2:

> As my mother risked very death to bring me into this world, our King was in another country, winning a bet on which he'd wagered the whole nation's future. All for your honour, Guildenstern. And after he had slain old Fortinbras and set up this substitute Norway in his place, did he return to his country to celebrate with his new born son and birth-torn queen? No. He continues on to Poland, where thousands more sons and fathers and uncles are made to die for his honour. (2010, Scene 2, p. 8)

In calling into question the behaviour of his father as both a ruler and a husband, Lesslie's Hamlet also provides a hint as to both Gertrude's reasons for marrying Claudius and the potential motives of the Danish populace in apparently electing him to the throne after Old Hamlet's death. Both of these elements are unexplained in Shakespeare's text, and have led to substantial critical discussion. Although Hamlet claims that Claudius is 'a cutpurse of the empire and the rule' (3.4.89), stealing the crown which should rightfully have been his, Denmark was, as many critics have pointed out, an elective monarchy, as is implied at 1.2.109, 4.5.106, 5.2.66 and 5.2.307–8. Certainly no one in the play, other than Hamlet, questions Claudius' right to rule, and thus, it appears that he has been chosen by the people (Edwards, 2003, p. 209). Lesslie's play implies that Claudius may have provided the people of Denmark with a welcome contrast to Old Hamlet, a possibility which is not inconsistent with Claudius's first speech in 1.2 *Hamlet*, which 'has been admired as a demonstration of his political skill' (Thompson and Taylor, 2006, p. 165) in dealing with young Fortinbras by writing to his uncle rather than by threatening war.

Gertrude's reasons for marrying Claudius are less transparent. Although the Ghost accuses Claudius of being an 'incestuous' and 'adulterous beast' (1.5.42), it is, as the Arden editors point out, 'notoriously unclear whether the Ghost means to say that his wife embarked on an adulterous relationship with his brother before his death' (Thompson and Taylor, 2006, p. 214). In Scene 2 of *Prince of Denmark*, Hamlet, contrary to his behaviour in Shakespeare's play, praises Claudius, both for his treatment of the people and his treatment of Gertrude:

> The only man who stayed behind to hold my mother's hand as she screamed for assurance. One who commands the love of the country he lives in, capable of making the whole populace laugh with a single smile. (Lesslie, 2010, Scene 2, p. 8)

These moments in Lesslie's play not only fill out some of the 'gaps' in Shakespeare's text, encouraging young audiences to question the apparently simple dichotomy between the two kings, but also exploit the potential for dramatic irony inherent in the awareness of some audience members of the characterization and events of *Hamlet*. Lesslie acknowledges that this is one of the pleasures in writing 'a stage adaptation of an already existing play' (2011). It is also one of the pleasures for audience members who are familiar with Shakespeare's play, and, as such, suggests that *Prince of Denmark* may have a particular appeal to those who have studied or are studying *Hamlet*.

The dramatic irony in Lesslie's play comes not only in the form of undermining the audience's expectations of events and characters, but also with exploiting their knowledge of certain features or traditional interpretations of particular characters. As Lesslie explains, his characterization of Reynaldo drew on the text and performance history of the character – the recognition that in his only scene in *Hamlet* (2.1) Reynaldo uses the words 'My lord' to Polonius in almost every line. This feature, which Alec Guinness reportedly used to make Reynaldo 'a more sinister spy-like figure' (Lesslie, 2011), is exploited by Lesslie, so that his Reynaldo uses the same address to Laertes in each line of the first scene of *Prince of Denmark*.

Just as Lesslie draws upon Reynaldo's characteristics, displayed in only one scene of Shakespeare's play, to flesh him out into a character who spies for and on everyone, he inflates Osric's features to make him the 'bumbling, be-hatted fool' (2010, Scene 1, p. 1) of *Prince of Denmark*. The Arden editors describe Osric's 'affected style of speech' as 'full of empty and repetitive formulas' (Thompson and Taylor, 2006, p. 441). Lesslie exaggerates the affectation, giving Osric a series of hyperbolic and pretentious adjectives:

> *Osric* Trepidatious woe, Laertes! Your sister is over-suitored! She spurns my cupidinous epistles with the obstinacy of – (Scene 1, p. 2)

Even the fact that Osric is, unlike the other characters, wearing a hat, is a comic touch which draws on his well-known exchange with Hamlet in Shakespeare's 5.2 in which his obsequiousness leads him to take his hat on and off a number of times.

In the theatre, Rosencrantz and Guildenstern have regularly been portrayed as practically indistinguishable, a feature ironically exploited by Tom Stoppard in *Rosencrantz and Guildenstern Are Dead*, in which the characters themselves prove unable to remember which is which:

> *Ros* My name is Guildenstern, and this is Rosencrantz.
>
> *(Guild confers briefly with him.)*
>
> *(without embarrassment)* I'm sorry – *his* name's Guildenstern, and *I'm* Rosencrantz. (Stoppard, 1967, p. 13)

Lesslie plays on it to similar comic effect, with Ophelia, in this case, unable to tell the men apart:

> *Ophelia* A servant passes them to one of his friends. Guildenstern, I think.
>
> *Laertes* Not Rosencrantz?
>
> *Ophelia* I can't tell. The lanky one. (Lesslie, 2010, Scene 1, p. 5)

Indeed, 'the biggest laugh of the night', which, according to Lesslie, always came when Rosencrantz and Guildenstern deliver two lines of evasion in unison (Lesslie, 2011), was surely the result of a familiarity with the common perception of the two characters as akin to a Shakespearean 'Tweedle-Dum and Tweedle-Dee':

> *Hamlet* My father? How does he know I've gone?
>
> *Ros. (Together with Guildenstern)*   I don't know.
>
> *Guild. (Together with Rosencrantz)* I've no idea. (2010, Scene 7, p. 27)

Dramatic irony is not merely exploited by Lesslie for the sake of humour, but also to reinforce some of the central themes of *Hamlet*. Hamlet's regularly commented upon tendency towards thought rather than action, for example, is foreshadowed in *Prince of Denmark*, both in Laertes' Scene 3 soliloquy, and in Hamlet's own ability to philosophize his way out of usurping his father. Laertes, railing against his fate, worries how Denmark would fare under Hamlet's rule:

> I have seen him in court, glowering and mumbling to himself as though his troubles would defy the comprehension of mortal men, and we imitate our monarchs as pets their masters. Thus will Denmark be reduced to a

nation of cowards, brooding solipsists so paralysed by soliloquy as to be blind to their social duty. (2010, Scene 3, p. 12)

The metatheatrical reference to 'soliloquy' clearly brings to mind Hamlet as portrayed in Shakespeare's play where he speaks seven major soliloquies[9] in which he speculates on his own situation and the human condition, and raises the question of his suitability as a successor to his father.

Hamlet's reaction to the players' performance of 'Dido and Aeneas', in *Prince of Denmark*, not only plays on this tendency to meditate, but also on the audience's knowledge of Claudius' reaction to 'The Murder of Gonzago' in *Hamlet*. One might assume, when Hamlet leaps up from the performance of 'Dido and Aeneas', that he has recognized his own father's death in that of Priam and is reacting in horror at this murder. However, Lesslie cleverly manipulates the parallel with *Hamlet* so that Hamlet is, in fact, like Claudius, identifying himself with the murderer:

Watching then my double stand as Pyrrhus, streaked with blood and raising his righteous sword above the tyrannical old king, it was as though the gods themselves had climbed down from Olympus and were charging me to earn my name of greatness. (2010, Scene 7, p. 22)

Hamlet is thus, ironically, in *Prince of Denmark*, contemplating the murder of the very man whose murder he must avenge in Shakespeare's play. However, despite feeling the urge to take action, he goes on to philosophize on the meaning of existence and the possibility of simultaneous time, finally concluding, 'What then does it matter whether I kill the King?' (Scene 7, p. 23). In placing thought over action, Lesslie's Hamlet fulfils the common perception of the character, as described by Laurence Olivier, as a man 'who could not make up his mind' (1948).

Lesslie's inclusion of the play of 'Dido and Aeneas', in which Hamlet explicitly identifies himself with Pyrrhus, serves not only as a means of mirroring the episode of the play-within-a play in Shakespeare's *Hamlet*, but also as a means of giving the characters 'a certain awareness of themselves as characters in a drama' (2011) and thus exploring the issues of fatalism and free will. The characters make a number of self-conscious metatheatrical references, which are dependent on the audience's appreciation of *Prince of Denmark* as a sequel to a preexisting text, and, in many cases, their prior knowledge of *Hamlet*. When Hamlet tells Ophelia about his reaction to the performance of 'Dido and Aeneas', she responds: 'It was only a play Hamlet', to which he counters: 'One still worth the telling some dozen centuries later. Perhaps if I am to merit such a permanent commemoration, I must do something equally terrible' (2010, Scene 7, p. 23). The irony of this comment resides in an audience's knowledge that Hamlet's actions will, indeed, be commemorated in a play which will be played many centuries later. A similar irony derives from

Ophelia's comment on her reflection in the brook in this same exchange – 'If that were Ophelia, she would be drowned' to which Hamlet replies 'In another story maybe she is' (Scene 7, p. 23). Again, a true understanding of the implications of this statement depends on the audience's knowledge of Ophelia's fate in *Hamlet*.

For an audience with a good knowledge of *Hamlet*, there is also pleasure to be gleaned from the echoes of Shakespeare's lines that Lesslie manages to work into his text – Laertes' 'This cannot come to good, Reynaldo' (Scene 1, p. 1), which echoes Hamlet's 'It is not nor it cannot come to good' (1.2.158); his 'Stand and unfold yourself!' (Scene 1, p. 2), which replicates Francisco's line in 1.1; and Laertes and Osric's exchange, a repeat of Hamlet and Horatio's lines in 1.4:

> *Laertes*   What hour now?
>
> *Osric*   I think it lacks of twelve. (Scene 6, p. 20)

In addition to broadly echoing some of the sentiments of 'To be or not to be', Laertes' soliloquy also echoes Hamlet's 2.2. soliloquy 'And all for nothing. For convention' (Scene 3, p. 12) recalling Hamlet's 'and all for nothing! / For Hecuba!' (2.2). Perhaps the wittiest verbal echo of *Hamlet* is Horatio's second to last line, 'The rest, Ophelia, is always violence' (Scene 7, p. 29), a clever pun on Hamlet's final line, 'The rest is silence' (*Ham.* 5.2.310), and one which neatly sums up the future we know is to come.

A full appreciation of the intertextuality, comedy and dramatic irony in *Prince of Denmark* is dependent on an audience's prior knowledge of Shakespeare's play, and, like Coxon's *The Eternal Not*, these features seem to fulfil Banks's criteria of 'bonus', rather than 'way in'. However, while some of those who booked to see *Prince of Denmark* may have been readily familiar with Shakespeare's play, the production became, as Banks explains, subject to the NT's marketing and education strategies, which elected to target the play predominantly to Key Stage 3 students. Many of these students are unlikely to have encountered *Hamlet* prior to seeing *Prince of Denmark*, since the curriculum demands the study of only one Shakespeare play up to this point, and, as Banks acknowledges, 'may have been too young to fully appreciate the play's nuances' (2011). The most obvious audience would have been A-Level, or even GCSE students, who were studying *Hamlet*, and thus would have benefitted from the reinterrogation of its themes and characters as well as appreciating the humour created by the dramatic irony.

The question then arises of how *Prince of Denmark* might provide a 'way in' for those without prior knowledge of *Hamlet* as well as a 'bonus' for those already familiar with the play. Banks suggests that the main way in which Lesslie's piece offers a 'way in' for young people is in enabling them to recognize that 'the problems facing them faced people 400 years ago'

(Banks), a similar strategy to MacDonald's *After Juliet*. Hamlet's battles with his father, Hamlet and Ophelia's burgeoning relationship and Laertes' intense jealousy of a boy who is wealthier and more advantaged than he is are all recognizable scenarios for contemporary teenagers.

Lesslie comments that part of the impulse behind making Laertes the protagonist of his play came from his recognition of the fact that 'so many young men see themselves as Hamlet' – the tormented young man, at odds with the world. In *Prince of Denmark* both Hamlet and Laertes are angst-ridden young men, Laertes frustrated by his lack of status in an unequal society, and Hamlet by his role as a prince. While Laertes muses on the possibility that a common man such as himself could rise to the status of a king – 'who is to say that a peasant could not be king? Who is to say not Laertes?' (Lesslie, 2010, Scene 3, p. 13), Hamlet desires freedom of equality – 'in Wittenberg, we may no longer be noble. There we may be taken for what we are, separated from role and royalty' (Scene 2, p. 9). A sense of frustration with one's social position and obsession with ideas of evading one's apparently pre-destined path are feelings that many experience in adolescence. Roberta Seelinger Trites writes that 'adolescents must learn their place in the power structure', learning 'to negotiate the many institutions that shape them' (1998, p. x). Such sentiments of social negotiation were thus no doubt familiar to a number of the young audience members, whether they identified with Hamlet and his desire for freedom or Laertes and his desire for power.

Although, like *Hamlet*, Lesslie's play is focused around the male characters, Lesslie, like the novelists whose work was discussed in the previous chapter, provides a fuller characterization of Ophelia, providing, perhaps, more of a way in for the young female members of the audience. Lesslie comments that he was surprised when his agent remarked that he had written a 'feminist reworking' of *Hamlet*, stating that this was not his intention (2011). However, it is, perhaps, inevitable, that in writing female characters in the twenty-first century, even when imagining them in a pseudo-Renaissance setting, writers will be influenced by the contemporary Western perception of women as having the potential to be of equal intelligence, assertiveness and perceptiveness as men. Lesslie's Ophelia is not as subservient to the male characters as her Shakespearean equivalent, questioning Osric's status as a suitable suitor and asserting her independence:

> *Ophelia*   A talking mushroom! I never knew a man with such a capacity to repulse and bore at same time, it's like being tortured with wet fruit. Honestly, I don't understand why you still speak to him.
> (Lesslie, 2010, Scene 1, p. 3)

> *Laertes*   Why didn't you tell me? You're my sister.
> *Ophelia*   I'm me. (Scene 1, pp. 3–4)
> *Ophelia*   I'm not yours to wager Laertes. (Scene 7, p. 25)

She is similarly confident and proactive in her relationship with Hamlet, countering his assertion, 'I'm the prince. You don't have a choice' with 'Yes I do' (Scene 7, p. 22). It is also Ophelia, rather than Hamlet, who instigates their first kiss:

> *Ophelia* What do you want, Hamlet?
>
> *Hamlet* Just you.
>
> *Ophelia* Then take me. (Scene 7, pp. 23–4)

As Nancy Groves' review comments, '[t]he play may be aimed at, and about, teenagers, but Lesslie is wise enough not to patronize his actors or audience. No need to relocate to a gritty urban housing estate. The affections and/ or disaffection of Elsinore's adolescents are recognisable enough' (2010). Lesslie's teenagers appear modern and relevant, while remaining firmly located in the world of pseudo-Elizabethan Denmark.

Lesslie's decision to write his play in modern prose certainly makes it more immediately accessible to young audiences who are apt to struggle with the archaisms of Shakespeare's language and its often complex syntax. Many of the characters' sentiments are expressed in plain and simple terms. However, like MacDonald, Lesslie does not patronize his potential spectators with an oversimplification of expression, often employing elements of imagery and rhetoric which recall those of Shakespeare. In addition to the direct echoes of lines from *Hamlet* and *Othello*, Lesslie draws on the phrasing of Shakespeare, most frequently in the extended metaphor:

> We do not elevate great ones to have them meddle in our affairs, they are above us to serve us, gilt pinions to our iron wheels. Should the pinion turn against the teeth that hold it, the whole machine will crack. (Lesslie, Scene 1, p. 1)
>
> Then perhaps in its ugliness it struck of truth! Decorum is the anaesthetic of our age, Guildenstern, a paint that distorts the thing it coats until every object is unrecognisable as its own being. (Scene 2, p. 7)

The NT's production of *Prince of Denmark* was accompanied by workshops advertised for students aged 10 and above, which purported, according to the publicity material, to 'explore the play and its connections to Shakespeare's original' (NT, 2010). However, these workshops mostly took the form of stage-fighting sessions since, as Banks explains, he felt that workshops centred around the play and its relationship to *Hamlet* might be the 'kiss of death' for the production (2011). Banks wanted his audiences to come and see the play fresh, and to experience it in its own right rather than with an awareness of its construction and a prescribed knowledge of *Hamlet*.

This then leads us to the question of whether Lesslie's play, despite its intricate and often witty intertextual references to *Hamlet*, is able to stand alone as a play in its own right. Certainly the piece feels more substantial than Coxon's *The Eternal Not*, with an independent story of Laertes tricking Osric into preventing Hamlet and Ophelia's relationship. Its very nature as a prequel rather than a sequel also means that it is not dependent on retrospective knowledge of the preceding events in the same way as Coxon's play.

Each of the three plays discussed has an intricate and often sophisticated relationship to its Shakespearean source, employing dramatic irony, witty intertextual references and a mixture of linguistic registers which draw both on Shakespeare's language and on modern day parlance. As a prequel rather than a sequel, Lesslie's play seems the most likely to be able to stand alone as an independent piece of drama, since, although an appreciation of much of its humour is dependent on a knowledge of *Hamlet*, an understanding of its plot and characters is not. *After Juliet*, with most of its characters being MacDonald's original creations, also has a life independent of *Romeo and Juliet*; however, an appreciation of the plot and its intricacies is largely reliant on an awareness of the identity of Rosaline and her relationship with Romeo; the feud between the Montagues and Capulets and its consequences as seen in the deaths of Romeo, Juliet, Tybalt and Mercutio and the involvement of the Nurse, Friar, apothecary and Peter in the events of Shakespeare's play. Coxon's play is the most heavily dependent on a knowledge of its Shakespearean source, somewhat ironically given that *AWW* is the play least likely to be familiar to a young audience. As such one imagines that it might have been better scheduled to play after the production of *AWW* in the Olivier rather than before, exploiting an audience's ready familiarity with Shakespeare's play.

All three plays encourage audiences to interrogate the themes of Shakespeare's plays in relation to the experiences of contemporary youth – in particular the themes of love, romantic relationships, youth violence, parental relationships, class and gender roles. In featuring as their protagonists the younger characters in Shakespeare's plays, in particular those who have little to say or do in the original, they are also part of the movement discussed in Chapter 7 of giving a voice to marginalized figures, in particular to female characters, who are often repressed in Shakespeare's tragedies and in Shakespeare's comedies ultimately subject to the constraints of patriarchal society and its expectations of conformity to marriage and childbearing. The plays also encourage the exploration of gaps and questions in the Shakespearean originals, inviting young audience members, performers or readers to think about the ambiguities inherent in much of Shakespeare's work, in particular in the perception of characters as either good or bad, culpable or blameless. Perhaps most importantly they have all been seen to reinvigorate Shakespeare's plays for contemporary teenagers who might otherwise perceive Shakespeare's work as either difficult or boring, encouraging them to tackle the originals afresh.

**Interview with Michael Lesslie, Author of Prince Of Denmark –
Conducted on 31 January 2011**

HOW DID YOU COME TO WRITE A PREQUEL TO *HAMLET*?

Anthony Banks who directed *Prince of Denmark* runs the NT Connections programme. I'd done a Connections play the year before which was set in a public school and was all about machinations of power and Anthony came to me and said that he had had a conversation with the Head of the Literary department and, having done *The Eternal Not* the year before, they wanted to do another adaptation of Shakespeare to run in conjunction with *Hamlet*. So, they asked me to write a prequel, maybe set 10 years before, but with the main thing being to use only the young characters.

WHY DID YOU DECIDE TO CONCENTRATE ON A PERIOD SOME TIME BEFORE THE START OF SHAKESPEARE'S PLAY RATHER THAN ON THE IMMEDIATE AND HIGHLY DRAMATIC EVENTS DIRECTLY PRECEDING THE PLAY?

They suggested 10 years before, because I think they thought that it would be interesting to see the characters (however old you posit Hamlet) young and forming the personas and formulating the decisions that lead to Shakespeare's play. There's the massive question of free will and fatalism in *Hamlet* which made me think that a prequel was going to be interesting. The very nature of doing a prequel, especially when the full play is running in parallel in the space nextdoor, is that you are calling into question the very nature of free will and fatalism, and so I wanted the characters to have a certain awareness of themselves as characters in a drama, which was partly why I incorporated the Pyrrhus sequence with the players.

Both Anthony and I also thought that there is so much pro-paternal angst in the play that it feels as though Hamlet is compensating for something. I played Hamlet at school and he is so obsessed with living up to his father. I thought that going back to a place where Hamlet hated his father and was more combustible and young and angry might sow the seeds for why he was sent to Wittenberg.

OLD HAMLET COMES OVER AS A RATHER NEGLECTFUL FATHER, OBSESSED WITH WAR

I did think that throughout *Hamlet* he is talked about as this military hero, and I was looking back at 1.1 and the backstory when Horatio says 'He wagered the entire nations' fortune on a one-on-one duel with Old Fortinbras', and I thought, this points to a real neglect of your own people; gambling on your own people's lives.

AND IT'S IN THE GRAVE-DIGGER SCENE IN 5.1, ISN'T IT, WHEN WE DISCOVER THAT THIS DUEL OCCURRED ON THE DAY THAT HAMLET WAS BORN

Exactly, and I thought that that sense of paternal abandonment was an interesting source of angst in Hamlet, and one of the things that I wanted to do, and like doing in a lot of the things that I write, was to explore the private reasons behind public, political decisions. There is no definitive backstory, and that is one of the joys, of course. But the multiplicity of interpretation and the ambiguity is what makes the text so rich. That's another thing that I wanted to draw out in *Prince of Denmark*.

THERE MUST BE A LEVEL OF FUN TO BE HAD WITH EXPLOITING A KIND OF DRAMATIC IRONY. YOU KNOW THAT YOUR AUDIENCE WILL BE THINKING – 'BUT WAIT A MINUTE, OLD HAMLET'S THE GOOD KING AND CLAUDIUS IS THE BASTARD'

Huge fun. I wanted to turn it on its head. The other thing about writing a stage adaptation of an already existing play is that you can use that dramatic irony to create humour. The biggest laugh of the night, every time, was when Marcellus says 'Hamlet, your father needs you back in court' and Hamlet says 'How does he know I've gone?' and Rosencrantz and Guildenstern at the same time say 'I've no idea'. You can play with prolepsis. You can count on the audience knowing things to a certain degree and that's great fun. My favourite gag in the whole thing is Reynaldo. In the one scene he appears in in *Hamlet* he has the words 'My lord' in every line. I read about the performance history of Reynaldo, and for years he was just seen as a deferential servant, but then, I think it was Alec Guinness who was playing it to Gielgud's Hamlet and realized that 'My lord' was in every line and used this exaggerated deference to create a more sinister spy-like figure. And I wanted to exploit that. It also made me think about the fact that one of the things about Elsinore in *Hamlet* is that there is never a private moment. Walls are listening.

WHAT LED YOU TO THE IDEA OF HAVING LAERTES AS THE PROTAGONIST?

When people think about *Hamlet*, so often they think about the brooding young man in practically every scene – it's a protagonist's play – so it's interesting to consider the reality of all the other characters that surround Hamlet. My main thing was looking back on the play and thinking 'Wait a minute, who is Laertes?' What also interested me is that so many young men see themselves as Hamlet. It's a kind of definitive position for young men to be in and I quite liked the idea that if we were going back to the time when they were all teenagers that all of the figures would see themselves as 'Hamlets', because it's a tendency of pretty much everyone to see themselves as the protagonist in their own drama. So, I wanted to give Laertes, in his central speech, the 'To be or not to be' reworking, because everyone has that moment. It wasn't the first thing that I wrote, but it was the centre point of how I imagined the play.

As well as drawing on *Hamlet* I also drew on other Shakespeare plays because I wanted to have that intertextual element – obviously there is the moment where Osric and Laertes start taking on the Roderigo and Iago lines and dynamic.

EVEN THE DEVICE OF DISGUISE AND OF SWAPPING CLOTHES IS A SHAKESPEAREAN ONE

Yes. There are lots of tropes that recur throughout the plays of character pairings and plot workings, which doesn't denigrate the plays as great individual works in themselves. It's interesting to look at these tropes when you are exploring a Shakespearean worldview, if such a coherent thing exists.

HOW DID YOU CHOOSE WHICH CHARACTERS TO HAVE IN THE PLAY? I UNDERSTAND THAT PART OF THE COMMISSION WAS TO EXCLUDE THE OLDER GENERATION BUT WHY DID YOU DECIDE, FOR EXAMPLE, TO EXPAND ON THE ROLES OF CHARACTERS LIKE REYNALDO AND OSRIC, WHO ARE UNDERDEVELOPED IN SHAKESPEARE'S PLAY?

I think that the role of the fool throughout Shakespeare is really interesting, and *Hamlet* is often seen as characterized by the lack of a fool. But I think that Osric is, to an extent, the fool, and as I was going for this Shakespearean mode in the play, incorporating a fool who can be the butt of a typically Shakespearean manipulation plot was (1) going to be really useful, but (2) a lot of young people today see *Hamlet* as oppressively serious and hard to approach, so throw a bit of comedy in, why not? Osric is a hilarious character. Also I think that the source of Osric's humour comes from what we have been saying about Elsinore. Here is a man who is insecure about his position within a structure which seems to allow social mobility, because his father is a landowner and this allows him access to court, but he doesn't always understand what he is saying because he is trying to fit into a social milieu. I think that is a rich source of comedy and as old as the hills, but it also rings true for the whole conception of Elsinore as this socially obsessed, scheming spy zone.

HORATIO IS A FAIRLY BIG PART IN *HAMLET* BUT IN YOUR PLAY HE'S A MINOR CHARACTER. WAS THE IDEA THAT HAMLET DOESN'T REALLY GET TO KNOW HIM UNTIL HE GETS TO WITTENBERG?

I was looking at the backstory of the play and it is kind of ambiguous as to when they started becoming friends. When one looks back at what Claudius and Gertrude say about Rosencrantz and Guildenstern, they seem to have been Hamlet's school mates, but Horatio Hamlet knows from Wittenberg and I wanted to explore the idea that that is a relationship that develops later when Hamlet is away at university and doesn't have to observe the social hierarchy of the court. That is the time when he can explore being a friend rather than being a prince.

Notes

1 Such plays include Tim Kochenderfer's *A Midsummer Vacation's Nightmare* (2008), James Venhaus's *Romeo and Juliet at Verona High* (2005) and Ken Preuss's *Juliet's Ghost* (2008).

2 *Prince of Denmark* © 2011 Michael Lesslie. All rights whatsoever in this play are strictly reserved and application for performance and so on, must be made before rehearsal to Casarotto Ramsay & Associates Ltd., 7–12 Noel Street, London W1F 8GQ. No performance may be given unless a licence has been obtained.

3 A 2-year study carried out between 1998 and 2000 showed that violent behaviour in young women was noticeably on the increase, with four out of ten teenage girls having been beaten up by another young person and 98.5 per cent having witnessed violent incidents (Burrell).

4 Brooke Kinsella, sister of murdered teenager Ben Kinsella, was commissioned by the Home Office to research ways of tackling knife crime among teenagers (Kinsella, 2011).

5 The play was performed at the Contemporary Urban Centre in Liverpool by Weaverham High School and at the Tobacco Factory in Bristol by Sir William Romney's School, Gloucestershire (http://www.ssf.uk.com/schools).

6 The internet is rife with discussion sites and forums about 'trapping' a man by getting pregnant.

7 In Marianne Elliott's National Theatre production (2009), which Coxon's *Eternal Not* played alongside, Diana, dressed in a sexy kitten costume, blindfolded Bertram, before Helena, dressed in a similar outfit took her place.

8 *Ham.* (5.1.168–9). See Chapter 2.

9 In the Q2 version of the text: 1.2.129, 1.5.92, 2.2.484, 3.1.55, 3.2.378, 3.3.73, 4.4.31 (Q2 only).

Web resources

Maxwell, Tom (2007), 'Keira's Helpful Prompt'. *Edinburgh Evening News*: http://living.scotsman.com/performing-arts/Keiras-helpful-prompt.3306002.jp

National Theatre, *Prince of Denmark*: www.nationaltheatre.org.uk/59868/productions/discover-prince-of-denmark.html

The Shakespeare Schools' Festival: www.ssf.uk.com

Stanford, Peter (2009), 'Lucinda Coxon: Return of the Prodigal Woman'. *Independent*: www.independent.co.uk/arts-entertainment/theatre-dance/features/lucinda-coxon-return-of-the-prodigal-woman-1693064.html

CHAPTER NINE

Film Adaptations of Shakespeare: *'Romeo and Juliet the Cartoon'* and 'High School Dreams'

Elizabeth Klett notes that in the wake of Baz Luhrmann's *Romeo + Juliet* (1996) 'the "Shakespeare teenpix" industry has flourished . . . with films like *Never Been Kissed* (1999, dir. Raja Gosnell, an adaptation of *As You Like It*), *10 Things I Hate About You* (1999, dir. Gil Junger, *The Taming of the Shrew*), *'O'* (2001, dir. Tim Blake Nelson, *Othello*), and *Get Over It!* (2001, dir. Tommy O'Haver, *A Midsummer Night's Dream*)' (2008, p. 71). Klett's list is by no means exhaustive, and one might add to it not only *Lost and Delirious* (2001, dir. Léa Pool) and *She's The Man* (2006, dir. Andy Fickman) adaptations of *Twelfth Night* about which Klett writes, but also *High School Musical* (2006, dir. Kenny Ortega, *Romeo and Juliet*) and *Were the World Mine* (2008, dir. Tom Gustafson, *A Midsummer Night's Dream*) all of which are set in High Schools and feature contemporary teenagers as their protagonists. In addition, Luhrmann's film cannot be held solely responsible for the phenomenon of adapting Shakespeare's plays for a teen audience. As Douglas Lanier notes, 'the success of Amy Heckerling's *Clueless* (1995)', an adaptation of Jane Austen's *Emma*, may also have had a role in the film industry's eagerness to exploit the 'putative educational value' of 'film adaptation of Shakespeare' 'to turn classrooms into additional marketing venues' (2002, p. 163).

It is difficult to define the genre of the teen movie, since, as Wheeler Winston Dixon comments, 'all films of the late 1990s might well be considered "teen" films for purposes of marketing alone, if for no other reason' (2000, pp. 126–7). However, for the purpose of this chapter I consider as 'teen' movies those films that focus predominantly on teenage characters, and are rated as suitable for teenage viewers.

The first section of this chapter looks at teen adaptations of *A Midsummer Night's Dream (AMD)*, examining *Get Over It!* by R. Lee Fleming, Jr, and *Were the World Mine* by Tom Gustafson, exploring their treatment of the themes, plots and characters of *AMD*, and considering their appeal to teenagers. The motivation behind such adaptations is also examined – the extent to which the films seem designed to mediate teenagers' experience of Shakespeare's plays or exploit Shakespeare's status as a cultural icon in order to give a perceived artistic value to films otherwise barely distinguishable from the staple Hollywood romantic teen comedy.

The second section of the chapter examines the trend for animated adaptations of Shakespeare aimed at a family audience. Disney's *The Lion King* (dir. Rob Minkoff and Roger Allers, 1994) is possibly the most famous of these 'cartoon' Shakespeares with its skilful revision of the central familial relationships of *Hamlet*. Less well known is the film's sequel *The Lion King 2* (dir. Darrell Rooney, 1998) which reworks *Romeo and Juliet* with the protagonists recast as young lions seeking to reconcile the differences of their opposing prides. Part 2 of this chapter looks not only at this film but also at two further animations that reenvisage Shakespeare's famous tragic lovers as non-human figures – *Romeo and Juliet: Sealed with a Kiss* (dir. Phil Nibbelink, 2006) in which the protagonists are a pair of sea lion cubs, and *Gnomeo and Juliet* (dir. Kelly Asbury, 2011) in which the central pair are garden gnomes.

Teen *'Dreams'*

The appropriation of Shakespeare as a repository for the examination of teenage concerns and relationships stems not only from the increasing dominance of teenagers as the prime consumers of main-stream cinema, but also from what Klett describes as the 'intersections between the traditional teen film genre and the Shakespearean canon' (2008, p. 71) – in particular in the theme of adolescent romance. With its pairs of young lovers, transfers of affection and childish squabbling, *MND* seems particularly appropriate for transposition to a High School setting, and it is no surprise that it is on this central theme of young love, confused and resolved, as opposed to on the subplot of the mechanicals or the nuptials of Theseus and Hippolyta, that *Get Over It!* and *Were the World Mine* focus, the latter combining this with the magical elements of the play.

Both films revolve around high school musical productions of *MND*, providing an explicit link to Shakespeare's play from the outset. However, the staging of the play is not the prime concern of the films. Rather, in both, the lives of the protagonists begin to mirror the lives of Shakespeare's characters, helping them, and by extension the viewer, to see the relevance of the play to contemporary adolescence. In setting up the convention of life imitating art, both films make use of imaginative sequences in which the line between the films' characters and their theatrical counterparts becomes blurred and the notion of the 'dream' as a locus for secret desire is brought to the fore.

Although sharing the structural devices of the play in performance and the fantasy dream sequence, the two films differ significantly from one another, departing in different ways, from certain common conventions of the 'Shakespeare teenpix' as identified by Klett, with its 'ultimate focus . . . on the achievement of heterosexual coupling in the face of parental or social opposition' and a focus on a female protagonist (2008, p. 72). In the first place, both *Get Over It!* and *Were the World Mine* revolve around male protagonists, Berke and Timothy respectively, and in doing so perhaps encourage a greater interest from male adolescents in what is traditionally perceived as a feminine genre (Evans, 2009, p. 27). Secondly, while Timothy encounters both parental and social opposition to his sexuality, which his mother refers to as his 'problem' (Gustafson, 2008), Berke has a mother and father who comically reverse the convention of the opposing parents, actively encouraging him to hold parties in their house, offering him condoms, and congratulating him on being caught underage, in a compromising position, in a sex club. Finally, and most notably, Timothy seeks not a 'heterosexual coupling' but a homosexual one.

Were the World Mine stands out among the teen adaptations cited at the start of this chapter, in using Shakespeare's work to explore the issue of adolescent homosexuality. In a clever twist on *MND*, Timothy, an openly gay student, cast as Puck in a school production of the play, uses a love potion, akin to Shakespeare's 'love-in-idleness', to turn the whole of the town, including the object of his desire, Jonathon, gay. In setting up a scenario where all the members of the town, contrary to their previous prejudices, become attracted to members of the same sex, Gustafson uses Shakespeare's theme of magically manipulated sexual desire to normalize gay relationships and question the role of choice in sexual attraction. Although, as in *MND*, the love juice is eventually lifted from the eyes of those affected, the dream-like recollections of their experiences lead to understanding and acceptance of Timothy's sexuality, in the place of disgust and intolerance.

The film also employs a further device from *MND* to ensure that queerness does not appear merely aberrant in the vein of Titania's attraction to Bottom as an ass. Drawing on Shakespeare's retention of Demetrius under the power of magic at the end of *MND*, the film ends with Jonathon, though seemingly released with everyone else from the spell of the love juice, persisting in his attraction to Timothy. Unlike Demetrius, however, Jonathon's desire for Timothy is portrayed not as the continuing result of magic, but as enlightenment – a realization of his true sexuality which has been hinted at earlier in the film when he squeezes Timothy's bottom during a game of basketball. This admission by the rugby playing jock of his homosexuality not only provides the film with comedy's requisite 'happy ending', but also counters perceptions of homosexuals as necessarily effeminate, forcing both the pair's classmates, and by extension the viewer, to question their preconceptions.

MND is not the most obvious of Shakespeare's plays through which to bring out the theme of homoerotic desire – it being a more evident feature of plays like *As You Like It*, *Twelfth Night* and *The Merchant of Venice*. However, like the swift transfers of affection from one object of desire to another, and the (albeit temporary) same-sex attractions in *Twelfth Night* and *As You Like It*, the love juice plot of *MND* suggests that love is inherently unstable and changeable, and offers up the possibility that sexual attraction is not always straightforwardly homo- or heterosexual. Indeed, Ms. Tebbit reinforces this theme when defending Shakespeare against a parent's accusation that 'He was gay' (and thus by implication responsible for their son's conversion to homosexuality), responding, 'It has never been proved that Mr. William Shakespeare was homosexual – bisexual perhaps' (Gustafson, 2008), an assertion that also refutes the 'them and us' culture which exists through most of the film.

It is, of course, also the case that in the Elizabethan theatre, where all roles were played by boys or men, all of the onstage pairings in *MND* would have appeared as same-sex pairings. Gustafson uses his setting of the film in an all-boys school to re-rehearse the debate about the potential homoeroticism inherent in the practice of cross-dressing on the Renaissance stage.[1] While the school principal Dr Bellinger and Coach Driscoll raise anxieties about the feminizing effect on boys of playing female roles – 'We're concerned about the tradition; members of the rugby team portraying females' (Gustafson, 2008) – Ms. Tebbit, the play's director, invokes the argument, as set out by Ejner J. Jensen, of boys playing women as a straightforward 'convention' (1975, p. 7) – a practical necessity in a culture where 'women were prohibited by law to act' (Gustafson, 2008). Her comment serves a dual purpose – contributing to the viewer's understanding of the conventions of the Renaissance theatre, and reinforcing the notion of sexuality as something biologically determined as opposed to influenced by external factors like theatrical transvestism.

In addition, although *MND* is not explicitly connected to the theme of homosexual relationships, Andrew John Buzny, writing about *Were the World Mine*, expresses his surprise 'that it has taken this long for queers to draw on *Dream*'s themes and imagery' (2010, p. 25). Buzny cites, in particular, the line 'Love looks not with the eye, but with the mind' (1.1.234), which Ms. Tebbit quotes to her students in an early scene, a line which, like her dismissal of the potentially damaging influence of theatrical performance on the sexuality of the rugby team, 'illustrates a concern central to queer theory' (p. 25): sexual orientation not as a choice, but as biologically determined. The play also, as Buzny notes, throws up phrases commonly used as slang signifiers for homosexuals, most notably the term 'fairy', which Timothy's mother plays upon in revealing her son's sexuality to Mrs Boyd, the church administrator:

Mrs. Boyd:	We'd love to have you stay for bible study.
Donna:	I have wings to make.
Mrs. Boyd:	It's a potluck!
Donna:	No, for my son. He's a fairy.
Mrs. Boyd:	A fairy?
Donna:	In a play.
Mrs. Boyd:	(said with relief) Oh!
Donna:	Well, in real life, too. He's gay. My son is gay . . . Or queer. But the wings are for the play.
Mrs. Boyd:	A man shall not lie with man – (Gustafson, 2008)

Although Gustafson appears to exploit this terminology by having Timothy cast in the role of the fairy Puck, he in fact subverts it. In eliding Timothy's persona with that of a fairy, not by endowing him with the perceived negative quality of effeminacy but with the magical ability to transform others, the metaphor becomes one of empowerment rather than diminishment.

Were the World Mine not only draws on *MND*'s themes of desire, transformation and reveries but also on the play's plot, characterization and, at times, language. Although the characters are not explicitly linked to Shakespeare's by name, obvious connections emerge in their situations and behaviour. Timothy, for example, is elided not only with the figure of Puck, but also with Helena as the figure who suffers from unrequited love until the magical transformation of the object of her desire. Indeed, the film takes its title from Helena's lines – 'Were the world mine, Demetrius being bated, / The rest I'd give to be to you translated' (1.1.190–1) – which Timothy sings as he dreams of charming Jonathon into falling in love with him. By extension, Jonathon is allied to Demetrius, while Max might be compared to Lysander – magically and accidentally influenced into rejecting his girlfriend (Frankie) to fall in love with another (Timothy) before returning to his former love. Ms. Tebbit, meanwhile, acts as a beneficent Oberon figure, instigating the creation of the love juice by giving Timothy an enchanted copy of *MND*, overseeing the effects of the potion with detached amusement and, finally, curtailing Timothy's 'fun' by instructing him with an approximation of Oberon's lines from 3.3 (367–72):

Crush this herb into [Lysander's] the lovers' eyes;
. . .
When they next wake, all this derision
Shall seem a dream and fruitless vision. (Gustafson, 2008)

In addition to these character parallels, lines from *MND* are used throughout the film, not only in episodes in which the characters read or quote from the play, but in the dream-sequence songs (many of which use Shakespeare's dialogue in their lyrics) and notably in the scene that resembles Shakespeare's lover's quarrel in 3.2, pushing the confusion further than does Shakespeare by having a love sextet – Frankie loving Max, who loves Timothy, who shares a mutual love with Jonathan, whose girlfriend and her best friend have fallen for Frankie. As the confusion reaches its height, the characters quote loosely from *MND*. Timothy tells Max – 'You love Frankie, you know I know' (Gustafson, 2008) – a line similar to Lysander's line at 3.2.164, while Jonathon's girlfriend turns on Frankie with the words 'Who is this goddess, nymph, perfect, divine' (Gustafson, 2008), an echo of Demetrius' line to Helena (3.2.138). Although in the first sequence of the film one of the boys voices the common complaint about Shakespeare's difficulty – 'Four hundred years old, it doesn't make sense' (Gustafson, 2008) – these character parallels, thematic echoes and quotations show that not only does Shakespeare's work come to 'make sense' to the characters, but becomes intimately related to their own experiences and even a part of their dialogue.

A similar strategy of having characters voice their difficulty in comprehending Shakespeare's work only to find their own lives mirroring elements of the plot is evident in *Get Over It!*. Berke's initial response to *MND* is 'I'm understanding about every other word of this shit' (Fleming, Jr, 2001), and yet, a few minutes later he is envisaging himself in the role of Lysander. In his eagerness to see his own romantic struggles mirrored in those of Shakespeare's characters, however, Berke actually twists the events of the play, corrupting the lovers' story to fit his own. As Kelly begins to narrate the story – 'Now, Hermia has everything a girl could ask for – cool clothes, nice complexion, and the pick of almost any guy she wants. But of all the guys in the greater Athens area Hermia's heart belongs to the handsome young nobleman Lysander' (Fleming, Jr, 2001) – Berke imagines his girlfriend Allison as Hermia, walking towards him in the wood, and kissing him. However, Kelly continues:

> This would all be perfect if it weren't for Demetrius – Hermia's father already promised her hand to him and he's just as charming and handsome as Lysander – maybe even more so. Not to mention Demetrius will stop at nothing to make Hermia his bride. This pretty much leaves Lysander screwed. (Fleming, Jr., 2001)

During this narration, rather than indicating Hermia's mutual devotion to Lysander and reluctance to marry Demetrius, Berke's dream sequence shows Allison happily leaping onto the back of Striker's horse and charging off across the forest with him. Although the corruption of the lovers' story may stem partly from Kelly's failure to mention Hermia's opposition to her father's will, and her elopement with Lysander, it is mainly the result of Berke's own desire to see himself in the figure of Lysander. Eventually cast as Lysander in the school production, Berke's self-identification with the character continues, even though it becomes increasingly apparent that he is more closely allied with Demetrius – his love for Allison unrequited while Kelly clearly dotes on him. It is not until the film's final moments, during the performance of *A Midsummer Night's Rockin' Eve*, that Berke eventually recognizes Kelly's unrequited love for him, and, moving from Lysander's lines (4.1.143–50) to words the sentiments of which more closely mirror those of Demetrius (4.1.161–73), appears to make the transition from the former character to the latter:

> I came with Hermia hither: our intent
> Was to be gone from Athens, where we might,
> Without the peril of the Athenian law.
> Be wed.
> However. My lord, we slept and slept, as well you know,
> Things did change, as love did grow.
> Although, in ways, fair Hermia's soul and mine
> Shall forever intertwine,
> Alas we must forever part,
> For lo, to another belongs this heart. (Fleming, Jr., 2001)

This twisting of the plot of *MND* may be seen as confusing – a misrepresentation of the events and relationships of Shakespeare's play. However, it may equally be perceived as a comment on the nature of adolescent self-fashioning – the eagerness of adolescents to forge their identities in the image of others, and the constantly shifting nature of such identity construction. Thus Berke's change in self-identification may be seen to represent both a movement towards a fuller understanding of Shakespeare's play and a journey towards self-discovery.

Although Berke appears to gain a greater insight into Shakespeare's work as the film progresses, this insight is a rather superficial one – his failure to engage with Shakespeare's language made evident in his attempts to personate Lysander – 'Oh fair Hermia, thou art so incredibly hot and stuff' (Fleming, Jr, 2001). As Richard Burt notes, the film 'explicitly thematizes Shakespeare's incomprehensibility' (2002, p. 210). However, it does not appear to do so with the aim of making his work more comprehensible to an audience of young people, but rather by evading its complexities, and most particularly its language. The production that the students stage is itself an adaptation of *MND*, with Shakespeare's words mostly replaced by musical numbers, the first of which foregrounds the issue of unintelligibility:

> Did you ever read a Shakespeare play
> And never understand a word they say?

Well tonight we're going to make things clear.
'Cos Shakespeare's dead but we're all here (Fleming, Jr., 2001)

The audience appear wowed not by Shakespeare's lines or even by his story, but by Dennis's dance moves and Kelly's song, the only Shakespearean lyric of which comes not from *MND* but from *Hamlet* ('To sleep, perchance to dream' (3.1.67)).

The question then arises as to the function of adaptations such as *Were the World Mine* and *Get Over It!*. Ariane M. Balizet suggests that Shakespeare-based teen films have a dual purpose of 're-cognition' – using a contemporary setting as a means through which to '*know again*' the Shakespeare play, and 'recognition-as-familiar' – using a Shakespeare play as a lens through which to view 'contemporary concerns' (2004, p. 123). The first criteria is applicable to films such as Luhrmann's *Romeo and Juliet* and Almereyda's *Hamlet* in which, as explored in Chapter 2, elements of the plot, themes, characterization and dialogue are illuminated through their transferral to a setting recognizable to the modern viewer. In the case of *Were the World Mine* and *Get Over It!* the play of *MND* is too peripheral to be recognizable. Both function more obviously on the level of recognition-as-familiar, using elements of *MND* to explore issues of adolescent identity. However, this criterion of recognition-as-familiar assumes in the viewer a familiarity with Shakespeare's play, something which neither film seems to pre-suppose. While the echoing of lines from *MND* and the concept of the love juice in the form of a purple flower in *Were the World Mine* might be more fully appreciated by those acquainted with *MND*, few features of *Get Over It!* are dependent on, or indeed likely to be enhanced by, an audience's knowledge of the play.

The main function that the Shakespearean framework seems to serve is one of authorization – sanctioning the validity of the events depicted, and suggesting their widespread relevance. In the case of *Were the World Mine* the connection of the film to Shakespeare – a universal cultural icon – helps to turn what might otherwise be perceived as a cult 'gay' movie into a film with wider appeal. Although the film's greatest success was at gay and lesbian film festivals, its awards for 'Best Narrative Feature' at the Florida Film Festival and 'Grand Prize Best Feature' at the Rhode Island International Film Festival are testament to its appeal beyond the gay community. In the case of *Get Over It!* as Balizet suggests, 'Shakespeare' 'serves as a legitimizing agent on the fickle love affairs of high school students' (2004, p. 132). While Balizet's assertion that 'the authority of "Shakespeare" offers profundity to the protagonists' interactions' (p. 132) seems somewhat hyperbolic, the association of their actions with those of the characters in *MND* gives them a certain validity and appeal beyond that of most teen romantic comedies. While it is difficult to imagine that either film's association with Shakespeare gives it a valid place in the classroom, as suggested by Lanier, it is easy to imagine that parents might be more inclined to encourage their children to watch such films, and teachers to endorse them, on the basis of their, albeit often tenuous, connection to Shakespeare.

Romeo and Juliet the cartoon

Richard Finkelstein, writing in 1999, asserts that 'since the late 1980s, Disney has quietly absorbed Shakespeare into its family': through its Miramax division which distributed *Shakespeare in Love* and three films from Kenneth Branagh's 'Shakespeare Film Company'; in the form of allusions to Shakespeare in Disney films including *Aladdin* and *The Quest for Camelot*; and most notably in *The Lion King* and *The Little Mermaid* which 'not only make isolated allusions to Shakespeare, but also involve plot structures and characters that consistently borrow from his work' (p. 181). *The Lion King* is, as Finkelstein points out, an adaptation of both *Hamlet* and 'the prodigal son story from *1 Henry IV*' (p. 181), while *The Little Mermaid* is partly based on *The Tempest*. In 1998, Disney produced a sequel to *The Lion King – The Lion King 2* – also based on a Shakespeare play, in this case *Romeo and Juliet*. Disney's use of classical literature as a basis for its animations is not new, a number of its animated features having based on canonical novels, a factor which has, in Finkelstein's view, distinguished Disney's productions from those of other animation companies, providing its films with 'cultural capital' and a perceived educational value which has put its 'products in a position to win the approval of critics . . . and thus the tickets of upper-middle-class, educated parents' (pp. 181, 183).

Like *The Lion King*, *The Lion King 2* draws only loosely on Shakespeare, and does not make explicit its debt to his work. The only overt Shakespearean reference in the entire film is Zira's line to Simba – 'If you need your pound of flesh', a reference to *The Merchant of Venice* likely to be lost on a high proportion of the film's young audiences. However, the film clearly takes its inspiration from the central theme of *Romeo and Juliet* – the love of two youngsters from opposing families (or prides). Juliet finds her equivalent in the young female lion cub, Kiara, and Romeo in the young male lion cub, Kovu. Some parallels with other characters are evident – Kiara's father, Simba, resembles Lord Capulet in his overprotectiveness of his daughter and Rafiki, the Mandrill is a shaman, a religious leader, who, like Friar Laurence, encourages the two lovers in their relationship in the belief that it will lead to the reconciliation of the prides.

Of equal and perhaps even greater interest than the correspondences are the ways in which the film departs from Shakespeare's play, many of the differences seemingly motivated by the intended audience of contemporary youngsters. One of the main differences is the greater focus on the female characters, who take a similarly proactive role to the male figures. This alteration in the gender balance was a notable feature of the contemporary adaptations discussed in Chapters 7 and 8. Marsha M. Sprague and Kara K. Keeling assert that in YA literature such an alteration is a necessary reflection of changes in expectations about female behaviour and helps to make the heroine more relevant to girls in the twenty-first century.[2] Unlike Shakespeare's Juliet, Kiara does not spend most of the story confined to her home. Indeed, she begins the film by disobeying her father and venturing into the Outlands – the territory of Kovu and the Outsiders – thereby reversing the action of 1.5 *Romeo and Juliet* where Romeo enters the Capulet house in defiance of the interfamily feud. Later in the film, rather than feigning death in order to escape her parents' demands, Kiara again departs from her homeland, following Kovu into exile and then persuading him to return home with her to effect the reconciliation of their parents. The more proactive role played by Kiara is in keeping with the trend identified by Rebecca-Anne C. Do Rozario in the development of Disney 'princesses' (2004, p. 35). Although, as many critics have contended, even the later Disney heroines remain subject to the demands of patriarchy, Do Rozario argues that they take 'an active role' in its 'disruption' (p. 57) – often defying their fathers as opposed to conforming to the passivity of their earlier counterparts. Do Rozario also sees in these later heroines a greater tendency towards athleticism and an inclination to 'run wild' (p. 57), descriptions which also fit with the character of Kiara, most notably when she jumps between Zira and her father to prevent them from fighting. Kiara's intervention in the fight marks another point at which she fulfils an action similar to that of Romeo – in this case, Romeo's intrusion into the fight between Mercutio and Tybalt. However, while Romeo's intervention leads to the death of his friend Mercutio, Kiara's leads to the salvation of her father and the death of his foe, Zira. The female protagonist is thus shown not only to be capable of actions assigned by Shakespeare to the male protagonist, but to be more adept in their execution. The presence of a feistier heroine in Disney films of the late twentieth and early twenty-first centuries is undoubtedly partly designed to combat perceptions of Disney films as perpetrating negative images of women as 'domestic', 'helpless' and valued more for 'appearance . . . than . . . intellect' (Towbin et al., 2004, p. 30) and to provide a more positive role model for young girls whose 'imaginations, desires, roles, and dreams' are liable, Henry A. Giroux and Grace Pollock argue, to be provoked and informed by their viewing of the animations (2010, p. 98).

However, while Kiara may provide a positive role model for young girls, the characters of Zira and Vitani (Kovu's mother and sister) epitomize the Disney tendency towards if not deifying, then demonizing women. Zira is the film's chief antagonist, confronting Simba at the start of the film and then attempting to manipulate Kovu into taking revenge on the Pride Landers. In many respects, Zira takes on the persona of the wicked queen (or stepmother) – a common convention of the Disney film from *Snow White* (1937) to *Tangled* (2010). The demonization of Zira leads to a more straightforward battle between the forces of good and ill than is present in Shakespeare's play – a 'moral simplification' that A. Waller Hastings identifies in other of Disney's films based on classic stories (1993).

Unlike in *Romeo and Juliet*, where the Montagues and Capulets are presented as equally culpable for the feud, and equally capable of violent behaviour, in *The Lion King 2* the Outsiders – in particular Zira and Nuka – are depicted as straightforwardly evil, with glowing eyes and cackling voices, while the Pride Landers are portrayed as far more attractive – either gentle and wise (Simba and Nala), or funny (Timon and Pumba). This is, of course, partly because as a sequel to *The Lion King*, based on *Hamlet*, the Pride Landers are descended from Mufasa, the beneficent Old Hamlet figure and the Outsiders from Scar, the evil Claudius figure. However, it is also part of a trend identified by Waller Hastings in Disney animations, to 'present a Manichean world of moral absolutes in eternal warfare, from which . . . good always emerges triumphant' (1993, p. 85). Thus, unlike in *Romeo and Juliet*, where there are casualties on either side, the only figures to die in *The Lion King 2* are the 'evil' Zira and Kovu's villainous brother, Nuka. Although Kovu is an Outsider, initially involved in plotting against Simba, unlike Romeo, he switches allegiance before the commencement of the bloodshed, and unlike Romeo, who avenges the death of Mercutio by murdering Tybalt, Kovu does not seek vengeance for the death of his brother. As the young hero, he thus remains innocent of murder, again delineating clearly between the good and evil characters.

Herein lies another difference from *Romeo and Juliet*, and *After Juliet* (discussed in Chapter 8). While in both Shakespeare and MacDonald's plays the younger generation are the chief perpetrators of the violence, in *The Lion King 2*, the violence is mainly enacted by the older generation – Zira and, to a lesser extent, Simba, both of whom are intent on keeping the division between the prides alive. The reconciliation of the two prides is instigated not by the parental figures as a result of the deaths of their children, but by the younger generation who insist that the fighting must end. Thus, rather than using Shakespeare's play, as MacDonald does, to expose and interrogate the prevalence of gang violence among young people, this film shows the young protagonists as idealized figures, preaching the need for tolerance and forgiveness, and thus setting a positive example to the young viewers.

The greatest difference between *Romeo and Juliet* and *The Lion King 2* is, therefore, that the reconciliation of the families is brought about without the young protagonists taking their own lives. While Shakespeare's play ends in tragedy, *The Lion King 2* follows one of the structural assumptions of Disney films, that 'while a certain amount of violence and danger help to keep children interested in the plot, all threats must be successfully banished, leading to a joyful, happy ending' (Booker, 2010, p. 2). The need for a happy ending is a common assumption in relation to all children's literature, apparently motivated by adult perceptions of children as 'innocent by nature, emotionally weak, and easily affected and upset' (Yun, 2007, p. 86). It also informs all three of the animations discussed in this chapter – all of which conclude with the young protagonists alive, the families reconciled and a sense of optimism about the future.

In 2011, the Disney Corporation released another *Romeo and Juliet*-based animation – *Gnomeo and Juliet*, a CGI film set in a pair of adjoining gardens and featuring a cast of garden gnomes. However, despite being an animated feature with a 'R' (United States) or 'U' (United Kingdom) rating, this film was controversially dropped by the Disney label, and released around 10 years after its initial conception by Touchstone Pictures – the 'adult-oriented' (Wasko, 2001, p. 31) wing of the company. This decision to release the picture under the Touchstone label seems to suggest its perceived appeal to the adult market as well as to children, at whom it was originally aimed. Certainly a number of features of the film may be seen to appeal to adult audiences, not least the choice of Elton John's popular 1970s hits for the soundtrack, as opposed to an original score like that composed by John for *The Lion King*. The adult appeal may also stem from the film's explicit acknowledgement of its status as an adaptation of Shakespeare, unlike *The Lion King 2* which does not advertise its Shakespearean connection in its title. The Shakespearean connection helps to enhance the perceived cultural value of the film, and is likely not only to attract adult viewers with an interest in Shakespeare, but also parents who view the film as having some educational potential, and teenagers studying the play in school.

Gnomeo and Juliet not only makes explicit its debt to Shakespeare in its title, but throughout the film in a series of Shakespearean puns and allusions. In the opening sequence, for example, a gnome appears (in the form of a prologue) to speak to the audience:

> The story you are about to see has been told before . . . a lot. And now we are going to tell it again . . . but different. It's about two star-crossed lovers kept apart by a big feud. No one knows how this feud started, but it's all quite entertaining. Unfortunately, before we begin, there is rather a long boring prologue which I will read to you now.

He unrolls a huge scroll, and begins – 'Two households . . .' before hooks appear from the wings and attempt to pull him off stage and finally a trapdoor opens beneath his feet. Though undoubtedly appealing to children in its element of slapstick, this opening sequence has a more sophisticated purpose, not only making explicit the film's status as an irreverent take on Shakespeare's play, but also locating it within a long tradition of adaptations.

Like Luhrmann's film, *Gnomeo and Juliet* contains a number of self-reflexive visual references to Shakespeare. When we first see the two houses, for example, the Montague house has the number 2b, and the Capulet house a 2b with a cross through it, a witty visual pun on Hamlet's famous 3.1 soliloquy. In addition, the moving firm that takes Featherstone's fellow flamingo is called 'Rozencrantz and Guildenstern' (another reference to *Hamlet*), the teapot company that nearly runs Romeo down is called

'Tempest Teapots', the interior of Featherstone's shed contains a ticket stub for a production of *As You Like It* and the glue used to secure Juliet to her pedestal is labeled 'The Taming of the Glue'. There are also a series of verbal echoes of Shakespeare's play – Featherstone's 'A weed by any other name is still a weed', Gnomeo's 'Red, I hate the word', and Juliet's 'What's in a gnome?' These references, though rather less witty than Luhrmann's 'Out Damned Spot' cleaners, serve as what Anthony Banks (Chapter 8) describes as a 'bonus' for Shakespeare aficionados, locating the film within the tradition of animations with a dual appeal to both adults and children.[3]

Despite the nod towards an adult audience, however, the film abounds in elements that are clearly designed to appeal to young children. The attractive garden gnomes and their animal friends have an obvious allure, in particular Juliet, who, like Kiara, is a feisty, proactive female protagonist, equally as capable as Gnomeo of engaging in physical and verbal combat. The most obviously child-friendly aspects are the absence of swordplay and bloody deaths, cutting of the suicides of the protagonists, and alteration of Shakespeare's tragic ending to one of joy. The alterations made recall some of those levelled at Disney's manipulation of classic stories, including Waller Hastings's description of the 'moral simplification' of Hans Andersen's *The Little Mermaid* and other Disney films. Such simplification is particularly apparent in terms of the 'Manichean' division between good and bad (Waller Hastings, 1993, p. 90) present in *Gnomeo and Juliet*, as it was in *The Lion King 2*. In the opening 'battle' – in this case a lawnmower race in which Tybalt and Romeo compete for their respective houses – Tybalt engages in foul play and destroys the Montague lawnmower. Tybalt is thus established from the outset as the villain, and, as in *The Lion King 2*, only villains die, and die through their own stubbornness or stupidity. Tybalt is killed when, in a fight with Romeo, he fails to acknowledge Romeo's warning and crashes into the wall. Although this episode somewhat mirrors that of Shakespeare's 3.1, it is significant for the straightforward dichotomy between good and evil that Gnomeo is not seen as being to blame for Tybalt's death. Indeed, like Kiara in *The Lion King 2* who attempts to save Zira from falling to her death, Gnomeo attempts to save Tybalt – 'Tybalt, the wall!'. It is also significant that unlike in *Romeo and Juliet* where Mercutio is 'hurt under [Romeo's] arm' (3.1.103), in *Gnomeo and Juliet* there is no Mercutio character and Gnomeo is not culpable for the deaths of any of his friends. None of the Montagues are killed and Gnomeo seeks vengeance not 'for Mercutio's soul' (*Rom.* 3.1.126) but for the slicing off of Benny's hat with a trowel ('a hat for a hat'). Thus, Tybalt is the only character to die, and, even then, he appears in the film's final dance number, as if miraculously resurrected (or reconstructed), contributing to the film's happy ending.

The film's happy ending has encountered criticism, with Stephen Holden in the *New York Times* remarking that 'fiddling with the ending to make it a brighter family-friendly lark has its costs' (2011) while Mike Leader comments – 'to commit to tragedy would be to aspire to a higher ideology – of fate, of romance, of poetry, whereas *Gnomeo and Juliet* prefers to be predictable' (2011). However, while the devastating consequences of prejudice and hatred, and hence the 'moral intention' of the original, are lost along with the potential for tragic catharsis, *Gnomeo and Juliet* explicitly acknowledges its alteration of its source's ending, playing with the notion of dramatic irony to create complicity with the viewer familiar with both Shakespeare's tale and the convention of the happy ending in children's animations. In the most obviously self-reflexive and metadramatic episode in the film, Shakespeare himself appears as a talking statue (played in another 'in-joke' by well-known Shakespearean actor Patrick Stewart) who comments with surprise on the similarities between Gnomeo's tale and that of his own tragedy and predicts that all will end in disaster. Thus, Gnomeo's comment at the end of the film – 'I think this ending is much better' – is not only the triumphant cry of a character who has escaped their apparently predetermined tragic destiny, but also an ironic comment on the film's manipulation of genre.

A similar effort to create a dual appeal to children and adults by balancing sentimentality and parody is evident in Phil Nibbelink's *Romeo and Juliet: Sealed with a Kiss*. The film starts with a more serious prologue than *Gnomeo and Juliet*, apparently setting it up as an earnest adaptation of the story, and in some respects *Sealed with a Kiss* does seem to take its status as an adaptation quite seriously, closely following the plot of *Romeo and Juliet* and including a number of apparently sincere verbal echoes of the play, in particular in the equivalent of the balcony scene (2.1) which includes a close approximation of Shakespeare's lines:

Juliet   Who's there?
Romeo   I don't know how to tell you who I am my love, because my name and my colour are your enemy.
Juliet   My ears haven't heard you bark a hundred words and yet I recognize the sound of your sweet voice. (Nibbelink, 2006)

However, it also includes a number of Shakespearean allusions that suggest a degree of irony in Nibbelink's approach. The main source of Shakespearean puns in the film is Mercutio – an overtly comic character with a broad Bronx accent, whose speech is peppered with archaisms and who plays on lines from *Romeo and Juliet* and from other of Shakespeare's plays. When Romeo, for example, keen to enter the Capulet party cries 'Let's party', Mercutio responds in a travesty of one of Juliet's lines – 'Partying is such sweet sorrow' (Nibbelink, 2006). Mercutio seems, in particular, to self-consciously and satirically ally himself with Hamlet, quoting (or misquoting) lines from Hamlet's soliloquies in a melodramatic fashion – 'O Benvolio, I knew him well'; 'To be, or not to be, that is the question' and, when returning, apparently from death, to discover the other seals gathered at what he believes to be a party, 'Ah. To suffer the slings and arrows of outrageous . . .' (Nibbelink, 2006). As in *Gnomeo and Juliet*, these playful intertextual references are evidently intended to appeal to viewers familiar with Shakespeare's dramatic works – most obviously to adults viewing the film alongside children. However, the character of Mercutio has a simultaneous appeal for young children, with his slapstick physical comedy and his repertoire of ridiculous anti-Capulet jokes – 'What do you have when a Capulet is buried up to his neck in sand? . . . Not enough sand'; 'What do you call five hundred dead Capulets at the bottom of the ocean? . . . A good start' (Nibbelink, 2006).

Similar to *Gnomeo and Juliet* a number of elements of the film are clearly designed with a young audience in mind. The characters are correspondingly attractive, either in their cuteness (the huge-eyed seal-pup protagonists, who look far too young to be married) or their comic foulness (the elephant seal Prince who emits toxic green burps) and, as in *Gnomeo and Juliet* where the Montagues are blue gnomes and the Capulets red, the two 'families' are distinguished by colour – the Montagues brown sea lions and the Capulets white – a straightforward semiotic that makes apparent the allegiances of the various characters. Also like *Gnomeo and Juliet*, the film contains appealing songs, some childish humour and ubiquitous cartoon chase sequences. The most extensive of these chase sequences – in which the sea-otter Friar is pursued by the Shark – comes at the point when Romeo is about to encounter the apparently dead Juliet, diffusing the dramatic tension of his discovery, and delaying the climax. As if anticipating adult frustration at this essentially pointless episode Nibbelink includes a self-conscious comment from Friar Lawrence – 'Is this what we really need, another shark chase?' This comment, like that of Gnomeo on the ending of *Gnomeo and Juliet*, allows an adult audience to become complicit acknowledging the child-oriented aspects of the film, involving rather than alienating them.

Unlike *The Lion King 2* and *Gnomeo and Juliet* in which at least one character dies, the happy ending of *Sealed with a Kiss* is brought about without any deaths. Even Mercutio, who appears to fall to his death, is miraculously revealed in the film's final moments to have survived. The film's ending follows quite closely the plot of Shakespeare's *Romeo and Juliet*, more so than either of the other animations – Juliet feigns death in order to escape her marriage to the Prince (who in the animation also serves the function of Paris, and to an extent Tybalt), taking a sleeping draught given to her by the Friar; the Friar (doubling the function of Friar Laurence and Friar John) arrives too late to tell Romeo of their plan; and Romeo rushes, distraught to Juliet's tomb. However, unlike in Shakespeare's play where Romeo, believing his lover to be deceased, poisons himself, in *Sealed with a Kiss*, as he kisses her apparently lifeless body, he ingests some of the sleeping draught, making him too seem dead. Thus, the *apparent* death of both protagonists is achieved with the audience remaining fully aware that both are in fact alive. This allows for a similar moment to that at the end of *Romeo and Juliet*, where the two families come together to lament their loss, regret their fighting and forge a reconciliation. However, it subsequently allows for the reawakening and reunion of the two young protagonists, and an ending in which the two families of seals dance happily together and even the foul Prince succeeds in finding an equally foul elephant seal bride.

The notion of retelling the story of Shakespeare's most romantic tragedy in the form of a whimsical comedy about garden gnomes seems at first bizarre and even foolhardy. However, the success of *Gnomeo and Juliet* – grossing $189,967,670 worldwide (Box Office Mojo, 2011) – bears testament to its public appeal, despite some rather negative critical responses which bemoaned the film's 'hackneyed' (Leader, 2011) and 'discombobulated grab bag' of jokes (Holden, 2011). The audiences for *The Lion King 2* and *Sealed with a Kiss* were far smaller, the former being released only on Video/DVD, and the latter playing to only 27 screens in the United States at its widest release (Box Office Mojo, n.d.). Both films also received little critical attention, although *Sealed with a Kiss* encountered severe criticism from *Los Angeles Times* critic Sam Adams, who described it as 'a genuine tragedy', 'an unending torture, 77 minutes that feel longer than an uncut *Hamlet*', criticizing it for its 'nearly unintelligible dialogue' and its appropriation of 'racist jokes', which in Adams' view rendered the film 'suitable for no one' with its only educative function being to teach 'children a long list of schoolyard taunts' (2006). This onslaught from Adams may appear vitriolic, but it makes clear the dangers inherent in creating an animation that seeks to appeal to both children and adults and ultimately appeals to neither.

And so we return to the questions asked of *Get Over It!* and *Were the World Mine:* what is the function of these Shakespearean adaptations and do they have the potential to serve an educational purpose? If we revert to Balizet's categories of recognition and recognition as familiar, these are less easy to justify in relation to the animations. In none of these cases can the viewer be said to '*know again*' the Shakespeare play, and it is difficult to see what 'contemporary concerns' are illuminated as a result of the animations' Shakespearean connections. It may be true that the story of *Romeo and Juliet* provides a moral framework of acceptance and forgiveness; however, these concepts are by no means exclusive to Shakespeare's tragedy, and the fact that all three animations feel the need to manipulate the events of the play in order to provide a happy ending for their young viewers suggests that the story is not perhaps the most appropriate conduit for these messages of tolerance and understanding.

Again, a prime function of the Shakespearean connection seems to be, as Finkelstein suggests in relation to Disney's use of 'high art', one of 'cultural capital' – an effort to raise the artistic status of the animations by linking them with a canonical literary text. In the case of *Gnomeo and Juliet* and *Sealed with a Kiss* there also seems to be a certain pleasure on the part of the filmmaker in parodying classical literature in order to generate a degree of adult comedy.

In addition to proving satisfying to 'the Shakespeare fans out there' (Asbury), the identification of verbal and visual references to *Romeo and*

Juliet and other of Shakespeare's plays in the animations might form the
basis of some educational exercises, stimulating discussions on the themes,
characters and genre and the notions of parody, literary allusion and
adaptation. Teacher Rosemarie Gavin explains how she fruitfully used
The Lion King alongside *Hamlet* to encourage discussion of 'characters,
conflicts, themes, and ending scenes' and to consider the concept of the
'archetype' of the 'exiled child' (1996, p. 55). These films might equally be
used to explore archetypes such as the star-crossed lovers, love at first sight
and loss of innocence. Study notes produced by Film Education as part of
National Schools Film Week also suggest ways in which *Gnomeo and Juliet*
might be used in the classroom as early as Key Stage 1 and 2 (prior to pupils
having studied *Romeo and Juliet*) in 'History, Literacy, Numeracy and DT'
(Poyton, 2011, p. 1). Although partially geared to a study of gardening and
gnomes, these study notes encourage the use of the animation as inspiration
for research into Shakespeare: his life and work, use of the oxymoron as
illustrated in Juliet's line 'Parting is such sweet sorrow' and a consideration
of Comedy, Tragedy and History in relation to the film's source play (p. 2).
It may be difficult to imagine children at Key Stage 1 discussing dramatic
genres or having any interest in researching the life and times of a writer
with whose plays they are unfamiliar; however, it is possible to see how an
awareness among children that what they are watching is an adaptation
(albeit a lose one) of a story by William Shakespeare may help to inspire a
greater enthusiasm for, and interest in his drama when they do eventually
encounter it.

Notes

1 Lisa Jardine (1983) cites the beliefs of Dr John Rainoldes and other Renaissance
   anti-theatricalists that men dressing as women on stage would lead to sexual
   perversion and encourage homosexuality (pp. 9, 17).
2 See discussion in Chapter 7.
3 See Chris Hildrew (2007) – a study of modality, address, reading and response
   in contemporary children's film'.

Web resources

McAvoy, James (2011), 'Interview: James McAvoy Talks "Gnomeo and Juliet" &
   Animated Filmmaking'. *Screenrant*:
   http://screenrant.com/james-mcavoy-gnomeo-juliet-interview-rothc-101237/
Poyton, Matthew (2011), 'Gnomeo and Juliet: Study Notes'. *Film Education*.
   www.filmeducation.org/pdf/resources/primary/Gnomeo%20&%20
   Juliet%282%29.pdf

BIBLIOGRAPHY

Films

Almereyda, Michael, dir. (2000), *Hamlet* [DVD]. USA: Miramax/Buena Vista Entertainment.

Asbury, Kelly, dir. (2011), *Gnomeo and Juliet* [DVD]. USA: Rocket Pictures/ Touchstone Pictures.

Edzard, Christine, dir. (2001), *The Children's Midsummer Night's Dream* [DVD]. UK: Sands Films.

Fickman, Andy, dir. (2006), *She's the Man*. USA: Dreamworks.

Fleming Jr., R. Lee, writer (2001), *Get Over It!* [DVD]. USA: Miramax.

Gosnell, Raja, dir. (1999), *Never Been Kissed*. USA: Fox 2000.

Gottlieb, Lisa, dir. (1985), *Just One of the Guys*. USA: Columbia Pictures.

Gustafson, Tom, dir. (2008), *Were the World Mine* [DVD]. USA: Speakproductions.

Heckerling, Amy, dir. (1995), *Clueless*. USA: Paramount.

Junger, Gil, dir. (1999), *10 Things I Hate About You*. USA: Jaret/Mad Chance/ Touchstone.

Luhrmann, Baz, dir. (1996), *William Shakespeare's Romeo + Juliet* [DVD]. USA: Twentieth Century Fox.

Minkoff, Rob and Allers, Roger dirs. (1994), *The Lion King*. USA: Disney.

Moorhouse, Jocelyn, dir. (1997), *A Thousand Acres*. USA: Touchstone Pictures.

Morrissette, Billy, dir. (2001), *Scotland Pa*. USA: Lot 49 Films.

Nelson, Tim Blake, dir. (2001), *'O'*. USA: Lions Gate.

Nibbelink, Phil, dir. (2006), *Romeo and Juliet: Sealed with a Kiss* [DVD]. Phil Nibbelink productions.

O'Haver, Tommy, dir. (2001), *Get Over It!* [DVD]. USA: Miramax.

Ortega, Kenny, dir. (2006), *High School Musical*. USA: Disney.

Polanski, Roman, dir. (1971), *Macbeth* [DVD]. USA: Columbia Pictures.

Pool, Léa, dir. (2001), *Lost and Delirious*. USA: Lions Gate.

Rooney, Darrell, dir. (1998), *The Lion King 2*. USA: Disney.

Van Sant, Gus, dir. (1991), *My Own Private Idaho*. USA: New Line.

Waters, Daniel, dir. (2001), *Happy Campers*. USA: DiNovi Pictures.

Television

Anderson, Mike B., dir. (2002), *The Simpsons,* 'Tales from the Public Domain'. [TV]. Twentieth Century Fox.

Baeza, Carlos, dir. (1992), *The Simpsons,* 'Treehouse of Horror III'. [TV]. Twentieth Century Fox.

Gamburg, Effim, dir. (1992), *Romeo and Juliet: Shakespeare: The Animated Tales*. [DVD]. USSR/UK/Wales: Shakespeare Animated Films Ltd./Christmas Films/Soyuzmultfilm.

Karayev, Alexei, dir. (1994), *As You Like It: Shakespeare: The Animated Tales*. [DVD]. Russia/UK/Wales. Christmas Films/S4C.

Kulakov, Yuri, dir. (1994), *Julius Caesar: Shakespeare: The Animated Tales*. [DVD]. Russia/UK/Wales. Christmas Films/S4C.

Muat, Mariya, dir. (1992), *Twelfth Night: Shakespeare: The Animated Tales*. [DVD]. USSR/UK/Wales: Shakespeare Animated Films Ltd./Christmas Films/Soyuzmultfilm.

Orlova, Natalie, dir. (1992), *Hamlet: Shakespeare: The Animated Tales*. [DVD]. USSR/UK/Wales: Shakespeare Animated Films Ltd./Christmas Films/Soyuzmultfilm.

— (1994), *Richard III: Shakespeare: The Animated Tales*. [DVD]. Russia/UK/Wales. Christmas Films/S4C.

Oswald, Gerd, dir. (1966), *Star Trek*, 'The Conscience of the King'. [TV]. US: Desilu Productions/Norway Corporation.

Palmer, Charles, dir. (2007), *Doctor Who*, 'The Shakespeare Code'. [TV]. BBC Wales.

Persi, Raymond S., dir. (2009), *The Simpsons,* 'Four Great Women and a Manicure'. [TV]. Twentieth Century Fox.

Sahakyants, Robert, dir. (1992), *A Midsummer Night's Dream: Shakespeare: The Animated Tales*. [DVD]. USSR/UK/Wales: Shakespeare Animated Films Ltd./Christmas Films/Soyuzmultfilm.

Serebryakov, Nikolai, dir. (1992), *Macbeth: Shakespeare: The Animated Tales*. [DVD]. USSR/UK/Wales: Shakespeare Animated Films Ltd./Christmas Films/Soyuzmultfilm.

— (1994), *Othello: Shakespeare: The Animated Tales*. [DVD]. Russia/UK/Wales: Christmas Films/S4C.

Sokolov, Stanislav, dir. (1992), *The Tempest: Shakespeare: The Animated Tales*. [DVD]. USSR/UK/Wales: Shakespeare Animated Films Ltd./Christmas Films/Soyuzmultfilm.

— (1994), *The Winter's Tale: Shakespeare: The Animated Tales*. [DVD]. Russia/UK/Wales: Christmas Films/S4C.

Ziablikova, Aida, dir. (1994), *The Taming of the Shrew: Shakespeare: The Animated Tales*. [DVD]. Russia/UK/Wales: Christmas Films/S4C.

Theatre productions

The Comedy of Errors (2009 and 2010), by William Shakespeare. [Performance] RSC. Dir. Paul Hunter.

The Eternal Not (2009), by Lucinda Coxon. [Performance] National Theatre. Dir. Anthony Banks.

FairyMonsterGhost (2011), by Tim Crouch. [Performance] Bristol Old Vic Theatre and Company of Angels. Dir. John Retallack.

Hamlet (2010), by William Shakespeare. [Performance] RSC. Dir. Tarell Alvin McCraney.

I, Malvolio (2011), by Tim Crouch. [Performance] RSC. Dir. Tim Crouch.

I, Peaseblossom (2011), by Tim Crouch. [Performance] RSC. Dir. Tim Crouch.

Macbeth (2009), by William Shakespeare, adapted by Carl Heap. [Performance] National Theatre. Dir. Carl Heap.

Macbeth (2010), by William Shakespeare. [Performance] Shakespeare's Globe. Dir. Bill Buckhurst.

Macbeth (2011), by William Shakespeare. [Performance] Shakespeare's Globe. Dir. Bill Buckhurst.

Macbeth: Reimagined for Everyone Aged Six and Over (2010), by William Shakespeare. [Performance] Regent's Park Open Air Theatre. Dir. Steve Marmion.

The Magician's Daughter (2011), by Michael Rosen. [Performance] Little Angel Theatre Company in association with the RSC. Dir. Peter Glanville.

A Midsummer Night's Dream (2008), by William Shakespeare, adapted by Carl Heap. [Performance] National Theatre. Dir. Carl Heap.

A Midsummer Night's Dream: Reimagined for Everyone Aged Six and Over (2008), by William Shakespeare. [Performance] Regent's Park Open Air Theatre. Dir. Dominic Leclerc.

A Midsummer Night's Dream (2011), by William Shakespeare, adapted by Christopher Geelan. [Performance] 17 January 2011, Bush Hill Park Primary School. Dir. Christopher Geelan.

Much Ado About Nothing (2007), by William Shakespeare. [Performance] Shakespeare's Globe. Dir. Jo Howarth.

Much Ado About Nothing (2008), by William Shakespeare. [Performance] Shakespeare's Globe. Dir. Jo Howarth.

Pericles (2006), by William Shakespeare, adapted by Carl Heap. [Performance] National Theatre. Dir. Carl Heap.

Pericles: Reimagined for Everyone Aged Six and Over (2011), by William Shakespeare. [Performance] Regent's Park Open Air Theatre. Dir. Natalie Abrahami.

Pocket Dream (2011), by William Shakespeare, adapted by Propeller. [Performance] 30 April 2011. Dir. Edward Hall.

Prince of Denmark (2010), by Michael Lesslie. [Performance] National Theatre: Cottesloe. Dir. Anthony Banks.

Romeo and Juliet (2007), by William Shakespeare, adapted by Carl Heap. [Performance] National Theatre. Dir. Carl Heap.

— (2009), by William Shakespeare. [Performance] Shakespeare's Globe. Dir. Bill Buckhurst.

Such Tweet Sorrow (2010), Royal Shakespeare Company and Mudlark. [Performance] RSC. Dir. Roxanne Silbert.

The Taming of the Shrew (2011), by William Shakespeare. [Performance] RSC. Dir. Tim Crouch.

The Tempest: Reimagined for Everyone Aged Six and Over (2009), by William Shakespeare. [Performance] Regent's Park Open Air Theatre. Dir. Liam Steel.

Twelfth Night (2010), by William Shakespeare, adapted by Carl Heap. [Performance] National Theatre. Dir. Carl Heap.

Books, articles and interviews

Adams, Sam (2006), 'Romeo and Juliet: Sealed with a Kiss'. *Los Angeles Times* [Online] 27 October. Available at: www.calendarlive.com/printedition/calendar/cl-et-romeo27oct27,0,5475419.story [Accessed 18 September 2011].

Almereyda, Michael (2000), *William Shakespeare's Hamlet*. London: Faber and Faber.

Alsup, Janet (2010), *Young Adult Literature and Adolescent Identity Across Cultures and Classrooms*. Oxford: Routledge

Anderegg, Michael (2003), 'James Dean Meets the Pirate's Daughter: Passion and Parody in William Shakespeare's Romeo + Juliet and Shakespeare in Love' in Richard Burt and Lynda E. Boose (eds), *Shakespeare, the Movie II: Popularising the Plays on Film, TV, Video and DVD*. London: Routledge, pp. 56–71.

Appignanesi, Richard (adpt.), Deas, Robert (ill.) (2008), *Manga Shakespeare: Macbeth*. London: SelfMadeHero.

AQA and Nelson, Thornes (2010), 'Overview of Syllabus'. *AQA* [Online]. Available at: http://store.aqa.org.uk/resourceZone/pdf/english/AQA-4710-W-TRB-U1-OVERVIEW-OF-SYLLABUS.PDF [Accessed 9 June 2011].

Arizpe, Evelyn, Styles, Morag and Rokison, Abigail (2010), 'Discontinuous Knowledges: Some Neglected Dimensions of Children's Literature' in David Rudd (ed.), *The Routledge Handbook of Children's Literature*. London: Routledge.

Arts Council (2009), 'Hip Hop Shakespeare Company'. *Arts Council England* [Online]. Available at: www.artscouncil.org.uk/our-work/hip-hop-shakespeare-company/ [Accessed 19 October 2011].

Atwood, Margaret (1992), 'Gertrude Talks Back' in Margaret Atwood, *Good Bones*. Toronto: Coach House Press.

Aughterson, Kate (1995), *Renaissance Woman: A Sourcebook: Constructions of Femininity in England*. London: Routledge.

Babula, William (1977), 'The Character and the Conclusion: Bertram and the Ending of *"All's Well that Ends Well"'*. *South Atlantic Bulletin*, 42:2, 94–100.

Balizet, Ariane M. (2004), 'Teen Scenes: Recognizing Shakespeare in Teen Film' in James R. Keller and Leslie Stratyner (eds), *Almost Shakespeare: Reinventing His Works for Cinema and Television*. London: McFarland, pp. 122–36.

Banks, Anthony (2011), *Interview*. By Abigail Rokison, 28 February, National Theatre, London.

Banks, Fiona (2008a), 'The Best Possible Shakespeare: Playing Shakespeare at Shakespeare's Globe'. *English Drama Media*, 10, 15–16.

— (2008b), 'Learning with the Globe' in Christie Carson and Farah Karim-Cooper (eds), *Shakespeare's Globe*. Cambridge: Cambridge University Press, pp. 155–65.

Barber, B. L. (2006), 'To Have Loved and Lost . . . Adolescent Romantic Relationships and Rejection' in A. C. Crouter and A. Booth (eds), *Romance and Sex in Adolescence and Emerging Adulthood: Risks and Opportunities*. Mahwah, NJ: Lawrence Erlbaum Associates, pp. 29–40

Barnes and Noble (n.d.), *'No Fear Shakespeare Graphic Novels: Macbeth'* [Online]. Available at: http://search.barnesandnoble.com/Macbeth/SparkNotes-Editors/e/9781411498716/?itm=2&USRI=no+fear+macbeth [Accessed 9 June 2011].

Barone, Diane M. (2010), *Children's Literature in the Classroom: Engaging Lifelong Readers*. New York: Guilford Press.

Bartels, Emily C. (1994), 'Breaking the Illusion of Being: Shakespeare and the Performance of Self'. *Theatre Journal*, 46:2, 171–85

Barton, Chris (2009), Email message to the author. 13 March.

Bate, Jonathan and Rasmussen, Eric (eds) (2007), *Complete Works: The RSC Shakespeare*. Basingstoke: Macmillan.

Beckerman, Bernard (1962), *Shakespeare at the Globe, 1599–1609*. New York: Macmillan.

Billington, Michael (2010), 'Hamlet'. *Guardian* [Online] 22 January. Available at: www.guardian.co.uk/stage/2010/jan/22/hamlet-review [Accessed 12 June 2011].

Birch, Beverley (1997), *Shakespeare's Stories* (ill. James Mayhew). Hove: MacDonald Young Books.

— (2002), *Shakespeare's Tales* (ill. Stephen Lambert). London: Hodder Children's.

Blackwood, Gary (1998), *The Shakespeare Stealer*. New York: Penguin.

— (2000), *Shakespeare's Scribe*. New York: Penguin.

— (2003), *Shakespeare's Spy*. New York: Penguin.

Blau, Rosie (2007), 'The New Prints of Denmark'. *Financial Times* [Online] 23 February. Available at: www.ft.com/cms/s/2/e55f3c96-bfeb-11db-995a-000b5df10621.html#axzz1MQIFA6XW [Accessed 9 June 2011].

Bloom, Harold (2005), *Bloom's Guides: William Shakespeare's Romeo and Juliet*. Philadelphia: Chelsea House.

— (2010), *All's Well That Ends Well: Bloom's Shakespeare through the* Ages. Paul Gleed (ed.). New York: Infobase.

Booker, Keith M. (2010), *Disney, Pixar, and the Hidden Messages of Children's Films*. Santa Barbara: Praeger.

Bottoms, Janet (1999), 'Familiar Shakespeare' in Eve Bearne and Victor Watson (eds), *Where Texts and Children Meet*. London: Routledge, pp. 11–25.

— (2001), 'Speech, Image, Action: Animating Tales from Shakespeare'. *Children's Literature in Education*, 32, 3–15.

Box Office Mojo (2011), 'Gnomeo and Juliet'. *Box Office Mojo* [Online]. Available at: http://boxofficemojo.com/movies/?id=gnomeoandjuliet.htm [Accessed 18 September 2011].

— (n.d.), 'Romeo and Juliet: Sealed with a Kiss'. *Box Office Mojo* [Online]. Available at: http://boxofficemojo.com/movies/?id=sealedwithakiss.htm [Accessed 18 September 2011].

Bradley, Lynette and Bryant, Peter (1991), 'Phonological Skills Before and After Learning to Read' in Susan A. Brady and Donald Shankweiler (eds), *Phonological Processes in Literacy*. Hillsdale, NJ: Erlbaum Associates, pp. 37–45.

Branagh, Kenneth (1996), *Hamlet: Screenplay, Introduction and Film Diary*. London: W. W. Norton.

Brenner, Robin E. (2007), *Understanding Manga and Anime*. Westport, CT: Libraries Unlimited.

Brooke, Arthur (1562), *The Tragical History of Romeus and Juliet*. London.

Brooke, Nicholas (ed.) (1998), William Shakespeare, *Macbeth*. Oxford: Oxford University Press.

Bruckner, Christine (1992), *Desdemona, If Only You Had Spoken!* (trans. Eleanor Bron). London: Virago.

Bryant, Clive (2011), Private conversation with Abigail Rokison. May 2011.

Buchanan, Judith (2005), *Shakespeare on Film*. Harlow: Longman.

Buckhurst, Bill (2010a), *Interview*. By Abigail Rokison, 17 November 2010.

Buckhurst, Bill and Layton, Russell (2010), 'Porter's Speech' in *Macbeth*. Globe Education. Unpublished.

Buckman, Irene (1963), *Twenty Tales from Shakespeare*. London: F. E. Bording.

Bulman, James C. (1984), 'The BBC Shakespeare and "House Style"'. *Shakespeare Quarterly*, 35:5, 571–81.

Burdett, Lois (1994), *Shakespeare Can Be Fun!: Twelfth Night*. New York: Firefly.

— (1999), *Shakespeare Can Be Fun!: The Tempest*. New York: Firefly.

— (2000), *Shakespeare Can Be Fun!: Hamlet*. New York: Firefly.

— (2002), 'All the Colours of the Wind' in Naomi J. Miller (ed.), *Reimagining Shakespeare for Children and Young Adults*. London: Routledge, pp. 44–55.

Burrell, Ian (2000), 'Violence among Teenage Girls Is an "Everyday" Event, Study Reveals'. *Independent* [Online] 2 October. Available at: www. independent.co.uk/news/uk/home-news/violence-among-teenage-girls-is-an-everyday-event-study-reveals-634524.html [Accessed 2 April 2011].

Burt, Richard (2002), 'Slammin' Shakespeare in Acc(id)ents Yet Unknown: Liveness, Cinem(edi)a, and Racial Dis-integration'. *Shakespeare Quarterly*, 53, 201–26.

Burton Raffel (1996), 'Who Hear Rhymes, and How: Shakespeare's Dramaturgical Signals'. *Oral Tradition*, 11:2, 190–221.

Buzny, Andrew John (2010), *Queer Alchemy: Fabulousness in Gay Male Literature and Film*. Unpublished dissertation [Online] August 2010. Available at: http://digitalcommons.mcmaster.ca/opendissertations/4485/ [Accessed 18 September 2011].

Cadden, Mike (2010), 'Genre as Nexus: The Novel for Children and Young Adults' in Shelby Anne Wolf, Karen Coats and Christine A. Jenkins (eds), *Handbook of Research on Children's and Young Adult Literature*. Oxford: Taylor and Francis, pp. 302–12.

Can of Worms (n.d.), 'Can of Worms Press' [Online]. Available at: www. canofwormspress.co.uk/cartoonshakespeare1.html [Accessed 11 June 2011].

Carroll, Tim (2008), 'Practising Behaviour to His Own Shadow' in Christie Carson and Farah Karim-Cooper (eds), *Shakespeare's Globe*. Cambridge: Cambridge University Press, pp. 37–44.

Carter, Thomas (1910), *Stories from Shakespeare* (ill. Gertrude Demain Hammond). London: G. G. Harrap.

— (1912), *Shakespeare's Stories of the English Kings* (ill. Gertrude Demain Hammond). London: G. G. Harrap.

Cartmell, Deborah (2000), *Interpreting Shakespeare on Screen*. Basingstoke: Macmillan.

— (2004), 'Fin de Siecle Film Adaptations of Shakespeare' in Eckart Voigts-Virchow (ed.), *Janespotting and Beyond*. Tubingen: Narr.

Cartwright, Kent (1991), *Shakespearean Tragedy and Its Double: The Rhythms of Audience Response*. University Park, PA: Pennsylvania State University Press.

Catty, Emma (2008), 'A Midsummer Night's Dream'. MusicOMH [Online]. Available at: www.musicomh.com/theatre/midsummer_0708.htm [Accessed 12 June 2011].

Ceesay, Babou, Leigh, Vince and Williams, Tam (2011), *Interview*. By Abigail Rokison, 17 November 2010.

Chambers, Colin (2004), *Inside the Royal Shakespeare Company: Creativity and the Institution*. London: Routledge.

Chapman, Diane L. (2005), 'Mystery and Detective Stories' in Bernice E. Cullinan and Diane Goetz Person, *The Continuum Encyclopedia of Children's Literature*. London: Continuum, pp. 572–4

Chenery, Julian and Gimblett, Matt (2007), 'Tryzone: *Hamlet*' [Online]. Available at: www.shakespeare4kidz.com/tryzone-s4k-hamlet.html [Accessed 12 June 2011].

— (1997–2011a), 'Welcome'. *Shakespeare 4 Kidz* [Online]. Available at: www.shakespeare4kidz.com/welcome/welcome-2.html [Accessed 12 June 2011].

— (1997–2011b), 'Why "Shakespeare 4 Kidz"?' *Shakespeare 4 Kidz* [Online]. Available at: www.shakespeare4kidz.com/welcome/why-shakespeare-4-kidz.html [Accessed 12 June 2011].

Chute, Marchette (1960), *Stories from Shakespeare*. London: John Murray.

Classical Comics (n.d.), 'Education'. *Classical Comics* [Online]. Available at: www.classicalcomics.com/education/index.html [Accessed 9 June 2011].

— (n.d.), 'Testimonials'. *Classical Comics* [Online]. Available at: www.classicalcomics.com/testimonials.html [Accessed 9 June 2011].

— (n.d.), 'Text Versions'. *Classical Comics* [Online]. Available at: www.classicalcomics.com/textversions.html [Accessed 9 June 2011].

Claybourne, Anna (2004), *Usborne Stories from Shakespeare* (ill. Elena Temporin). London: Usborne.

Codden, Karin S. (1989), 'Such Strange Desygns: Madness, Subjectivity and Treason in *Hamlet* and Elizabethan Culture'. *Renaissance Drama*, 10, 51–75.

Connor, Sheila (2008), 'A Midsummer Night's Dream by William Shakespeare, Re-imagined for Anyone Aged 6 and Over'. *British Theatre Guide* [Online]. Available at: www.britishtheatreguide.info/reviews/OAkidsdream-rev.htm [Accessed 12 June 2011].

Cooney, Caroline (2007), *Enter Three Witches*. New York: Scholastic Press.

Cooper, Susan (1999), *King of Shadows*. London: Bodley Head Children's Books.

Coxon, Lucinda (2009), *The Eternal Not*. Unpublished.

Coville, Bruce (1997), *William Shakespeare's Macbeth* (ill. Gary Kelley). New York: Dial.

— (2004), *William Shakespeare's Hamlet* (ill. Leonid Gore). New York: Dial.

Crago, Hugh (1999), 'Can Stories Heal?' in Peter Hunt (ed.), *Understanding Children's Literature: Key Essays from the International Companion Encyclopedia of Children's Literature*. Oxford: Routledge, pp. 163–73

Crouch, Tim (2011), *I, Shakespeare: I, Caliban; I, Banquo; I, Peaseblossom; I, Malvolio*. London: Oberon.

Crowl, Samuel (2003), *Shakespeare at the Cineplex*. Athens: Ohio University Press.

Daily Mail (2011), 'Half of Men Don't Know the Date of Their Wedding Anniversary (and One in Four Buy Their Flowers at a Petrol Station)'. *Daily Mail* [Online] 29 April. Available at: www.dailymail.co.uk/news/

article-1382044/Survey-reveals-half-men-know-wedding-anniversary.html [Accessed 27 June 2011].

Dane, Gabrielle (1998), 'Reading Ophelia's Madness'. *Exemplaria: A Journal of Theory in Medieval and Renaissance Studies,* 10, 405–23.

Davies, Caitlin (2009), 'The Play's the Thing: Can Young Children Be Vowed by Shakespeare?' *Independent* [Online] 5 February 2009. Available at: www.independent.co.uk/news/education/schools/the-plays-the-thing-can-young-children-be-wowed-by-shakespeare-1545624.html [Accessed 19 October 2011].

Dekker, Thomas (1609), *The Guls Horne-booke.* London.

Department for Children, Schools and Families (2008), 'Shakespeare for All Ages and Stages' [Online]. Available at: http://publications.education.gov.uk/eOrderingDownload/ShakespearesBooklet.pdf [Accessed 9 June 2011].

Department for Education (2009a), 'Audio Transcript: Romeo and Juliet at the Globe Theatre 2009 – Interview with the Director, Bill Buckhurst'. *National Strategies* [Online]. Available at: http://nationalstrategies.standards.dcsf.gov.uk/node/173930 [Accessed 9 June 2011].

— (2009b), 'Secondary English Newsletter – Summer 2009'. *National Strategies* [Online]. Available at: www.teachfind.com/national-strategies/teaching-shakespeare [Accessed 9 June 2011].

— (2010a), 'Macbeth: From the Globe to the Classroom'. *National Strategies* [Online]. Available at: http://nationalstrategies.standards.dcsf.gov.uk/node/431031 [Accessed 9 June 2011].

— (2010b), National Strategies, 'Macbeth: From the Globe to the Classroom – Bill Audio Clip Transcript'. *National Strategies* [Online]. Available at: http://nationalstrategies.standards.dcsf.gov.uk/node/432361 [Accessed 9 June 2011].

— (2010c), 'Macbeth: from The Globe to the classroom – James audio clip transcript'. *National Strategies* [Online]. Available at: http://nationalstrategies.standards.dcsf.gov.uk/node/432373 [Accessed 9 June 2011].

Desmet, Christy and Sawyer, Robert (1999), *Shakespeare and Appropriation.* London: Routledge.

Dessen, Alan (2008), '"Original Practices" at the Globe: A Theatre Historian's View' in Christie Carson and Farah Karim-Cooper (eds), *Shakespeare's Globe.* Cambridge: Cambridge University Press, pp. 45–54.

Dickins, Rosie, Claybourne, Anna, Sims, Lesley, Mason, Conrad and Stowell, Louie (ill. Christa Unzner, Jana Costa and Serena Riglietti) (2010), *Usborne Illustrated Stories from Shakespeare.* London: Usborne.

Discover: Primary and Early Years (2010), *Primary Classics Report 2010: Twelfth Night.* Unpublished.

Dixon, Wheeler W. (2000), '"Fighting and Violence and Everything, That's Always Cool": Teen Films in the 1990s' in Wheeler W. Dixon (ed.), *Film Genre 2000: New Critical Essays.* Albany: State University of New York Press, pp. 125–43.

Dominguez, Robert (2000), 'A Renaissance Man Tackles Shakespeare'. *Daily News* [Online] 11 May. Available at: http://articles.nydailynews.com/2000–05–11/entertainment/18140524_1_ethan-hawke-hamlet-gattaca [Accessed 9 June 2011].

Do Rozario, Rebecca-Anne C. (2004), 'The Princess and the Magic Kingdom: Beyond Nostalgia, the Function of the Disney Princess'. *Women's Studies in Communication,* 27, 34–59.

Draper, Sharon M. (2001), *Romiette and Julio*. New York: Simon Pulse.

Duncan, Lois (1978), *Killing Mr Griffin*. Boston: Little, Brown.

Dusinberre, Juliet (1975), *Shakespeare and the Nature of Women*. London: Macmillan.

Eason, Gary (2007), 'Shakespeare Gets Comic Treatment'. *BBC News* [Online] 11 May. Available at: http://news.bbc.co.uk/1/hi/6647927.stm [Accessed 9 June 2011].

Edmondson, Paul (2005), 'Macbeth: The Play in Performance' in Niels Bugge Hansen and Sos Haugaard (eds), *Angles: Charting Shakespearean Waters*. Copenhagen: Museum Tusculanum Press, pp. 121–34.

Edwardes, Jane (2008), 'New Playwrights at the RSC'. *Time Out* [Online] 18 February. Available at: www.timeout.com/london/theatre/features/4271/New_playwrights_at_the_RSC.html [Accessed 2 April 2011].

Edwards, Lee R. (1979), 'The Labors of Psyche: Toward a Theory of Female Heroism'. *Critical Inquiry*, 6:1, 33–49.

Edwards, Philip (ed.) (2008), *Hamlet*. Cambridge: Cambridge University Press.

Elgin, Kathy (2001), *Julius Caesar* (ill. Tony Morris). London: Hodder Wayland.

Evans, Beth Bingham (2009), 'Electronic Media as Entertainment: Film' in Andi Stein and Beth Bingham Evans (eds), *An Introduction to the Entertainment Industry*. New York: Peter Lang, pp. 15–36.

Fiedler, Lisa (2003), *Dating Hamlet*. London: Collins Flamingo.

— (2006), *Romeo's Ex: Rosaline's Story*. New York: Henry Holt.

Figaro Digital (2011), 'Case Study: Mudlark – "Such Tweet Sorrow"'. *Figaro Digital* [Online]. Available at: www.figarodigital.co.uk/case-study/Mudlark.aspx [Accessed 19 October 2011].

Film 4 (1996), 'Romeo + Juliet: Review' [Online]. Available at: www.film4.com/reviews/1996/william-shakespeares-romeo-juliet [Accessed 9 June 2011].

Finkelstein, Richard (1999), 'Disney Cites Shakespeare: The Limits of Appropriation' in Christy Desmet and Robert Sawyer (eds), *Shakespeare and Appropriation: Accents on Shakespeare*. London: Routledge, pp. 179–96.

Finlayson, J. Caitlin (2010), '*The Tempest*: Re-imagined for Everyone Aged Six and Over (Review)'. *Shakespeare Bulletin*, 28:2, 291–97.

Fischlin, Daniel and Fortier, Mark (2000), *Adaptations of Shakespeare: A Critical Anthology from the 17th Century to the Present*. London: Routledge.

French, Emma (2006), *Selling Shakespeare to Hollywood: The Marketing of Filmed Shakespeare Adaptations from 1989 into the New Millennium*. Hatfield: University of Hertfordshire Press.

Friedman, Michael D. (2008), '"To think o' th' teen that I have turned you to": The Scholarly Consideration of Teen Shakespeare Films'. *Shakespeare Bulletin*, 26:2, 1–7.

Fuchs, Cynthia (2000), 'Interview with Michael Almereyda'. *Pop Matters* [Online]. Available at: www.popmatters.com/pm/interviews/almereyda-michael.shtml [Accessed 9 June 2011].

Gallagher, Catherine and Greenblatt, Stephen (2001), *Practicing New Historicism*. Chicago: University of Chicago Press.

Gardner, Lyn (2008), '*A Midsummer Night's Dream*'. *Guardian* [Online] 16 July. Available at: www.guardian.co.uk/stage/2008/jul/16/theatre.shakespeare [Accessed 12 June 2011].

— (2009), 'The Comedy of Errors'. Guardian [Online] 20 May. Available at:
www.guardian.co.uk/stage/2009/may/20/review-comedy-of-errors [Accessed
12 June 2011].

Garfield, Leon (1985), Shakespeare Stories (ill. Michael Forman). London:
Gollancz.

— (1992), 'A Present for Mr Patten'. Books for Keeps, 77, 36.

Gavin, Rosemarie (1996), 'The Lion King and Hamlet: A Homecoming for the
Exiled Child'. English Journal, 85:3, 55–7.

Gearhart, Stephanie (2007), '"Faint and Imperfect Stamps": The Problem with
Adaptations of Shakespeare for Children'. Journal of Comparative Poetics, 27,
44–67.

Giblin, James Cross (2005), 'Awards: Publishing Trends' in Bernice E. Cullinan
and Diane Goetz Person, The Continuum Encyclopedia of Children's
Literature. London: Continuum, pp. 53–8.

Gibson, Mel (n.d.), 'Graphic Novels in the Curriculum'. Learning and Teaching
Scotland [Online]. Available at: www.ltscotland.org.uk/resources/g/
graphicnovels/studyofcomics.asp?strReferringChannel=resources&strReferrin
gPageID=tcm:4–396281–64 [Accessed 9 June 2011].

Gilbertson, Irvyn G. (2003), 'Death and Dying in Children's Literature' in
Bernice E. Cullinan and Diane Goetz Person, The Continuum Encyclopedia of
Children's Literature. London: Continuum, pp. 221–23.

Gilmore, Kate (1990), Enter Three Witches. Boston: Hougton Miffin.

Giroux, Henry A. and Pollock, Grace (2010), The Mouse That Roared: Disney
and the End of Innocence. Plymouth: Rowman and Littlefield.

Globe Education (2011a), 'Character and Motivation: Lady Macbeth'. Playing
Shakespeare [Online]. Available at: http://2010.playingshakespeare.org/
node/5/42#comment-42 [Accessed 9 June 2011].

— (2011b), 'Character and Motivation: Lady Macduff'. Playing
Shakespeare [Online]. Available at: http://2010.playingshakespeare.org/
node/20/12#comment-12 [Accessed 9 June 2011].

— (2011c), 'Character and Motivation: Macbeth'. Playing Shakespeare [Online].
Available at: http://2010.playingshakespeare.org/character-and-motivation/
macbeth [Accessed 9 June 2011].

— (2011d), 'Character and Motivation: Malcolm'. Playing Shakespeare [Online].
Available at: http://2010.playingshakespeare.org/character-and-motivation/
malcolm [Accessed 9 June 2011].

— (2011e), 'Character and Motivation: Murderers'. Playing Shakespeare [Online].
Available at: http://2010.playingshakespeare.org/node/22/10#comment-10
[Accessed 9 June 2011].

— (2011f), 'Character and Motivation: The Witches'. Playing Shakespeare
[Online]. Available at: http://2010.playingshakespeare.org/
node/21/43#comment-43 [Accessed 9 June 2011].

— (2011g), 'Director's Notes on Act 5 Scene 4'. Playing Shakespeare [Online].
Available at: http://2008.playingshakespeare.org/directors_notes_on_act_5_
scene_4/ [Accessed 9 June 2011].

— (2011h), 'Performance: The Student's View'. Playing Shakespeare [Online].
Available at: http://2008.playingshakespeare.org/text_in_performance/
item/17/ [Accessed 9 June 2011].

— (2011i), 'Playing Shakespeare with Deutsche Bank' *Playing Shakespeare* [Online]. Available at: www.playingshakespeare.org/ [Accessed 9 June 2011].

— (2011j), 'Romeo and Juliet (2009 Playing Shakespeare)'. *Playing Shakespeare* [Online]. Available at: www.globe-education.org/discovery-space/plays/romeo-and-juliet-2009-playing-shakespeare [Accessed 9 June 2011].

— (2011k), 'Text in Performance – Music'. *Playing Shakespeare* [Online]. Available at: http://2008.playingshakespeare.org/text_in_performance/item/6/) [Accessed 9 June 2011].

— (2011l), 'The Director'. *Playing Shakespeare* [Online]. Available at: http://2008.playingshakespeare.org/text_in_performance/item/4/ [Accessed 9 June 2011].

— (2011m), 'Themes and Issues'. *Playing Shakespeare* [Online]. Available at: http://2008.playingshakespeare.org/themes_and_issues/ [Accessed 9 June 2011].

Goldson, Barry (2011), *Youth in Crisis?: Gangs, Territoriality and Violence.* Oxford: Routledge.

Gordon, Sarah (n.d.), *The Young Shakespeare Company: A Midsummer Night's Dream: Follow up Materials.* London: Young Shakespeare Company.

Graff, Gerald and Phelan, James (2000), *The Tempest: A Case Study in Critical Controversy.* Basingstoke: Palgrave MacMillan.

Grande, Troni (2010), 'Manga Shakespeare and the Hermeneutic Problems of "Double Access"'. *Queen City Comics* [Online]. Available at: http://hdl.handle.net/10294/3091 [Accessed 9 June 2011].

Gratz, Alan M. (2006), 'Alan's Worst Kept Secret'. *Gratz Industries* [Online] 28 July. Available at: http://gratzindustries.blogspot.com/2006/07/alan-worst-kept-secret.html [Accessed 19 June 2011].

— (2007), *Something Rotten.* New York: Dial.

— (n.d.), *Something Rotten: Discussion Guide* [Online]. Available at: www.files.alangratz.com/rotten_readers_guide.pdf [Accessed 18 August 2009].

— (2008), *Something Wicked.* New York: Dial.

Graves, Joseph (c.1840), *Dramatic Tales founded on Shakespere's* [sic] *Plays.* London: J Duncombe.

Greaves, Simon (2003a), *Shakespeare Comic Books: Macbeth.* Shrewsbury: Timber Frame Publications.

— (2003b), *Shakespeare Comic Books Teacher's Book: Macbeth.* Shrewsbury: Timber Frame Publications.

Greenblatt, Stephen (2001), *Hamlet in Purgatory.* Princeton, NJ: Princeton University Press.

Grimley, Terry (2009), 'Review of *The Comedy of Errors*'. *Birmingham Post.* Available at: www.toldbyanidiot.org/reviews/detail/terry_grimley_on_the_comedy_of_errors [Accessed 12 June 2011].

Groves, Nancy (2010), 'Prince of Denmark'. *What's Onstage* [Online] 24 October. Available at: www.whatsonstage.com/reviews/theatre/off-west+end/E8831287941808/Prince+of+Denmark.html [Accessed 2 April 2011].

Guest, Katy (2009), 'Young, Gifted and Big Fans of Sonnet 18', *Independent* [Online] 27 February 2009. Available at: www.independent.co.uk/arts-entertainment/books/features/katy-guest-young-gifted-and-big-fans-of-sonnet-18–1632965.html [Accessed 19 October 2011].

Haig, Matt (n.d.), 'A Conversation with Matt Haig'. *Penguin.com* [Online].
    Available at: http://us.penguingroup.com/static/rguides/us/dead_fathers_club.
    html [Accessed 19 June 2011].
— (2006), *The Dead Fathers Club*. London: Jonathan Cape.
Hall, Edward (2011), 'About Pocket Propeller: An Introduction from Edward
    Hall'. *Propeller* [Online]. Available at: www.propeller.org.uk/education
    [Accessed 12 June 2011].
Hammond, Anthony (ed.) (1981), *King Richard III*. London: Arden.
Hapgood, Robert (1999), *Hamlet*. Cambridge: Cambridge University Press.
Harper, Karen (2009), *Mistress Shakespeare*. New York: Penguin.
Harper, Suzanne (2008), *The Juliet Club*. New York: Harper Collins.
Harrison, G. B. (1938), *New Tales from Shakespeare*. London: T. Nelson & Sons.
Hassinger, Peter W. (2004), *Shakespeare's Daughter*. New York: Harper Collins.
Hatchuel, Sarah (2004), *Shakespeare: From Stage to Screen*. Cambridge:
    Cambridge University Press.
Hatchuel, Sarah and Vienne-Guerrin, Nathalie (2004), 'Producing the Children's
    Midsummer Night's Dream (2001): A Discussion with Olivier Stockman' in
    Sarah Hatchuel and Nathalie Vienne-Guerrin (eds), *Shakespeare on Screen:
    A Midsummer Night's Dream*. Rouen: Publications de l'Université de Rouen,
    pp. 115–28.
Heap, Carl (n.d.), 'Discovering Shakespeare'. Unpublished essay.
— (2009a), *A Midsummer Night's Dream*. London: Oberon.
— (2009b), *Pericles*. London: Oberon.
— (2009c), *Romeo and Juliet*. London: Oberon.
— (2010), *Twelfth Night*. London: Oberon.
Hermes, Myrlin Abrosia (2010), *The Lunatic, the Lover and the Poet*. New York:
    Harper Collins.
Herz, Sarah K. and Gallo, Donald R. (1996), *From Hinton to Hamlet*. Westport,
    CT: Greenwood Press.
Higgins, Charlotte (2010), 'A Plague on the Twitter Romeo and Juliet'. *Guardian*
    [Online] 27 April 2010. Available at: www.guardian.co.uk/culture/2010/
    apr/27/romeo-juliet-twitter-rsc [Accessed 19 October 2011].
Hildrew, Chris (2007), '*Wallace and Grornit: The Curse of the Were-Rabbit* –
    a Study of Modality, Address, Reading and Response in Contemporary
    Children's Film', *English in Education*, 41:2, 86–99.
Hindle, Maurice (2007), *Studying Shakespeare on Film*. Basingstoke: Palgrave
    Macmillan.
Hip Hop Shakespeare Company (2008), 'About'. *The Hip Hop Shakespeare
    Company* [Online]. Available at: www.hiphopshakespeare.com/site/about/
    [Accessed 19 October 2011].
Hoffman, Alice Spencer (1911), *The Children's Shakespeare: Being Stories from
    the Plays, with Illustrative Passages, Told and Chosen by A. S. Hoffmann*
    (ill. Charles Folkard). London: J. M. Dent & Sons.
Holden, Stephen (2011), 'A Kitsch-and-Tell Movie of Garden Variety Love'.
    New York Times [Online] 10 February. Available at: http://movies.nytimes.
    com/2011/02/11/movies/11gnomeo.html [Accessed 18 September 2011].
Holland, Peter (ed.) (1998), *A Midsummer Night's Dream*. Oxford: Oxford
    University Press.

Honegger, Thomas (2009), 'Wouldst Thou Withdraw Love's Faithful Vow?' in Harold Bloom (ed.), *William Shakespeare's Romeo and Juliet*. New York: Bloom's Literary Criticism, pp. 169–84

Hopkins, Lisa (2008), *Shakespeare's 'The Tempest': The Relationship between Text and Film*. London: Routledge.

Hulbert, Jennifer (2010), '"Adolescence, Thy Name Is Ophelia!": The Ophelia-ization of the Contemporary Teenage Girl' in Jennifer Hulbert, Kevin J. Wetmore, Jr, and Robert L. York (eds), *Shakespeare and Youth Culture*. New York: Palgrave Macmillan, pp. 199–220.

Hulbert, Jennifer, Wetmore, Jr, Kevin J. and York, Robert L. (2006), 'Introduction' in Jennifer Hulbert, Kevin J. Wetmore, Jr, and Robert L. York (eds), *Shakespeare and Youth Culture*. New York: Palgrave Macmillan, pp. 1–41.

Irish, Tracy (2011), Email message to the author. 16 September 2011.

Irvine, Chris (2009), '*Romeo and Juliet* Production Sparks Fears over Knife Crime'. *Telegraph* [Online] 11 February. Available at: www.telegraph.co.uk/culture/theatre/4592467/Romeo-and-Juliet-production-sparks-fears-over-knife-crime.html [Accessed 9 June 2011].

Isaac, Megan Lynn (2000), *Heirs to Shakespeare: Reinventing the Bard in Young Adult Literature*. Portsmouth: Boynton/Cook.

Jardine, Lisa (1983), *Still Harping on Daughters: Women and Drama in the Age of Shakespeare*. Brighton: Harvester Press.

Jensen, Ejner J. (1975), 'The Boy Actors: Plays and Playing'. *RORD*, 18, 5–11.

Jones, Ernest (1949), *Hamlet and Oedipus*. London: Gollancz.

Jones, Karl O., Reid, Juliet M. V. and Bartlett, Rebecca (2005), 'Student Plagiarism and Cheating in an IT Age' in CompSysTech (The International Conference on Computer Systems and Technologies. Technical University, Varna, Bulgaria, 16–17 June 2005. Available at: http://ecet.ecs.ru.acad.bg/cst05/Docs/cp/sIV/IV.8.pdf [Accessed 9 June 2011].

Jonson, Ben (1623), 'To the Memory of My Beloved, the Author Mr. William Shakespere and What He Hath Left Us' in William Shakespeare, *Mr William Shakespeares Comedies, Histories & Tragedies. Published according to the True Originall Copies*. London.

Kahn, Coppelia (1981), *Man's Estate: Masculine Identity in Shakespeare*. Berkeley: University of California Press.

Karim-Cooper, Farah (n.d.), 'Women'. *Playing Shakespeare* [Online]. Available at: http://2008.playingshakespeare.org/themes_and_issues/article/2334ca727e1101c9c0fa17ccf887f39e/ [Accessed 9 June 2011].

Kastan, David Scott (1985), '*All's Well That Ends Well* and the Limits of Comedy'. *ELH*, 52:3, 575–89.

Keller, James R. and Stratyner, Leslie (2004), *Almost Shakespeare: Reinventing His Works for Cinema and Television*. London: McFarland.

Kennedy, Maev (2010), 'Romeo and Juliet Get Twitter Treatment'. *Guardian* [Online] 12 April 2010. Available at: www.guardian.co.uk/culture/2010/apr/12/shakespeare-twitter-such-tweet-sorrow [Accessed 19 October 2011].

Kiernan, Pauline (2006), *Filthy Shakespeare: Shakespeare's Most Outrageous Sexual Puns*. London: Quercus.

King, Geoff (2002), *New Hollywood Cinema: An Introduction*. London: I. B. Tauris.

Kinsella, Brooke (2011), *Tackling Knife Crime Together – a Review of Local Anti-Knife Crime Projects. Home Office* [Online]. Available at: www. homeoffice.gov.uk/publications/crime/tackling-knife-crime-together/ [Accessed 2 April 2011].

Kipp, Jeremiah (2003), 'Michael Almereyda'. *Senses of Cinema* 25 [Online]. Available at: www.sensesofcinema.com/2003/great-directors/almereyda/ [Accessed 9 June 2011].

Kirwan, Peter (2010), '*Hamlet* (RSC Young People's Shakespeare) @ The Courtyard Theatre'. *Bardathon* [Online] 27 August. Available at: http://blogs. warwick.ac.uk/pkirwan/entry/hamlet_rsc_young/ [Accessed 12 June 2011].

Klein, Lisa M. (2006), *Ophelia*. London: Bloomsbury.

— (2009), *Ophelia*. London: Bloomsbury.

Klett, Elizabeth (2008), 'Reviving Viola: Comic and Tragic Teen Film Adaptations of *Twelfth Night*'. *Shakespeare Bulletin*, 26:2, 69–87.

Kochenderfer, Tim (2008), *A Midsummer Vacation's Nightmare*. New York: Playscripts.

Korman, Gordon (2002), *Son of the Mob*. New York: Hyperion.

Kott, Jan (1964), *Shakespeare Our Contemporary*. Translated from Polish by B. Taberski. London: Methuen.

Lamb, Charles and Lamb, Mary (1807), *Tales from Shakespeare*. London

Lamb, Susan (2002), 'Applauding Shakespeare's Ophelia in the Eighteenth Century: Sexual Desire, Politcs and the Good Woman' in Susan Shifrin (ed.), *Women as Sites of Culture: Women's Roles in Cultural Formation from the Renaissance to the Twentieth Century*. Aldershot: Ashgate, pp. 105–23.

Lambert, Chloe (2010), 'Macbeth, Murder and Mayhem'. *The Times* [Online] 11 March. Available at: www.timesonline.co.uk/tol/life_and_style/education/ young_times/article7057177.ece [Accessed 9 June 2011].

Lancelyn Green, Roger (1964a), *Tales from Shakespeare: The Comedies*. London: Victor Gollancz.

— (1964b), *Tales from Shakespeare: The Tragedies and Romances*. London: Victor Gollancz.

Lanier, Douglas (2002), *Shakespeare and Modern Popular Culture*. Oxford: Oxford University Press.

— (2006), 'Popular Culture: Will of the People: Recent Shakespeare Film Parody and the Politics of Popularization' in Diana E. Henderson (ed.), *A Concise Companion to Shakespeare on Screen*. Oxford: Blackwell.

Leader, Mike (2011), 'Review: *Gnomeo and Juliet*'. *Film Four* [Online]. Available at: www.film4.com/reviews/2011/gnomeo-juliet [Accessed 17 September 2011].

Leapfrog Research and Planning (2011), 'RSC: Such Tweet Sorrow'. *Leapfrog* [Online]. Available at: www.leapfrogresearch.co.uk/clients/rsc [Accessed 19 October 2011].

Lee, Veronica (2010), 'This *Hamlet* Was a Palpable Hit'. *Evening Standard* [Online]. Available at: www.thisislondon.co.uk/theatre/review-23798801-this-hamlet-was-a-palpable-hit.do [Accessed 12 June 2011].

Lehmann, Courtney (2001), 'Strictly Shakespeare? Dead Letters, Ghostly Fathers, and the Cultural Pathology of Authorship in Baz Luhrmann's William Shakespeare's Romeo + Juliet'. *Shakespeare Quarterly*, 52:2, 189–221.

Lerner, Richard M. and Steinberg, Laurence (2009), *Handbook of Adolescent Psychology: Contextual Influences on Adolescent Development*. New York: John Wiley and Sons.

Lesslie, Michael (2010), *Prince of Denmark*. Unpublished.

— (2011), *Interview*. Interviewed by Abigail Rokison. 31 January 2011.

Lewis, Barbara (1992), 'Bard Suffers Slings and Arrows'. *Sunday Telegraph*. 1 November 1992. 12

Linehan, Nancy Charles (2001), *A Midsummer Night's Dream or The Night They Missed the Forest for the Trees*. Illinois: Dramatic.

Lipmann, Stephen (1976), '"Metatheater" and the Criticism of the Comedia'. *MLN*, 91:2, 231–46.

Loehlin, James N. (2000), '"These Violent Delights Have Violent Ends": Baz Luhrmann's Millennial Shakespeare', in Mark Thornton Burnett and Ramona Wray (eds), *Shakespeare, Film, Fin-de-Siecle*. Basingstoke: Macmillan.

Logan, Robert A. (2007), *Shakespeare's Marlowe: The Influence of Christopher Marlowe on Shakespeare's Artistry*. Aldershot: Aldgate.

Luhrmann, Baz (1996), 'Commentary' to *Romeo + Juliet* [Film] Directed by Baz Luhrmann. USA: Bazmark Films and Twentieth Century Fox.

Luhrmann, Baz and Pearce, Craig (1996), *William Shakespeare's 'Romeo & Juliet': The Contemporary Film, the Classic Play*. New York: Bantam Doubleday.

Macauley, Elizabeth Wright (1822), *Tales of the Drama*. London.

McAvoy, James (2011), 'Interview: James McAvoy Talks 'Gnomeo and Juliet' & Animated Filmmaking'. *Screenrant* [Online]. Available at http://screenrant.com/james-mcavoy-gnomeo-juliet-interview-rothc-101237/ [Accessed 17 September 2011].

McCaughrean, Geraldine (1997), *Stories from Shakespeare*. London: Orion.

McDonald, John (adpt.) and Hayward, Jon (ill.) (2008a), *Classical Comics: Macbeth* 'Original Text' edition. Towcester: Classical Comics.

— (2008b), *Classical Comics: Macbeth* 'Plain Text' edition. Towcester: Classical Comics.

— (2008c), *Classical Comics: Macbeth* 'Quick Text' edition. Towcester: Classical Comics.

MacDonald, Sharman (1999), 'Writers' Diaries: 1999 – After Juliet' [Online]. Available at: www.writernet.co.uk/php2/news.php?id=323&item=86 [Accessed 1 April 2009].

— (2001), *After Juliet*. London: Faber and Faber.

McKeown, Adam (2008), *The Young Reader's Shakespeare: Julius Caesar* (ill. Janet Hamlin). New York: Sterling.

McLeod, Mary (1902), *The Shakespeare Story-Book*. London: Wells, Gardner and Co.

Malakh-Pines, Ayala (1998), *Romantic Jealousy: Causes, Symptoms, Cures*. London: Routledge.

Marchitello, Howard (2002), 'Descending Shakespeare: Toward a Theory of Adaptation for Children' in Naomi J. Miller (ed.), *Reimagining Shakespeare for Children and Young Adults*. London: Routledge, pp. 180–90.

Mark, Jan (2000), *Heathrow Nights*. London: Hodder Children's.

Marsden, John (2009), *Hamlet*. Cambridge, MA: Candlewick Press.

Martin, Jennifer L. (2002), 'Tights vs. Tattoos: Filmic Interpretations of "Romeo and Juliet"'. *English Journal*, 92:1, 41–6.

Maslen, R. W. (2006), '*Twelfth Night,* Gender, and Comedy' in G. A. Sullivan, P. Cheney and A. Hadfield (eds), *Early Modern English Drama: A Critical Companion.* Oxford: Oxford University Press, pp. 130–9

Maslin, Janet (1996), 'Soft! What Light? It's Flash, Romeo'. *New York Times* [Online] 1 November. Available at: www.nytimes.com/1996/11/01/movies/soft-what-light-it-s-flash-romeo.html [Accessed 9 June 2011].

Masters, Andrew (2000), *Hamlet* (ill. Stephen Player). London: Hodder Wayland.

Matthews, Andrew (2001), *The Orchard Book of Shakespeare Stories* (ill. Angela Barrett). London: Orchard Books.

— (2003), *The Tempest: A Shakespeare Story* (ill. Tony Ross). London: Orchard Books.

Maxwell, Caroline (1828), *The Juvenile Shakespeare: Adapted to the Capacities of Youth.* London.

Maxwell, Tom (2007), 'Keira's Helpful Prompt'. *Edinburgh Evening News* [Online] 20 July. Available at: http://living.scotsman.com/performing-arts/Keiras-helpful-prompt.3306002.jp [Accessed 2 April 2011].

Menzer, Paul (2006), 'Dislocating Shakespeare: Scene Locators and the Place of the Page'. *Shakespeare Bulletin*, 24:2, 1–19

Meyer, Carolyn (2006), *Loving Will Shakespeare.* New York: Harcourt Children's Books.

Miles, Bernard (1976), *Favourite Tales from Shakespeare* (ill. Victor Ambrus). London: Hamlyn.

— (1986), *Well-Loved Tales from Shakespeare* (ill. Victor Ambrus). London: Hamlyn.

Milner, Joseph and Milner, Lucy (2007), *Bridging English.* 4th edn. New Jersey: Prentice Hall.

Mudlark and the Royal Shakespeare Company (n.d.), *Such Tweet Sorrow* [Online]. Available at: www.suchtweetsorrow.com/cast-and-crew/laurence [Accessed 19 October 2011].

Muir, Kenneth (1984), *Macbeth.* London: Methuen.

Mullaney, Steven (1995), *The Place of the Stage: License, Play and Power in Renaissance England.* Michigan: University of Michigan Press.

Mulvey, Laura (1998), 'Visual Pleasure and Narrative Cinema' in Lizbeth Goodman (ed.), *The Routledge Reader in Gender and Performance.* London: Routledge, pp. 270–75.

Museum of Broadcast Communications (2011), '*The Simpsons*'. *Museum of Broadcast Communications* [Online]. Available at: www.museum.tv/eotvsection.php?entrycode=simpsonsthe [Accessed 19 October 2011].

National Theatre (2010), 'Prince of Denmark Workshops'. *National Theatre* [Online]. Available at: www.nationaltheatre.org.uk/60606/discover-events/emprince-of-denmarkem-workshops.html [Accessed 2 April 2011].

National Theatre Education (2006), *Programme Report Primary Classics 2005–2006 Pericles by William Shakespeare in a Version by Carl Heap.* Unpublished.

Nesbit, E. (1897), *The Children's Shakespeare.* London

Newman, Peter (1997), 'Luhrmann's Young Lovers as Seen by Their Peers'. *Shakespeare Bulletin*, 15:3, 36–7.

O'Hanlon, Jacqui (2011), Email message to the author. 20 September 2011.

Olivier, Laurence (1986), *On Acting*. Sevenoaks, Kent: Sceptre.

Orgel, Stephen (1996), *Impersonations: The Performance of Gender in Shakespeare's England*. Cambridge: Cambridge University Press.

Osborne, Laurie E. (1997), 'Poetry in Motion: Animating Shakespeare' in Richard Burt and Lynda E. Boose (eds), *Shakespeare the Movie – Popularizing the Plays on Film, TV, and Video*. London: Routledge, pp. 103–20.

— (2003), 'Mixing Media and Animating Shakespeare Tales' in Richard Burt and Lynda E. Boose (eds), *Shakespeare the Movie II: Popularizing the Plays on Film, TV, Video, and DVD*. London: Routledge, pp. 140–53.

Partridge, Eric (1947), *Shakespeare's Bawdy*. London: Routledge.

Paterson, Katherine (1977), *Bridge to Terabithia*. New York: Crowell.

Pearce, Craig (1996), 'Commentary' to *Romeo + Juliet* [Film] Directed by Baz Luhrmann. USA: Bazmark Films and Twentieth Century Fox.

Pipher, Mary (1994), *Reviving Ophelia*. New York: Putnam.

Ponton, Lynn (1998), *The Romance of Risk: Why Teenagers Do the Things They Do*. New York: Basic Books.

Powling, Chris (2000), *The Tempest* (ill. Tony Morris). London: Hodder Wayland.

Poyton, Matthew (2011), 'Gnomeo and Juliet: Study Notes'. *Film Education* [Online]. Available at: www.filmeducation.org/pdf/resources/primary/ Gnomeo%20&%20Juliet%282%29.pdf [Accessed 17 September 2011].

Preminger, Alex and Brogan, T. V. F. (eds) (1993), *The New Princeton Encyclopedia of Poetry and Poetics*. Princeton: Princeton University Press.

Preuss, Ken (2008), *Juliet's Ghost*. New York: Playscripts.

Prindle, Alison H. (2002), '"The Play's the Thing": Genre and Adaptations of Shakespeare for Children' in Naomi J. Miller (ed.), *Reimagining Shakespeare for Children and Young Adults*. London: Routledge, pp. 138–46.

Propeller (2011), 'Propeller' [Online]. Available at: www.propeller.org.uk/ [Accessed 12 June 2011].

— (n.d.), *Pocket Dream Education Pack* [Online]. Available at: www.propeller. org.uk/userfiles/files/POCKET%20DREAM%20EDUCATION%20 PACK%20WEBSITE.pdf [Accessed 12 June 2011].

Pyles, Marian S. (1998), *Death and Dying in Children's Literature: A Survey and Bibliography*. London: McFarland.

Qualifications and Curriculum Development Agency (2010), 'Active Shakespeare: Capturing Evidence of Learning'. *National Curriculum* [Online]. Available at: http://curriculum.qca.org.uk/key-stages-3-and-4/subjects/key-stage-3/english/ active-shakespeare/index.aspx [Accessed 9 June 2011].

Quiller-Couch, Arthur (1899), *Historical Tales from Shakespeare*. London: Edward Arnold.

Ravassat, Mireille (2007), 'Assessing and Translating the Ambiguities of Wordplay in Shakespeare's *Macbeth*'. *Bulletin de la Société de stylistique anglaise, 29* [Online]. Available at: http://stylistique-anglaise.org/document. php?id=64 [Accessed 9 June 2011].

Ray, Ratri (2007), *William Shakespeare's 'The Tempest'*. New Dehli: Atlantic.

Regent's Park Theatre (2003–10a), 'About Us'. *Regent's Park Open Air Theatre* [Online]. Available at: http://openairtheatre.org/about [Accessed 12 June 2011].

— (2003–10b), 'Workshops'. *Regent's Park Open Air Theatre* [Online]. Available at: http://openairtheatre.org/workshops [Accessed 12 June 2011].

Reisert, Rebecca (2001), *The Third Witch*. London: Flame.
— (2003), *Ophelia's Revenge*. London: Flame.
Resetarits, C. R. (2001), 'Ophelia's Emphatic Function'. *Mississippi Review*, 29:3, 215–17.
Rokison, Abigail (2010a), 'Authenticity in the Twenty-first Century: The Globe and Propeller', in Chris Dymokowski and Christie Carson (eds), *Shakespeare in Stages*. Cambridge: Cambridge University Press, pp. 71–90
— (2010b), '"Our Scene Is Alter'd": Adaptations and Re-Workings of Hamlet for Young People'. *Literature Compass*, 7:9, 786–97.
Rosenberg, Marvin (1992), *The Masks of Hamlet*. London: Associated University Press, 1995.
Rosenthal, Daniel (2007), *100 Shakespeare Films*. London: British Film Institute.
— (2008), *100 Shakespeare Films*. London: British Film Institute.
Rothwell, Kenneth S. (1999), *A History of Shakespeare on Screen: A Century of Film and Television*. Cambridge: Cambridge University Press.
Rozett, Martha Tuck (1997), 'When Images Replace Words: Shakespeare, Russian Animation, and the Culture of Television' in Ronald E. Salomone and James E. David (eds), *Teaching Shakespeare into the Twenty-First Century*. Athens, OH: Ohio University Press, pp. 208–14.
RSC (2008), 'Manifesto'. *Stand Up for Shakespeare* [Online]. Available at: www.rsc.org.uk/standupforshakespeare/downloads/rsc_sufs_manifesto_full.pdf [Accessed 1 April 2009].
— (2009), *Education Pack: Young People's Shakespeare, The Comedy of Errors* [Online]. Available at: www.rsc.org.uk/downloads/rsc_edu_coe_2009_full_pack.pdf [Accessed 12 June 2011].
— (2010), 'YPS Week 2010'. *RSC* [Online]. Available at: www.rsc.org.uk/education/yps/2010/yps-week.aspx [Accessed 12 June 2011].
Rutter, Carol (1988), *Clamorous Voices*. London: Women's Press.
Rylance, Mark (2008), 'Research, Materials, Craft: Principles of Performance at Shakespeare's Globe' in Christie Carson and Farah Karim-Cooper (eds), *Shakespeare's Globe*. Cambridge: Cambridge University Press, pp. 103–14
Scaglione, Joanne and Scaglione, Arrica Rose (2006), *Bully-Proofing Children: A Practical Hands-On Guide to Stop Bullying*. Lanham, MD: Rowman & Littlefield.
Schonmann, Shifra (2006), *Theatre as a Medium for Children and Young People: Images and Observations*. Dordrecht, The Netherlands: Springer.
Schwartz, Delmore (1952), 'Masterpieces as Cartoons' in Jeet Heer and Kent Worcester (eds), *Arguing Comics: Literary Masters on a Popular Medium*. Jackson: University Press of Mississippi (2004), pp. 52–62.
The Scotsman (2008), 'Is This a Manga I See?' *Scotsman* [Online] 19 July. Available at: http://thescotsman.scotsman.com/books/-Book-Worm-.4294753.jp [Accessed 9 June 2011].
Scragg, Leah (2005), '*All's Well That Ends Well* and the Tale of the Chivalric Quest' in Simon Barker (ed.), *Shakespeare's Problem Plays: 'All's Well That Ends Well', 'Measure for Measure', 'Troilus and Cressida'*. New Casebooks. London: Palgrave Macmillan.
SelfMadeHero (2011a), 'Manga Shakespeare: Free Resources'. *Manga Shakespeare* [Online]. Available at: www.mangashakespeare.com/free_resources.html [Accessed 8 May 2011].

— (2011b), 'Manga Shakespeare: Glossary, *Macbeth*'. *Manga Shakespeare* [Online]. Available at: www.mangashakespeare.com/glossary/MACBETH_ Glossary.pdf [Accessed 8 May 2011].

— (2011c), 'Manga Shakespeare: Press'. *Manga Shakespeare* [Online]. Available at: www.mangashakespeare.com/press [Accessed 8 May 2011].

Semenza, Gregory M. Colón (2008), 'Teens, Shakespeare, and the Dumbing Down Cliché: The Case of The Animated Tales'. *Shakespeare Bulletin*, 26:2, 37–68.

Serraillier, Ian (1964), *The Enchanted Island: Stories from Shakespeare* (ill. Peter Farmer). London: Oxford University Press.

Sexton, Adam, Grandt, Eve and Chow, Candice (2008), *Shakespeare's Macbeth: The Manga Edition*. Hoboken, NJ: Wiley.

Seymour, Mary (1880), *Shakespeare's Stories Simply Told*. London: T. Nelson & Sons.

Shakespeare Comics (2011), 'Shakespeare Comic Books on BBC Radio 4'. *Shakespeare Comic Books* [Online]. Available at: www.shakespearecomics. com/content/view/31/2/ [Accessed 9 June 2011].

Shakespeare's Globe, Press Release: 'Teenagers Go to Cinema Not Theatre, and Only One in Five Has Seen the Bard', 12 March 2010. Unpublished.

Showalter, Elaine (1994), 'Representing Ophelia: Women, Madness, and the Responsibilities of Feminist Criticism' in Susan Wofford (ed.), *Hamlet*. Boston: St. Martin's Press, pp. 220–40.

Sim, Adelaide Gordon (1894), *Phoebe's Shakespeare*. London: Bickers & Son.

Smallwood, Robert (1996), 'Directors' Shakespeare' in Jonathan Bate and Russell Jackson (eds), *The Oxford Illustrated History of Shakespeare on Stage*. Oxford: Oxford University Press, pp. 176–96.

Smith, Warren D. (1975), *Shakespeare's Playhouse Practice: A Handbook*. Hanover, NH: University Press of New England.

Snyder, Susan (ed.) (1998), *All's Well That Ends Well*. Oxford: Oxford University Press.

Sonnenmark, Laura A. (1990), *Something's Rotten in the State of Maryland*. New York: Scholastic.

SparkNotes (2003a), *No Fear Shakespeare: Hamlet*. New York: Spark.

— (2003b), *No Fear Shakespeare: Macbeth*. New York: Spark.

— (2011), 'About SparkNotes'. *SparkNotes* [Online]. Available at: www. sparknotes.com/about/ [Accessed 9 June 2011].

SparkNotes and Hoshine, Ken (ill.) (2008), *No Fear Shakespeare Graphic Novels: Macbeth*. New York: Spark.

Sprague, Marsha M. and Keeling, Kara K. (2007), *Discovering Their Voices: Engaging Adolescent Girls with Young Adult Literature*. International Reading Association.

SSF (n.d.), 'History of the Shakespeare Schools' Festival'. *Shakespeare Schools' Festival* [Online]. Available at: www.ssf.uk.com/about-us/history [Accessed 2 April 2011].

Stanford, Peter (2009), 'Lucinda Coxon: Return of the Prodigal Woman'. *Independent* [Online] 31 May. Available at: www.independent.co.uk/ arts-entertainment/theatre-dance/features/lucinda-coxon-return-of- the-prodigal-woman-1693064.html [Accessed 2 April 2011].

Starr, Chelsea (2003), 'Third-Wave Feminism' in Lorraine Code (ed.), *The Encyclopedia of Feminist Theories*. Oxford: Routledge, p. 474.

Stern, Tiffany (2004), *Making Shakespeare: The Pressures of Stage to Page*. London: Routledge.

Stoppard, Tom (1967), *Rosencrantz and Guildenstern Are Dead*. London: Faber and Faber.

Stuart, James (2007), Review of *The Dead Fathers Club* by Matt Haig in 'Sea Changed'. *Guardian* [Online] 21 April. Available at: www.guardian.co.uk/books/2007/apr/21/featuresreviews.guardianreview27 [Accessed 18 August 2009].

Sutherland, Tui T. (2004), *This Must Be Love*. New York: Harper Collins.

Teker, Gulsen Savin (2006), 'Empowered by Madness: Ophelia in the films of Kozintsev, Zeffirelli, and Branagh'. *Literature-Film Quarterly, 34*, 113–19.

Thomas, Kevin (2001), Review of Michael Almereyda's *Hamlet*. *LA Times*.

Thomas, Peter (1992), 'A Present for Mr Patten'. *Books for Keeps* 77, 37.

Thompson, Ann and Neil Taylor (eds) (2006), *Hamlet*. London: Arden.

Thornton Burnett, Mark (2002), '"Fancy's Images": Reinventing Shakespeare in Christine Edzard's the Children's Midsummer Night's Dream'. *Literature/Film Quarterly*, 30:3, 166–70.

Throne of Blood (1957), [Film] Directed by Akira Kurosawa. Toho Company and Kurosawa Production Company.

Tiffany, Grace (2003), *My Father Had a Daughter: Judith Shakespeare's Tale*. New York: Berkley Books.

Towbin, Mia Adessa, Haddock, Shelley A., Zimmerman, Toni Schindler, Lund, Lori K. and Tanner, Litsa Renee (2004), 'Images of Gender, Race, Age, and Sexual Orientation in Disney Feature-Length Animated Films'. *Journal of Feminist Family Therapy*, 15:4, 19–44.

Trites, Roberta S. (1998), *Disturbing the Universe: Power and Repression in Adolescent Literature*. Iowa: University of Iowa Press.

Trupe, Alice, (2006), *Thematic Guide to Young Adult Literature*. Westport, CT: Greenwood.

Turner, Helen, Mayall, Berry, Dickinson, Rachel, Clark, Alison, Hood, Suzanne, Samuels, Julia and Wiggins, Meg (2004), *Children Engaging with Drama: An Evaluation of the National Theatre's Drama Work in Primary Schools 2002–2004*. Social Science Research Unit, Institute of Education, University of London, London. Available at: http://eprints.ioe.ac.uk/2995/1/Turner2004Childrenengaging.pdf [Accessed 12 June 2011].

Updike, John (2000), *Gertrude and Claudius*. New York: A. A. Knopf.

Vaughan, Alden T. and Vaughan, Virginia Mason (1991), *Shakespeare's Caliban a Cultural History*. Cambridge: Cambridge University Press.

Venhaus, James (2005), *Romeo and Juliet at Verona High*. New York: Playscripts.

Von (ill.) (1982), *William Shakespeare's Macbeth: Graphic Shakespeare*. London: Can of Worms.

YSC (n.d.), 'Educational Aims of Key Stage 2 Work'. *Young Shakespeare Company* [Online]. Available at: www.youngshakespeare.org.uk/ks2aims.htm [Accessed 12 June 2011].

Wade, Barrie and Sheppard, John (1993), 'Shakespeare in the Curriculum: Direction by Content'. *Educational Studies*, 19:3, 267–74.

Walker, Peter (2009), 'Globe *Romeo and Juliet* Puts Spotlight on Knife
Crime'. *Guardian* [Online] 11 February. Available at: www.guardian.co.uk/
stage/2009/feb/11/globe-romeo-juliet-knife-crime) [Accessed 9 June 2011].

Waller Hastings, A. (1993), 'Moral Simplification in Disney's The Little
Mermaid'. *The Lion and the Unicorn*, 17:1, 83–92.

Wasko, Janet (2001), *Understanding Disney: The Manufacture of Fantasy.*
Cambridge: Polity Press.

Weiner, Stephen (2004), 'Show, Don't Tell: Graphic Novels in the Classroom'.
English Journal, 94:2, 114–17.

Wells, Stanley (1992), BBC 2, 'Animating Shakespeare', Jeff Morgan, producer,
broadcast, 2 November 1992.

— (1993), 'Tales from Shakespeare' in E. A. J. Honigmann (ed.), *British
Academy Shakespeare Lectures 1980–89*. Oxford: Oxford University Press,
pp. 185–213.

Wenborn, Karen (2009), *Classical Comics Teaching Resource Pack: Macbeth.*
Towcester: Classical Comics.

Werness, Hope B. (2004), *The Continuum Encyclopedia of Animal Symbolism in
Art*. London: Continuum.

Wertham, Fredric (1954), *Seduction of the Innocent*. New York: Rinehart.

Wetmore, Jr, Kevin J. (2006), '"The Amazing Adventures of Superbard":
Shakespeare in Comics and Graphic Novels' in Jennifer Hulbert, Kevin J.
Wetmore, Jr, and Robert L. York (eds), *Shakespeare and Youth Culture*. New
York: Palgrave Macmillan, pp. 171–98.

Williams, Marcia (1998), *Mr Williams Shakespeare's Plays*. London: Walker
Books.

— (2000), *Bravo Mr William Shakespeare!* London: Walker Books.

World Shakespeare Festival (2011), 'Education'. *World Shakespeare Festival
2012* [Online]. Available at: www.worldshakespearefestival.org.uk/education/
[Accessed 19 October 2011].

Worthen, W. B. (1998), 'Drama, Performativity, and Performance'. *PMLA*, 113:5,
1093–107.

Yun, Eunja (2007), *Postmodern Interrogation of Children's Literature and
Possibilities in Literacy Education by Means of Postmodern Picture Books.*
Pennsylvania: Penn State University.

INDEX